Transnational Tortillas

Race, Gender, and Shop-Floor Politics in Mexico and the United States

Carolina Bank Muñoz

ILR Press

AN IMPRINT OF

CORNELL UNIVERSITY PRESS

ITHACA AND LONDON

First published 2008 by Cornell University Press
First printing, Cornell Paperbacks, 2008
Printed in the United States of America

Library of Congress Cataloging-in-Publication Data

Bank Muñoz, Carolina.
   Transnational tortillas : race, gender, and shop-floor politics in Mexico and the United States / Carolina Bank Muñoz.
       p. cm.
   Includes bibliographical references and index.
   ISBN 978–0–8014–4649–8 (cloth : alk. paper) — ISBN 978–0–8014–7422–4 (pbk. : alk. paper)
   1. Tortilla industry—Mexico—Baja California (Peninsula) 2. Tortilla industry—California. 3. Factory system—Mexico—Baja California (Peninsula) 4. Factory system—California. 5. Industrial relations—Mexico—Baja California (Peninsula) 6. Industrial relations—California. 7. Women—Employment—Mexico—Baja California (Peninsula) 8. Alien labor, Mexican—California. I. Title.
   HD9330.T753M612   2008
   338.4'7664752—dc22

                                                                    2008011611

Cornell University Press strives to use environmentally responsible suppliers and materials to the fullest extent possible in the publishing of its books. Such materials include vegetable-based, low-VOC inks and acid-free papers that are recycled, totally chlorine-free, or partly composed of nonwood fibers. For further information, visit our website at www.cornellpress.cornell.edu.

Cloth printing   10 9 8 7 6 5 4 3 2 1
Paperback printing   10 9 8 7 6 5 4 3 2 1

TRANSNATIONAL TORTILLAS

For immigrants in the United States who work in the shadows;
For workers in Mexico who fight for survival;
And for my parents, whose struggle has been a source of inspiration.

CONTENTS

Acknowledgments

I am deeply indebted to all of the workers, managers, and organizers who participated in this study and allowed me into the factory and into their homes and lives. I am especially grateful to the production workers who took risks in speaking with me about their working conditions. Their willingness to tell me about their lives showed great courage. Without their participation, this book would not have been possible.

I have been working on this project for most of my academic career. In that time I have benefited from a rich intellectual community that has encouraged and shown enthusiasm for the project from its inception. I thank Edna Bonacich, Ellen Reese, Chris Chase-Dunn, and Karen Pyke, who always pushed me to sharpen my analysis. Michael Burawoy expressed excitement in the initial stages of the project and gave me the confidence to pursue it. Enrique de la Garza Toledo and Huberto Juárez Núñez in Mexico were always willing to talk to me about Mexican politics and labor law reform. I am grateful to them for the time they took to help me deepen my analysis of the situation in Mexico.

During my time in graduate school I was lucky to meet Erika Gutiérrez, who helped me collect some of the data in Mexico. I feel privileged to have met Erika's grandmother, who opened her home to me in Mexico and allowed us to stay with her on several occasions (feeding us amazing food, I might add). I was also fortunate to participate in a writing group with students at the University of Southern California. Belinda Lum, Rigoberto Rodríguez, and Lorena Muñoz always gave me insightful and critical feedback and forced me to be accountable to both them and myself. I am grateful for grants and fellowships I received from The Institute for Labor and Employment Dissertation Fellowship, The Ernesto Galarza Research Center, Women in Coalition, and the graduate division and the sociology department of the University of California at Riverside.

At the UCLA Labor Center, I was surrounded by a community of amazing activists and intellectuals. I thank Kent Wong, Linda Delp, and Stephanie Arellano for providing me with support and the space to finish my research and writing. I especially thank Juan DeLara, who read many drafts with a critical eye and helped me sharpen my analysis. I have also really valued his friendship and the friendship of his partner, Veronica Carrizales, and their daughter, Ixchel, over the past six years.

At Brooklyn College–City University of New York I benefited enormously from a writing group with fellow CUNY faculty. I especially thank Karen Miller, Nicole Trujillo Pagan, and Celina Su, who spent hours reading every chapter and providing valuable feedback.

Many others helped make this book possible. Ralph Armbruster-Sandoval, Rachel Sherman, Johanna Brenner, Kelly Moore, Beverly Silver, and participants in the CUNY Faculty Fellowship Publication Program, especially Virginia Sánchez Korrol, all provided insightful comments.

I am also grateful to the staff at Cornell University Press, especially Fran Benson. The first time I met Fran she sat with me for an hour and listened to me talk about my project. She has been an extremely patient editor and has been encouraging throughout the process. I also thank the two anonymous reviewers who gave the book manuscript a careful reading and offered insightful and specific comments for revision.

I am indebted to Ruth Milkman and Edna Bonacich. Ruth's keen insights, sharp critique, and advice about writing style have significantly influenced my work. Edna has read the manuscript more times than she probably cares to remember! I have benefited tremendously from her big-picture analysis and her example of integrating theory and practice. I have known Edna for thirteen years, and I consider her not only a friend and mentor but also a part of my family.

At Brooklyn College I have been fortunate to receive junior faculty release time and three PSC-CUNY grants to support the completion of this project. I thank my current and former colleagues in the sociology department for providing encouragement: Alex Vitale, Tim Shortell, Kelly Moore, and Aviva Zeltzer Zubida.

My friends have given me unwavering support during this long road. I especially thank Andrea Gallelli, Paula Alonso, Kay Pih, Scott Melzer, Lisa Gallegos, Tara Marray, Erin Small, Catherine Sameh, Charlie Post, Teresa Stern, Nathalia Jaramillo, Stephanie Luce, and Mark Brenner. Participating in the faculty union at CUNY kept me motivated during the revisions of the manuscript. In that context I've made numerous friends whom I cherish and respect deeply. Thanks especially to Karen Miller, Penny Lewis, Nikki McDaniel, Pat Lloyd, and Scott Dexter for being such wonderful union activists.

Daisy Rooks has been one of my greatest supporters in this eight-year journey. Not only has she read the manuscript, but she has also provided me with encouragement and laughter during difficult times. She is also a fantastic conference partner and a wonderful friend.

Most important, I thank my parents. They have led incredibly difficult lives as immigrants in the United States. It is from them that I first learned about inequality, and it is from them that I get my passion for social justice. From a very young age they instilled in me the value of human life. For that I am forever grateful. I am also deeply thankful to my family in Chile for their warmth and closeness despite great distances, and to my in-laws Karen and Bill Levine, who have always shown interest in my work. Finally, this book would not have been possible without the love, support, and patience of my husband, Ted Levine. He has offered excellent critiques and praise, and he has been a wonderful copy editor. I have so much admiration for his work in labor and social justice and look forward to raising our first child together.

C.B.M.

Brooklyn, New York

TRANSNATIONAL TORTILLAS

1

The Tortilla Behemoth and Global Production

José and Eugenio—Hacienda CA

Hacienda California (CA) is a factory in the United States owned by Tortimundo, a Mexican transnational tortilla manufacturing corporation.[1] The factory is one of the largest tortilla manufacturing plants in the world. Workers at the factory labor in a highly regimented and monitored work environment. The California factory is surrounded by security cameras that watch workers' every move, and strict discipline is enforced on the shop floor. The workforce in the factory is composed predominantly of men, and managers at Hacienda CA specifically construct the work as "men's work."

José and Eugenio are two production workers at Hacienda CA. Despite working in the same factory, for the same length of time, José and Eugenio's work and family lives are vastly different. The central explanation of this difference is the fact that José is undocumented whereas Eugenio is not.

Eugenio is a documented worker who has been at the factory for eight years. He works the day shift from 6 A.M. to 2 P.M. and earns $10.50 an hour. He started as a production worker but was promoted to line leader four years later. His position as line leader gives him flexibility and the power to report absenteeism, tardiness, and behavioral issues on the line. He also has the power to determine when workers can take bathroom and lunch breaks. While he does not love his job, he feels satisfied with it and the opportunities it has given him. After work he goes to the corner taco stand with friends from the surrounding neighborhood and some people from his shift. He then drives to pick up his kids from school and rests at home for the remainder of the day. His wife gets home from her job in a nearby factory at 5 P.M. Their dual income has allowed them to purchase a modest home in a working-class Latina/o neighborhood.

José has also been at Hacienda CA for eight years. He has been working the graveyard shift (10 P.M.–6 A.M.) for six years and earns $8.15 per hour. He has watched younger Latino men whom he calls "Los Chicanos" come and work during the graveyard shift and get moved or promoted in three months. But year after year he is stuck in the same shift. José thinks that managers won't give him the day shift or promote him because of his immigration status.

When José first applied for the job at Hacienda CA, managers asked him about his immigration status. They told him that they did not care if he was undocumented but that they needed to know if he was so that they would be able to protect him from the Immigration and Naturalization Service (INS).[2] Managers told José that, as a Mexican company in a hostile U.S. climate, they were committed to protecting their compatriots. According to José, telling managers about his status was the worst mistake he ever made. He is treated like a second-class citizen in the workplace. José is consistently denied wage increases and shift changes. Managers constantly remind him that they have taken a risk in hiring him and that they cannot adequately protect him unless he works the night shift.

For José, working in the factory is difficult for another reason as well: he does not know whom he can trust. Women do not trust men; undocumented workers are afraid of being deported and rarely associate with anyone in the factory; and more established Mexicans look down on newer migrants. As a result of this environment, José has very few friends in the factory. After work, José drives home, greets his family, showers and rests for a few minutes before he has to leave for his second job at a nearby res-taurant, where he works from 9 A.M. to 2 P.M. preparing vegetables (wash-ing, chopping, etc.). He earns minimum wage at the restaurant. After his second job, he drives home, enjoys time with his family, eats, and then goes to sleep until 9 P.M., when he has to get ready to go back to Hacienda.

For José it is a struggle to survive in California on $1,500 per month (after taxes). However, he is proud that he has managed to support his fam-ily. José's wife, Irma, doesn't work outside the home. She is primarily re-sponsible for taking care of the children and running the household. Irma is also undocumented, and the low wages she would receive for working in a garment factory or as a domestic worker would not compensate her enough to pay for child care. She also believes that staying at home will ensure that her children do not become involved with the local gang.

Both documented and undocumented workers at Hacienda CA labor in a racially charged and gendered environment. However, documented workers are treated better, paid higher wages, and can look forward to modest upward mobility within the factory, whereas undocumented work-ers endure poor treatment, low wages, and little internal factory mobility.

Despite a highly controlled work environment, workers at Hacienda CA have nonetheless engaged in resistance struggles. José and others at-tempted a union-organizing drive for production workers. This drive took place at the same time that truck drivers for the company were striking over their contract. The strike and the internal organizing drive were car-ried out by the Manufacturing Organizing Project (MOP), which consisted of a coalition of unions, including the Teamsters.[3] Although the campaign eventually failed, it is significant because even though workers did not win a union, conditions for all workers in the factory improved.

María and Antonio—Hacienda BC

A short one hundred miles away in Mexico, workers are churning out tor-tillas at Hacienda Baja California (BC), also owned by Tortimundo. How-ever, the work environment in this factory is markedly different from that in its counterpart in the United States. Here there are no security cameras monitoring workers, nor are there strict disciplinary policies. Workers casually walk into the factory, often laughing and conversing with their co-workers. However, women workers in this factory endure chronic sexual harassment and compete with each other for job stability. The workforce is predominantly female, and the work is constructed as "women's work."

Like Eugenio and José, their counterparts in the United States, María and Antonio have worked in the same factory for the same length of time, but their working conditions and family lives are very different. The central cause of division between these two workers is gender and the feminized labor regime at Hacienda BC.

Antonio works as a machine operator earning $3 per hour. He was raised in Baja California and has been working in the factory for four years. Before entering his current job, he worked in a variety of different industries in the region. He does not consider his job stressful. He likes the factory environment and considers himself relatively well paid. Antonio has a reasonable amount of independence and is essentially left alone by shop-floor supervisors and managers. When he leaves his job at 8 P.M., he takes the bus home, where his family awaits him. Antonio's wife stays at home and takes care of their two children and other household responsibilities. They have a large and supportive family network and live comfortably in a house with his parents.

María has a very different experience. She has also been working at Hacienda BC for four years, but as an assembly line worker she earns only $1 per hour. She is a single mother with three children. Her husband, Ignacio, crossed the border to get a better job, and she has not heard from him since. She does not know if he died crossing the border or if he lives another life in the United States. She and Ignacio and the children migrated to Baja California from Jalisco. María comes from a family of corn farmers. Her great-grandfather, her grandfather, and her father all worked the same land. Her brothers were going to follow in their father's footsteps but were forced to migrate to Mexico City to find jobs when María's father lost the family farm. María attributes the loss of the farm to unfair competition from American corn that flooded the Mexican market after the passage of the North American Free Trade Agreement (NAFTA).

After moving to Baja California, Ignacio found a job in an auto parts maquiladora and María stayed home, took care of the children, and sold food from their home. After a year they decided they would try to cross the border into the United States. However, they learned that it would be extremely dangerous for the entire family to cross, so Ignacio crossed alone. María was left with no money and no familial networks in Baja California. Having no resources, María began working in maquiladoras that produce garments, but the industry was very unstable, so she went to work for Hacienda BC.

María leaves her house at 5:30 A.M. to catch the bus that gets her to work by 6 A.M. She arrives at the factory with several friends who take the same bus. When she arrives on the production line, she is immediately greeted by a male supervisor who hugs her around the waist and kisses her on the cheek. María squirms uncomfortably. The manager laughs and moves to the next woman on the line.

María's working conditions are different from José's at Hacienda CA. Immigration status is, of course, not an issue at Hacienda BC. María has some friends whom she trusts in the workplace. Even the pace of work is different from that at Hacienda CA. However, she is confronted with more health and safety hazards, such as open flames shooting out of un-covered machines. The problem that most distresses her is the rampant sexual harassment on the shop floor. She says that production managers and supervisors are constantly harassing her. They stand next to her while she is working and touch her. They invite her to dinner, and if she rejects the offer, they treat her unfairly the next day or dock her pay for being late, which they would not ordinarily do. María also complains that managers pit darker- and lighter-skinned women against each other. She is tired of managers' advances and favoritism, but she does not feel that she can af-ford to lose her job because steady employment in Baja California is hard to find.

Unlike José and Eugenio at the Hacienda CA factory, María and An-tonio are represented by a union. However, they have never seen a union representative. María describes the union as a "ghost union." It exists, but it is not there to defend or protect workers. Changes in workplace conditions are negotiated by individual workers and managers.

As a single mother earning only $1 per hour, María finds it extremely challenging to live in Baja California, where the cost of living is higher— because of proximity to the United States—than in other parts of Mexico. Her single salary is insufficient to cover the costs of rent, child care, trans-portation, food, and clothing. Fortunately, her neighbor is a retired older woman who does not charge her very much to take care of the children. María hopes to cross the border some day when her children are older and the border is less dangerous and to obtain a higher paying job in the United States.

At Hacienda BC, women, who are often single mothers, are forced to compete with each other for job stability. They earn substantially lower wages than men and have to endure extensive sexual harassment. The few men who work there, on the other hand, have different job titles and the possibility of upward mobility. They earn significantly higher wages and have more independence.

José, Eugenio, María, and Antonio are linked by their transnational employer, and yet they do not know of the others' existence. They lead very different work and family lives despite the fact that they work in factories owned by the same corporation. José and Eugenio work under regular vigilance and strict discipline. However, unlike Eugenio, José is constantly intimidated because of his immigration status. María and Antonio work in a factory with more flexibility and less enforced discipline. However, María constantly has to endure sexual harassment and favoritism.

Why do two different kinds of factory regimes emerge despite the factories being owned by the same corporation and producing the same product? This book examines transnational production by comparing the shop floors of this Mexican transnational tortilla manufacturer on both sides of the U.S.-Mexico border. I refer to the transnational corporation as Tortimundo; the two subsidiaries in each country are TortiUS and TortiMX. The U.S. factory is Hacienda CA, and the Mexican factory is Hacienda BC. I explore how the mass production of tortillas has both led to the erosion of traditional tortilla-making techniques and created new forms of labor exploitation. I also expose the fundamental role of the state, labor markets, and race, class, and gender dynamics in the construction of factory regimes. The stories of the workers sketched above reflect the different ways in which managers at Hacienda exercise labor control. The existing literature on the labor process, state, and transnational production all provide some insight that can help explain the differences in the two Hacienda factories.

The Labor Process

Scholars of the labor process have traditionally sought to understand the organization and nature of work by viewing it through a class lens. This theoretical approach has concentrated on the process of labor control. Karl Marx argued long ago·that employers are able to extract surplus value from workers because of the inherently coercive nature of work organization under capitalism: workers have no alternative but to sell their labor power. Because there were no worker protections enforced by the state at the time of Marx's writing, there was no buffer between workers and employers. This led to fundamentally coercive factory regimes.

In his landmark book, *The Politics of Production,* Burawoy (1985) theorizes the relationship between the state and the shop floor. He argues that through different stages of economic development different kinds of factory or production regimes have emerged to extract labor from workers. A *factory regime,* according to Burawoy (1985, 8), comprises both the labor process (the organization of work) and the political and ideological apparatuses of production (those that regulate production). In capitalist labor relations, the character of these factory regimes has shifted from *despotic* to *hegemonic,* and finally to *hegemonic despotism.* Nineteenth-century sweatshops are the quintessential example of a despotic regime (one operated primarily through coercion). However, Burawoy (1985) argues that with new worker protections, such as unemployment insurance and the legal right to unionize, which was initiated by the state in the early to mid-twentieth century, employers could no longer be as unscrupulous as they had been previously. Workers now had mechanisms by which to hold employers to a certain standard of decency. If employers acted in overly coercive ways, workers could file grievances or leave their jobs and receive welfare benefits; thus, employers had to find new ways of maintaining labor control. They did so by shifting to hegemonic regimes operated by consent instead of coercion. Such hegemonic factory regimes obscure the relations of exploitation and the extraction of surplus value by making workers complicit in their own exploitation. The next shift occurred with the advent of globalization. Under hegemonic despotism, despite worker protection policies, employers could extract concessions from workers by threatening to shut down the factory and move offshore. Burawoy (1976, 1985) identifies one industry that has not shifted from despotic to hegemonic work arrangements: California agriculture. The reasons, he argues, are that agriculture has largely been exempt from federal labor legislation and that workers in the industry are often undocumented. In this industry we still witness substantial despotism.

Burawoy provides us with an insightful analysis of the state and factory regimes, but his class-only approach overlooks the complexity of race and gender on the shop floor. In this book, I argue that the processes of racialization and gender are intimately connected at the point of production, where workers' and managers' subjectivities produce and reproduce these notions on the shop floor. I also expand on Burawoy's analysis of the state to show how punitive state policies shape contemporary factory regimes. Finally, I broaden his analysis of immigrant farm workers by arguing that despotic control has, and continues to be, a dominant form of labor control in other industries that employ significant numbers of undocumented workers.

In *Gender and the South China Miracle,* Lee (1998) compares a factory in Hong Kong and a factory in Shenzhen, China, both owned by the same transnational electronics manufacturer. Different production regimes emerge across the border. The regime in Hong Kong is one of "familial hegemony," whereas the one in Shenzhen is characterized by "localistic despotism." She poses the question, "Why do two regimes of production emerge, given so many similarities across the two factories?" (Lee 1998, 9). Lee challenges Burawoy's argument about the role of the state in the labor process by arguing that the state in Hong Kong is noninterventionist and the state in Shenzhen does not have the capacity to regulate enterprises. She argues that it is the labor market much more than the state that shapes the two different factory regimes in her study. Lee also forcefully shows, unlike Burawoy (1985), how gender is central to the production process.

Lee's (1998) work was one of the first inspirations for this book. I found her argument about the state very provocative, and I wanted to see what I could find in the context of the U.S.-Mexico border. Lee's main contribution to this theoretical tradition is to consider how labor markets and gender, not simply the state, produce variations in factory regimes. While I find her arguments about the labor market convincing, I fear she may have too hastily dismissed the role of the state in her case studies. I argue that, in fact, state nonintervention or indirect intervention is a strategic policy of the state, one that plays a role in shaping labor markets and shop-floor regimes.

In *Genders in Production,* Salzinger (2003) also argues that gender is produced at the point of production. She expands the analysis by bringing to light the variability of gender in global production. Salzinger studied three

factories in Ciudad Juarez and one in Santa María. In each of these factories, gender is produced and reproduced differently based on the strategies of managers and the agency of workers. At Panoptimex, workers
most closely resemble the stereotypes of the "typical" maquiladora worker,
namely "docile women." At Particimex, the gendered regime is structured
around women's independence and decision-making ability. The An-
dromex factory employs a mix of female and male labor, but in this case,
the gendered regime is constructed around masculinized production. Finally, at Anarchomex the workforce is predominantly male, but the shop-
floor environment is such that managers feminize the work of all workers.
One of her main contributions to this subject is to show that the image of
docile, nimble-fingered women in global assembly plants is not a reality.
Rather, it is a managerial fantasy.

Salzinger (2003) provides a very insightful analysis into the ways in which
managers use gendered discourses to produce different kinds of gendered
regimes. However, she does not elaborate on why this is important or why
this makes a difference in the context of the four factories she studied.
Furthermore, she largely leaves out the role of the state and race/ethnicity
in the production of her four case studies. This book expands on her work
by illustrating how the different ways gender is produced on the shop floor
and between factories give managers different opportunities for coercive
or hegemonic control.

In his study of high-tech factories in the Philippines, McKay (2006) ana-
lyzes the interaction between states, labor markets, and gender. He argues
that technological change, competition, and contradictions in production
generate a range of organizational strategies beyond the despotic, hegemonic dichotomy. At Allied-Power, the work is labor intensive and the
regime is despotic. The regime at Storage Ltd. is panoptic, because of its
heavy surveillance of the workforce, but the company offers relatively high
wages and benefits. Integrated Production operates by using a "peripheral
human resource work regime." Here, control is facilitated by a combination
of surveillance and technology mixed with a human resources approach
of positive incentives. Finally, Discrete Manufacturing has a "collectively
negotiated work regime," where labor-intensive work organization is negotiated with a highly unionized workforce. McKay (2006) also contends
that the restructuring of work has broadened and extended labor control
outside the factory. Finally, he maintains that industry and the state shape

local labor markets to reproduce "the social and gendered relations of flexible accumulation" (McKay 2006, 4).

McKay (2006) comes closest to weaving together all of the factors that create variation in labor regimes. He argues, as I do, that variation in factory regimes must be viewed by bringing together an analysis of the state, labor market, and gender. Here I add an analysis of how racialization of labor is intimately tied to these other factors.

In short, this book provides two main contributions to the labor process literature. First, I address the issue of how race and immigration status are produced at the point of production. Second, I illustrate the dynamic interaction between the state, labor markets, and race, gender, and class in the production of labor regimes. In particular, I illustrate the unique role of the state in the context of the U.S.-Mexico border.

The State: Powerful or Weak?

The recent literature on the labor process and women and work, with the exception of McKay (2006), has generally failed to problematize the role of the state. Salzinger (2003), Lee (1998), Davies (1990), and other scholars whose studies build on Michael Burawoy's work on the labor process have largely ignored or downplayed the role of the state in their analyses of factory regimes. The state, however, is central to Burawoy's key distinction between despotic and hegemonic factory regimes.

Since the 1990s, debates have raged over the significance of the state. Many globalization theorists, as well as heads of transnational corporations, have predicted the demise of the nation-state (Ohmae 1996; Strange 1996; Cox 1996). Globalization, in their view, has created worldwide economic integration, leading to the decline of the state. These scholars argue that the declining power of the state is inevitable in today's globalized world.

Others have argued that the state has retained its primacy.[4] This strong state theory argues that accounts of globalization have been greatly exaggerated and that nation-states are in fact critical players in the process of economic development. Weiss (1998) argues that, in a vein similar to that explored by Skocpol (1985), there is unevenness in state capacity to respond to different pressures, but that "far from becoming an anachronism, state capability has today become an important advantage in international competition" (Weiss 1998, 5).

However, as Robinson (2004, 4) points out, it is simplistic to view the state in such dualistic terms. As he argues, "the nation-state is neither retaining its primacy, nor disappearing, but becoming transformed and absorbed into the larger structure of a transnational state."[5] While I agree with Robinson (2004) that the state is being transformed, in my view the state operates both within the context of transnational structures and locally. Borders do matter.

Transnational Production and Border Studies

The border is a muddled region, where the beginning of one nation-state and the end of another gets lost in the flurry of people and goods crossing over it every day. As border scholars have shown, this arbitrary line also marks the difference between higher wages and lower wages; a highly developed infrastructure (good roads, safe water, etc) and a less developed infrastructure; and different legal, social, political, and economic climates.[6] When scholars began looking at the new international division of labor (Fröbel, Kreye, and Heinrichs 1980) in the late 1970s and 1980s, the U.S.-Mexico border region and the Global South in general provided rich sites through which to explore globalization and the exploitation and feminization of labor (Fernandez Kelly 1983; Fuentes and Ehrenreich 1983; Ruiz and Tiano 1987). These scholars produced landmark studies that brought the severe exploitation of women workers in the Global South to the attention of the American public. Since their ground-breaking works first appeared, the amount of literature on transnational production and border studies has exploded. Hundreds of books have been written about maquiladoras and export-processing zones worldwide.[7] This book contributes to and expands on the vast literature on transnational production by looking at how a factory owned by the same transnational employer on both sides of the U.S.-Mexico border constructs different kinds of factory regimes.

In short, the scholars in the labor process, state, and transnational production literatures, all tell part of the story and leave other parts of the story out. In this book, I combine these areas of study in an attempt to provide a more comprehensive look at transnational production and managerial control. In what follows, I present my theoretical framework.

Two Tortilla Factory Regimes

In this book I seek to demonstrate the state's central role in the labor process by looking at racialized and gendered aspects of state policies, especially in the U.S.-Mexico border region.[8] In the era of global capitalism—marked by the rise of neoliberalism[9] and concomitant dismantling of the Keynesian state—Tortimundo draws on state policies, racialized and gendered labor markets, and race, class, and gender dynamics produced on the shop floor to create different ways of maintaining labor control. Particularly central to labor control on both sides of the U.S.-Mexico border is immigration policy, which serves to create a vulnerable group of undocumented men at Hacienda CA and a vulnerable group of single mothers at Hacienda BC.

Unlike in most of the literature on the labor process, here I argue that the factory regimes at Hacienda CA and Hacienda BC rely on hegemonic and despotic control coexisting on the shop floor. This provides a more nuanced analysis of labor control. The main logic of control in both factories is therefore "divide and conquer." We see this especially in how different types of workers are pitted against each other by gender, race, and immigration status on the shop floor. I have named the labor regime in each factory according to the main axis of division and control.

Figure 1 presents my theoretical framework. On the U.S. side of the border, state policies shape both the local labor market and the factory regime at Hacienda CA (both through and independent of its effects on the labor market). At the meso-level, the local labor market is segregated and stratified along racial and gendered lines.[10] This kind of stratification also influences managerial opportunities for labor control. However, the influence of the labor market on employers is not unidirectional. Employer preferences for a predominantly male immigrant workforce also shape the local labor market by producing demand for these particular kinds of workers. At the micro-, shop-floor level, managers' and workers' racialized and gendered ideas give managers the opportunity to divide and conquer, therefore weakening solidarity among workers. Hacienda CA is

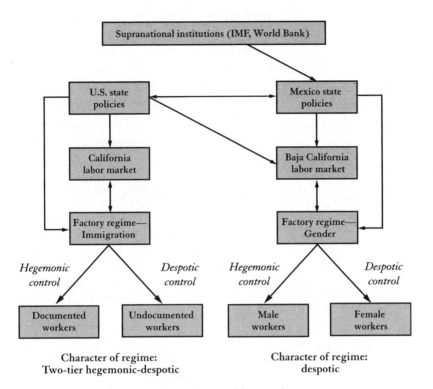

Figure 1. Theorectical framework

characterized by what I call an *immigration regime.* Managers use immigration policy, the immigrant status of workers, and a racialized labor market to enforce two kinds of labor control on the shop floor. Managers use hegemonic control with documented workers at Hacienda CA, whereas they use despotic control with undocumented workers in the factory. This leads to a two-tier regime in which hegemony and despotism coexist.

Let us briefly examine the immigration regime at Hacienda CA. Labor control at Hacienda CA is characterized by an immigration regime because managers use state policies such as Social Security Administration's No-Match letters[11] and the militarization of the border (Parenti 1999; Nevins 2002) to their benefit. Managers also rely on a segmented labor market, where a majority of immigrants are pushed into the secondary labor market (Gordon, Edwards, and Reich 1982), as well as the racialized status of immigrants in the United States, ironically a status that managers themselves occupy (Chang 2000; Glenn 2002; Maher 2002). These factors are used to pit documented and undocumented workers against each other and relegate undocumented workers to the lowest-paid jobs and the worst shifts in the factory. Pitting workers against each other is possible and effective, not only because of state policies and labor market conditions but because of the gendered and racialized notions held by managers and workers regarding how work should be organized, who should be treated well, and what is considered appropriate in the factory environment. As I have argued, a two-tier structure is created inside the factory where documented workers make higher wages and labor under better working conditions and undocumented workers are at the bottom of the barrel.

Unlike Burawoy's (1985) model of the shift from despotism to hegemony to hegemonic despotism, the two-tier structure of labor control at Hacienda CA illustrates how, within one factory regime, despotism and hegemony can operate simultaneously.

On the Mexican side of the border, at the macro-level, Mexico's state policies are strongly influenced by supranational institutions such as the International Monetary Fund (IMF) and World Bank, U.S. and Mexican negotiated policies such as the North American Free Trade Agreement (NAFTA), U.S. immigration policy, and internal political dynamics. These policies both directly and indirectly impact the local labor market and the factory regime (both through and independent of the labor market) at Hacienda BC. At the meso-level, the local labor market is stratified by gender (Cravey 1998), and at Hacienda BC, this creates one of the primary opportunities for coercive labor control practices. Employer preferences for single women and single mothers also affect the labor market by producing demand for the highly coveted managerial fantasy of a docile, female workforce. At the micro-level, the interaction between state policies and the gendered and racialized subjectivities of the managers and workers also produce various opportunities to control labor. This factory is typified by what I call a *gender regime*. Managers draw from a feminized labor market (in part created by neoliberal economic policy), U.S. immigration policy, and Mexican labor law to produce a regime where women are sexually harassed and have to compete with each other for job stability. Similar to the California factory, managers at Hacienda BC use hegemonic control with male workers and despotic control with female workers. However, because of the predominance of women workers in production, the area of the factory in which labor control is most central, the overall character of the regime is despotic.

Let us look at how these processes work in practice at the Mexico factory. Hacienda BC is characterized by a gender regime because the central mode of control in this factory has been to force women to compete with each other over job stability. Managers have taken advantage of a feminized labor market and created a sexualized and racialized work environment whereby women are competing with each other for managerial attention and dark- and light-skinned women are pitted against each other. When women do not respond positively to managers' advances, they are disciplined. Many women feel that they are at risk of losing their secure employment. Despite legal protection against sexual harassment, the institutionalized structure of labor law in Mexico makes it difficult for women to contest it.

Hacienda BC is interested in hiring a predominantly female workforce because women are the most vulnerable in the Baja California labor market. Ninety percent of the women workers at Hacienda BC come from other parts of Mexico, often as a direct result of NAFTA. After the United States flooded Mexico with cheap imported corn, many families lost farms and were forced to migrate. As a result of the increased militarization of the border, many husbands of the workers at Hacienda BC crossed the border, and as a result, women were left as single mothers in Baja California with no familial networks. Most women in the factory had previously worked in the maquiladora industry, but because of competition with China and other countries with even cheaper labor, the maquiladora industry grew unstable.[12] These women sought work in stable national industries such as tortilla production.

Managers at Hacienda BC understand (and have helped construct) women's vulnerable position in the labor market. They know that many of the women in the factory are single mothers who need stable jobs. Furthermore, they have created a sexualized work environment in which women feel they must participate to stabilize their positions in the factory.

As previously stated, Hacienda BC also has hegemony and despotism operating side by side, but the factory regime is overwhelmingly coercive. The regime is centered on hiring women to work on the assembly line, paying them low wages, and forcing them to compete with each other for job stability. Coercion is prevalent because of women's labor market vulnerability, which compels them to sell their labor power because no protective direct state intervention gives them real alternatives to withhold it (Burawoy 1979, 1985; Piore 1979; Gordon, Edwards, and Reich 1982). Men are largely invisible in the factory regime at Hacienda BC.

In short, the dynamic interaction between the different levels of analysis, the state, labor market, and shop-floor politics in each country provides managers of each factory different opportunities to control labor, opportunities that differ between the two factories as well as within each factory location. I am not suggesting that these particular state policies, labor market conditions, and shop-floor politics can produce only these two kinds of factory regimes; I am simply illustrating how and why the convergence of this variety of factors give managers varied opportunities to construct different kinds of factory regimes. By producing two different factory regimes at Hacienda CA and Hacienda BC, managers at Tortimundo are able to capitalize on what each country has to offer in order to maintain the corporation's competitive edge in the world market and expand its profit margin.

Methodology

This book was the result of my interest in the struggles of immigrant workers. Before entering graduate school, I was an organizer for the Union of Needletrades Industrial and Textile Employees (UNITE). At the union I worked with immigrant garment workers from across Latin America. Being an immigrant myself, I found their struggles deeply compelling. After entering graduate school in 1997, I wanted to continue doing work related to immigrant worker struggles, focusing on immigrant workers in manufacturing, in an industry that had been relatively unexplored. The idea of studying the tortilla industry came to me after talking to people who had been involved with the Manufacturing Organizing Project (MOP). Initially, I intended to concentrate on the potential for organizing in this industry.

As I was beginning to do my research, I read Ching Kwan Lee's (1998) book *Gender and the South China Miracle: Two Worlds of Factory Women* and became intrigued with her research design, which explored one corporation on both sides of a border. After finishing her book, I commented on the project to an organizer at MOP, who then told me that Tortimundo was a transnational company and operated on both sides of the U.S.-Mexico border. I could hardly restrain my excitement and decided to refocus the project as a binational comparison of the industry. I had read many studies of U.S. corporations that operated in Mexico, but I had not come across a comparison of a Mexican transnational operating on both sides of the U.S.-Mexico border. Furthermore, the two cases were particularly interesting, not only because of the variation across the border but also because of the variation of labor control strategies within each factory.

Although Tortimundo has many plant locations, I chose to study its California and Baja California (Mexico) factories for several reasons. First, these two factories represent the largest tortilla-manufacturing plants that the corporation owns (in each country). They are, in effect, flagship factories. Second, both are located in cities that are in the heart of global production. This is an important factor for studying the role of the state, race, and gender. Third, although access to this corporation was difficult, and they were hesitant to give me access to more than one plant in each country, based on numerous conversations with management, I believe that the California and Baja California plants are representative of other Hacienda tortilla factories in each region.

In developing the project design, I felt that the most suitable methodology was going to be ethnographic fieldwork along with in-depth interviews and document analysis.[13] I wanted to conduct participant observation because this method would allow me to observe shop-floor dynamics in both factories that would not otherwise be captured by interviews (because of various limitations of interview data). However, I also wanted to gain a complex picture of the factory and the industry through interviews (that I would not be able to capture with observation) with industry officials, managers, supervisors, line leaders, and workers. Observations and interviews occurred between October 2001 and December 2003, with follow-up interviews as late as 2005.

I conducted in-depth interviews with two of Tortimundo's senior executives (in the United States and Mexico) and four factory-level managers (in both countries). I had informal conversations and interviews with six supervisors and line leaders between the two locations. I interviewed twelve production workers and four truck drivers at the Hacienda CA plant and ten production workers and two warehouse workers at the Hacienda BC plant. I also interviewed two people at the Tortilla Industry Association, a specialist at a union prevention consulting group, and five organizers with MOP. Each of the interviews lasted between two and four hours.

I spent three months at Hacienda CA and nearly three months at Hacienda BC conducting shop-floor observations. Even though I was not allowed to work in these factories and experience the working conditions myself, I was able to spend full days (from two to four days per week) observing the shop floor at each location. During the fieldwork, I also attended two national Tortilla Industry Association meetings, where I learned about key players, labor practices, and technology in the tortilla industry. I was also able to make contacts with smaller tortilla manufacturers.

I also had access to and analyzed a wide variety of documents. These included internal company files, the company's website, newspaper articles, and organizing files for the MOP. Internal company documents included financial statements, recruitment materials, productivity calculations, and the company's employee newsletter. Data sources on manufacturing wages as a whole for the cities where the two plants are located were gathered from the Census of Manufactures 1997, Instituto Nacional de Estadística Geografía e Informática,[14] and the Bureau of Labor Statistics Current Population Survey.

Ethnographic research presents many difficulties, some of which include gaining access to the research site, ethical considerations about the impact of the research on people that one observes and interviews, and the ability to generalize results.

Despite my extensive experience working with immigrant workers and usually feeling comfortable in that position, I stuck out like a sore thumb in the California factory and even more so at the Baja California factory. What was a light-skinned Latina from Chile doing studying predominantly Mexican immigrant male tortilla workers in California and female tortilla workers in Baja California, Mexico? We don't even eat tortillas in Chile! It took several months of being subsumed in the research before I became more comfortable (but never entirely) with my position in the factory vis-à-vis managers and workers.

I gained access to Tortimundo almost by sheer luck. I had no previous relationship or contacts with the corporation, so it was very difficult to be taken seriously. I spent three months calling the U.S. corporate headquarters every day. I spoke to the same secretary daily. When I was just about to give up on this project, the secretary managed to get me an interview with one of the senior executives at Tortimundo. Frankly, I think she was probably sick and tired of me harassing her for so long. Before she could change her mind, I was on a plane to corporate headquarters. The senior executive I met with was enthusiastic to have a Latina study a Mexican corporation. He reiterated many times that he thought that the industry was understudied. He also expressed frustration that more researchers were not interested in successful Mexican companies. I used his enthusiasm to my advantage and immediately asked for access to the California and Baja California factories. We were able to negotiate a relationship with the California factory almost immediately. Baja California was a little harder because I had to communicate directly with a senior executive in Mexico.

Eventually, I was granted access to both locations. The one condition of my right of entry was that I would not have access to workers. This created a serious problem for me. If I interviewed workers first, and then began the shop-floor observations, I would run the risk that the company would find out that I had spoken to workers and therefore deny me access to the shop floor. On the other hand, if I conducted shop-floor observations first, and then interviewed workers, I would run the risk those workers would see me as a company spy. There was no good solution to the problem. However, access to the shop floor was a must, so I began with factory observations and gained access to workers later.

Gaining access to workers proved to be just as difficult as I thought it would be. Many workers distrusted me because they had already seen me walking around the factory with management. In some ways I never gained full access to the lives of some of the workers with whom I built relationships. Nevertheless, workers opened up to me despite it being a risky proposition. In California I had an easier time gaining access to workers than in Baja California because of the union. Several of the unionized truck drivers that I interviewed had contacts inside the factory. I was able to meet with workers in their homes, coffee shops, and at ceviche stands in California. On numerous occasions, workers would meet me at the factory and then drive me to some undisclosed location. This was a bit intimidating at first, but I slowly grew accustomed to uncertainty. They were all taking serious risks in talking to me, so I in turn had to be flexible about where and how I was going to get the information. Several truck drivers were bold enough to take me on their distribution routes.

At the Hacienda BC factory, I had no direct access to workers. Managers at the plant told me early on that I could observe the shop floor and talk to them, but I could not talk to the workers. This forced me to stand in the streets near the factory and near bus stops where I could access the factory workers. Many workers were quite suspicious of me at first. They had already seen me talking to managers inside the plant. After about a month, I was able to get interviews with four workers. All of these interviews were conducted on side streets near the factory or at their homes, away from managers. After these initial interviews and after gaining their trust, these workers gave me their cell phone numbers and recruited a few more workers from the plant to talk to me. The second round of interviews were conducted in small taquerias, on the bus, and on side streets. I also conducted follow-up interviews by phone with all of the Hacienda BC workers.

Toward the end of my fieldwork at Hacienda BC, managers became hesitant about my access to the factory. I started having difficulty getting into the factory whenever I wanted, my phone calls were not being returned, and eventually I was denied entry into the factory. Fortunately, I had completed most of my fieldwork, but I was about two weeks short of completing three months in the factory. I have never been able to determine why the company denied me access. However, my suspicion is that one of the workers I interviewed told managers that I was interviewing them outside the factory. Managers might have viewed this as a violation of the agreement, but the agreement never stated that I would not have access to workers outside of the workplace, only that I could not talk to them during work hours. When I went to do follow-up interviews with managers at Hacienda CA, I was also given the cold shoulder, and phone calls were never returned.

In any sociological study, whether qualitative or quantitative, there are problems and limitations with the data. This project is certainly no exception. Building relationships with workers and having them agree to interviews was extremely difficult, and this created numerous problems. First, I was not able to interview as many workers as I would have liked. Second, at Hacienda CA I was only able to interview workers who had connections with the truck drivers. Because truck drivers knew mostly pro-union workers, this might have created some bias in the interviews. Third, I paid workers at both factories a small stipend for their participation. This may have led them to answer my questions more favorably than they would have otherwise.

I tried to correct for these limitations in the interview data through ethnographic observations. I did a significant amount of observation in both factories, during different shifts and in different areas of production. Most of my interviews were consistent with my own observations of dynamics on the shop floor. Because I did fieldwork first and interviews later, I was not as influenced by individuals' accounts of shop-floor dynamics. My extensive research on the industry overall also helped to correct for bias in interviews with managers as well as workers. I was also able to get a broader picture of workers at Hacienda CA through archival data from the 1990 organizing campaign from MOP.

I have several regrets with regard to this project. I wish I had pushed for more access to important meetings between different managers and supervisors. I also wish I had pressed to obtain an interview from the CEO of Tortimundo. I think both of these steps would have added to the richness to the analysis. I also regret not being able to engage in actual work inside the factory. The company was worried about liability implications and therefore would not allow me to work on the assembly line. Despite these limitations, I am confident about the overall analysis presented in this book.

Difficult ethical issues are embedded in qualitative research, and I have had to navigate through many of them. I have protected the identity of all interviewees—managers, supervisors, line leaders, workers, organizers, and industry officials—by using pseudonyms and changing the identifying details such as job titles. However, confidentiality, in terms of the corporation, has been most difficult. The tortilla industry is relatively small, and this corporation is one of the larger players. I was careful to explain the project and possible risks of participating in interviews to all of the people I interviewed. I am confident that these workers and managers understood what they were getting into. Furthermore, managers and supervisors were given explicit permission from the corporation to contribute to this study. Since there are fewer managers/supervisors than workers, they are at greater risk of being identified. As a result, I have alternated between the terms manager and supervisor so that their identities are more protected.

In this book I have attempted to link the micro-level processes of shop-floor dynamics and labor control with the macro-level process of neoliberal globalization by using the extended case method. This is "a method which deploys participant observation to locate everyday life in its extralocal and historical context" (Burawoy 1998). Through this methodology, I have extended the theoretical analysis in the already rich labor-process literature by once again including the state and also theorizing the role of race, gender, and class at the point of production.

Organization of the Book

In the following chapters, I discuss the ways in which the state, race, class, and gender produce differently despotic factory regimes on both sides of the U.S.-Mexico border.

In Chapter 2, I explore the historical development of the corn and tortilla industry in Mexico and the rise of Tortimundo. Changes in this industry due to a shift toward neoliberal policy in Mexico in the 1980s substantially shaped the ability of Tortimundo to grow into a transnational operation. At the same time, the growing Latina/o population in the United States and the reinvention of the tortilla from an ethnic food to a more versatile product led to the increasing popularity of the tortilla in the United States. Tortimundo was able to successfully situate itself in this growing market.

Chapter 3 provides both a historical and contemporary overview of racialized and gendered state policies in the United States and Mexico. Additionally, I discuss the relationship between the United States and Mexico, with a particular focus on colonialism. This chapter sets the context for understanding the role of the state in the two different factory regimes that are situated along the U.S.-Mexico border.

Chapters 4 and 5 are the two factory case studies, Hacienda CA and Hacienda BC. These chapters describe the working conditions in each factory and the different managerial control strategies that result in two different kinds of labor regimes. Using data from observations inside the factories and in-depth interviews with managers and workers, I argue that control at Hacienda CA is dominated by a despotic immigration regime in which immigration status is used to force undocumented immigrant workers into the least desirable positions. Despotism at Hacienda BC, on the other hand, is dominated by sexualized control. Women on the shop floor are constantly sexually harassed and are pitted against each other.

Chapter 6 examines workers' resistance to their oppressive work environments. I discuss both individual and collective action. I also evaluate the political environments in California and Baja California, Mexico, that lend themselves to different organizing strategies in each factory. Chapter 7 sums up the findings of the study. I return to the original research questions and discuss the broader implications of the study.

2

The Political Economy of Corn and Tortillas

Enlightened elites used corn in this sense: as a contemptible object subject to discrimination. Corn carried the stigma of being alien, strange, poor. The wealthy judged corn and declared it to be guilty. The poor, on the contrary, opened their doors to it, embraced it, and adopted it. Corn shared the fate of the poor, of those mixed race, of the unchaste. (Warman 2003, xiii)

The Tortilla and Corn Flour Industry in Mexico

Tortillas are a staple in Mexico with a long and rich tradition in indigenous culture. The essential character of corn as a food staple and as a cultural symbol makes the production of corn, corn flour, and tortillas critical to the Mexican economy. In fact, the corn–tortilla industry currently makes up 1 percent of Mexico's gross domestic product.

For centuries tortillas have been produced by traditional methods. First, the dried corn is washed and cooked in water and powdered limestone. After this mixture sits for twelve hours, it is rinsed to remove the skin. This processed corn is called the *nixtamal* (corn that has been cooked in limestone). The nixtamal is then ground. The ground corn mixture is called *masa,* and this is the raw tortilla dough that is cooked on a comal (clay or metal griddle) to make tortillas (Bendesky 2005). Historically, tortillas have been produced by women in their homes or in small street corner tortillerias. Since the 1970s this process has been facilitated by the invention of nixtamalized corn flour. This corn flour is a manufactured product that only needs the addition of water to achieve the masa stage. It can then be cooked just like masa prepared in the traditional way. Tortilla production in the home and in tortillerias across Mexico and Latin America has been revolutionized because of nixtamalized corn flour. Between 1991 and 1998 alone, the share of corn tortillas produced from nixtamalized corn flour increased from 21 percent to 51 percent (Rosas Peña 2005). This increase can be explained in part by the durability of dried corn flour, which lasts roughly five months, versus fresh dough, which lasts only a couple of hours.

Because corn and tortillas are essential to the Mexican economy and diet, tortilla manufacturing has long been subsidized by the Mexican government. Food agencies were created in postrevolutionary Mexico as part of the welfare state. These agencies ensured that producers were given a good price for their harvest and that staple foods, such as tortillas, were available to consumers at affordable prices (Ochoa 2000). At its peak in the 1970s and 1980s, the state food agency Compañía Nacional de Subsistencias Populares (CONASUPO) was involved in grain purchases, retail food stores, corn milling, milk reconstitution, wheat milling, rural development, storage, rural training, food-processing plants, wholesale food stores, and retail fresh fruit stores (Ochoa 2000).

In times of economic crisis, such as the 1982 peso crisis, CONASUPO subsidized food products so that millions of Mexican families could continue to put food on the table despite staggering drops in real wages and increases in unemployment. Enrique Ochoa (2000, 8) correctly points out that "food policy serves as an indirect subsidy to the private sector as well as an object of social welfare." During the economic crisis, CONASUPO instituted various programs to help low-income groups (those making less than two times the minimum wage). At first, CONASUPO reduced the price of tortillas in government stores by 25 percent. In 1986 the program was refined to give low-income families coupons with which to purchase tortillas at a reduced rate. In 1989 the government changed the program once again. Under the new program, CONASUPO gave tortillas to 3.2 million poor families and began liberalizing the price of tortillas for the general public (Ochoa 2000).

From the mid-1980s onward, Mexico pursued a neoliberal strategy to end its economic problems. This policy included attracting foreign investment, opening Mexico to the world market, and rapid privatization.

Many of CONASUPO's industries were privatized, while others were eliminated altogether. The elimination of price controls on corn forced CONASUPO to purchase imported corn at higher levels in order to continue subsidizing tortillas and other food products (Ochoa 2000). The North American Free Trade Agreement (NAFTA) facilitated the importation of U.S. corn to Mexico. In fact, the United States is the largest producer and exporter of corn in the world, and 25 percent of corn consumed in Mexico comes directly from the U.S. market (Warman 2003; Ribeiro 2005). After the passage of NAFTA in 1993, and with the complete dismantling of the food agency CONASUPO in 1996, the Mexican corn market was privatized and flooded with corn from firms such as Arthur Daniels Midland and Cargill-Monsanto.[1]

The results have been disastrous for Mexican corn farmers. Not only have hundreds of thousands of Mexican corn farmers been displaced (Malkin 2005), but the privatization has also taken a serious toll on the economy. According to Ribeiro (2005, 6)

> although NAFTA originally created quotas and tariffs on the importation of corn to protect [Mexican] national production, the imports of subsidized corn from the U.S. were favored by the elimination of these restrictions even before the agreed time frame. Between 1994 and 2002, the amount of corn Mexico imported from the U.S. exceeded the quotas by more than 15 million tons. The fiscal loss resulting from the exemptions from tariffs in this period totaled US$2,790,000,000, equivalent to more than double the subsidies from Procampo [the national agency supporting the agro-food industry] in 2002.[2]

The loosening of quotas and tariffs on corn in Mexico has led small corn farmers to buy more imported corn. At the same time, the government began to lift the price controls on tortillas. As a result of these two interrelated policies, the price of tortillas inched up between 1994 and 1999. As a final blow to the poor and working-class citizens of Mexico, in 1999 the Mexican government ended the historic subsidy of tortillas, which for decades had totaled approximately MX$1 billion per year (Aspin 1996; Thompson 1999). The price of tortillas has risen dramatically. According to Rosas Peña (2005), the price of tortillas (per kilo) has gone from MX$0.75 in 1995 to between MX$4.80 and MX$8.00 in 2005 (the price varies regionally).

The latest tortilla crisis occurred in early 2007, when tortilla prices increased by 40 percent in one month (Enriquez 2007). Tortillas went from MX$6 per kilo in December to MX$10 per kilo in January (Orsi 2007). The result has been disastrous; many one wage-earner families have had to spend a third of their income on tortillas (Roig-Franzia 2007). The cause for the latest spike in tortilla prices is believed to be a result of increased international demand for corn to be used to make ethanol (especially by the United States) and monopolistic practices by Mexico's largest corn and tortilla producers (McKinley 2007; Roig-Franzia 2007; Orsi 2007). In 2007 thousands of people marched in Mexico City to protest the dramatic increases in the price of tortillas and call for price controls (BBC News 2007; Associated Press 2007). As a result of the massive protest and fear of growing inflation, Felipe Calderón, the newly elected president of Mexico, struck a bargain with Mexico's largest corn and tortilla producers, U.S. corn corporations in Mexico, and large supermarkets. In the pact these corporations agreed to cap tortilla prices at MX$8.5 per kilo. This price is still significantly more than the cost of tortillas a few months back. It is important to note that Calderón did not implement price controls; rather, he and corporations essentially made a "gentleman's agreement" (McKinley 2007, Roig Franzia 2007). Many smaller producers of tortillas have not abided by the agreement, and as a result, in numerous communities the price of tortillas remains high.

Today, approximately 225,000 people work in the corn flour and tortilla industries. It is one of the largest industries in Mexico. There are currently some 45,000 tortillerias across Mexico (Rosas Peña 2005). Despite the large numbers of tortillerias, a significant minority of the tortilla industry and a majority of the corn flour industry are in the hands of a few Mexican transnational corporations that have benefited from neoliberal policies, especially the widespread privatization of food industries formally under CONASUPO. When the industries under CONASUPO were sold, these few transnational corporations were able to buy them for bargain prices and turn them into very successful profit-generating ventures.

Today, a large percentage of tortillas in Mexico are made from nixtamalized corn flour, or powdered masa (Warman 2003). In fact, approximately half of the tortillerias use powdered masa to produce their tortillas. This is a huge labor- and cost-saving tactic. By using the powdered masa, the tortilla makers need only add water, then form and cook the tortillas, rather than use the elaborate traditional method. Even though powdered masa is more expensive than corn, because small tortillerias can produce more tortillas quickly, they save time and money. While this labor- and cost-saving technique is efficient, the quality and taste of the tortilla change drastically. It is generally accepted that a tortilla produced using the traditional method tastes much better than one made with powdered masa. While the country and the Mexican government have been moving in the direction of mass-produced tortillas, there is still some resistance to powdered masa, particularly because of a concern about genetically modified foods. In some instances powdered masa has been found to contain genetically modified corn (from the United States). There is a growing movement against genetically modified corn and toward the preservation of traditional methods. A group of small- and medium-sized Mexican corn producers has taken matters into its own hands and founded an organization called Nuestro Maíz (Our Corn). These farmers are committed to producing corn in Mexico free of any genetically modified seeds. They have also set up a network of over 131 tortillerias that are committed to producing tortillas using the traditional method and 100 percent Mexican corn (Velázquez 2005). The organization has a long struggle ahead of it, particularly given the economic and political power wielded by transnational Mexican corporations such as Tortimundo. Nuestro Maíz is a very small social movement and has not yet had an impact on large transnational corn and tortilla producers.

How have changes in the corn and tortilla industry facilitated the growth and success of Tortimundo?

Tortimundo and Its Factories

Tortimundo is a publicly held corporation that owns dozens of tortilla factories, corn and wheat flour mills, and tortilla machine manufacturing plants throughout the United States, Mexico, Central America, South America, and Europe. Tortimundo also opened a tortilla factory in Asia in 2005. This transnational corporation is almost entirely vertically integrated, producing everything from tortilla production machinery to fried tortilla products.

The owner of the corporation, whom I will call Don Enrique Hernandez, had humble beginnings. He came from a working-class family.

Don Enrique entered the Mexican corn flour industry in the 1940s, but it was not until the mid-1970s that his small business grew into the empire it is today.

In the 1970s Tortimundo entered the corn flour market in Central America, the tortilla market in California, and the tortilla machinery market in Mexico. By the mid-1990s Tortimundo could claim to be one of the largest tortilla manufacturers in the world (Major Metropolitan Newspaper 1996a).[3] It was also a significant player in corn and wheat flour production. The corporation had its first public offering of stock in the Mexican Stock Exchange in the mid-1990s, and a few years later Tortimundo opened its first tortilla-manufacturing plant in Europe. In 2003 the corporation's net sales were in the billions of U.S. dollars, and gross profit was nearly US$1 billion (Annual Report 2003).

As the chief executive officer of a profitable Mexican transnational corporation, Don Enrique is firmly situated within the emerging structures of the transnational capitalist class. He exerts economic control in the workplace and is very involved in Mexican politics, international politics (promoting NAFTA), and in spreading the consumption of the tortilla around the world. Thanks to his phenomenal business success, Hernandez has a lavish lifestyle, including the ownership of a private jet (not unlike other Mexican elites).

However, despite Hernandez's global orientation, his empire grew in large part because of a deal negotiated with the Mexican state. Tortimundo has derived power from the subsidies, laws, and regulations of both the U.S. and Mexican governments. It would be simplistic to argue that Tortimundo has acquired all of its wealth and power *entirely* from the state, but the state played a very important role in the growth of this corporation.

Don Enrique Hernandez's lucrative tortilla manufacturing operations grew out of his corn flour empire. Tortimundo has a majority of the corn flour market share in Mexico. In part, this empire was built on the political connections between Hernandez (and other corn giants) and former Mexican President Carlos Salinas de Gortari. According to a major metropolitan newspaper, Hernandez "persuaded the Mexican government to promote his tortilla made from dehydrated corn flour instead of fresh dough." Hernandez benefited so much from the Salinas years that his "business has skyrocketed from hundreds of thousands of tons of corn flour a year in 1988 to millions of tons" (Major Metropolitan Newspaper 1996b). These subsidies totaled some US$300 million (Major Metropolitan Newspaper 1996b). Tortimundo's wealth, in part due to increased corn flour production, facilitated the process of expansion into other industries such as tortilla manufacturing, tortilla machine manufacturing, and other operations.

According to Francisco Gutiérrez, a senior executive at TortiMX (the Mexican subsidiary of Tortimundo), opening tortilla production facilities in Mexico seemed impossible in the 1970s and 1980s.

> Mexican people have their traditions. They like their tortillas and they like them fresh. In the 1970s and 1980s there were too many small corner tortillerias. Families would have their girls go to the corner to buy fresh tortillas or make them at home. At that time women weren't working as they are today. Nobody would have bought packaged tortillas.

In the early 1990s, with the potential for a new trade agreement (NAFTA), a modern Mexico, and the rapid rise of the maquila industry, the idea of opening tortilla-manufacturing plants in Mexico seemed to have tremendous potential. Gutiérrez states, "Hernandez is a visionary. He saw the potential for tortilla manufacturing in Mexico. The increasing number of maquilas would need them in their lunchrooms. Modern families with two people working, but not earning enough to hire a maid, would resort to supermarket tortillas, and NAFTA would make it easier for us to export to the U.S. market. This was his vision."

TortiMX opened tortilla-manufacturing plants throughout Mexico, beginning in 1994. The Baja California factory produces corn and wheat flour tortillas, as well as fried products such as tostadas. Its corn and wheat flour operations total dozens of plants throughout the country. Unfortunately for the corporation, tortilla manufacturing in Mexico was not as lucrative as expected. In 2004 only three of the nine tortilla-manufacturing plants remained open. According to Francisco Gutiérrez, "as Mexicans we are not ready for the product. Many people still rely on the small tortillerias. Many women still stay at home. Things are changing, so we are certain that in the near future we will be able to expand the tortilla-manufacturing industry once again. While many middle-class families do not buy our bagged tortillas, they do eat our fresh tortillas in the supermarkets and purchase our fried products."

Francisco and managers that I spoke to in Mexico were determined to change the Mexican palate. Their determination is interesting because it demonstrates how this company operates. The basic dilemma is that not enough Mexicans are eating store-bought tortillas. The lack of popularity of packaged tortillas represents a significant loss of potential profit. Tortimundo is particularly concerned about this loss of profit because they have seen the potential profits derived from tortilla production in the United States. Therefore, Tortimundo is interested in the modernization of Mexico and in changing Mexican taste. Francisco has pointed out, "We want to bring Mexico into the twenty-first century." For Tortimundo (and Francisco), bringing Mexico into the twenty-first century specifically means several things: free trade, women moving into the paid labor market, and two-income families.

Managers at Hacienda BC and executives at TortiMX argue that NAFTA has not gone far enough. From their vantage point, NAFTA must treat both U.S. and Mexican corporations the same, and in 2008 the United States is benefiting most from this trade agreement. Francisco said, "You know how the Americans are. They fight for their interests first, and we have to fight for every little piece of the pie." There is no doubt that Tortimundo would operate only in Baja California if it could, because labor costs in Mexico are cheaper than those in the United States and regulations are more lax. However, Tortimundo cannot manufacture its product in Baja California for the U.S. market because it is on the wrong side of the U.S.-Mexico border. While NAFTA may have opened the border for U.S. firms to come into Mexico, it has not sufficiently opened the border for Mexican firms to come into the United States. Long lines at border checkpoints and the perishability of the product make it impossible for Hacienda BC to adequately supply the U.S. market. They hope that in the near future restrictions for Mexican companies exporting across the border will be loosened, but until then they must use secure cheap labor in the United States.

For Tortimundo, part of modernizing Mexico is to bring women workers into the paid labor market. Tortimundo's vision of a modernized labor market is similar to that of the United States and other industrialized countries. Tortimundo wants to see an economy in which maintaining a middle-class lifestyle depends on a two-income household. Francisco says, "what we need is for there to be more two-income households who earn enough to buy things like packaged tortillas, but who don't have enough money to hire a domestic worker. The reason tortillas are so popular in the U.S. is that people don't have time to prepare them themselves but also don't have the money to hire a domestic worker to prepare them. In Mexico, middle-class families often have servants that will make fresh tortillas." This quote demonstrates their careful analysis of how the Mexican economy must change in order for their product to be as successful in Mexico as it is in the United States. Tortimundo sees its profit line as intricately linked to modernizing the economy, which will ultimately help them change the Mexican palate.

Changing the Mexican palate in the absence of such an economic transformation is difficult. In the United States Tortimundo is very much focused on adapting their product to American tastes. According to Roberto Echeverría, a senior executive for TortiUS (the U.S. subsidiary of Tortimundo), "this was very easy because in the U.S. people are used to eating processed and packaged foods. That revolution happened in the 1950s with frozen entrees." When TortiUS started producing tortillas in the United States, the concern was how to popularize an ethnic food rather than how to market a packaged product. In Mexico the problem is the opposite. The company's greatest need is to convince consumers that packaged products can be as good, if not better, than fresh ones. Instead of catering to Mexican tastes, what TortiMX (the Mexican subsidiary of Tortimundo) is trying to do is to reinvent the Mexican palate. Tortimundo was successful at the mass production of tortillas in the United States, and they appear to be using a U.S.-style business plan in Mexico. It seems that Tortimundo is a Mexican company trying to impersonate a U.S. company that is impersonating Mexican culture. Because making these changes in the absence of economic change is difficult, until that change happens TortiMX must find different methods of selling and promoting their product.

Ironically, the strategy of reinventing the Mexican palate has not worked. In fact, changes in the Mexican economy, including the elimination of tortilla subsidies, have caused the consumption of tortillas to decline by 15 percent in Mexico while consumption has grown around the world. The increased price of tortillas, coupled with the lower quality of the product, have driven middle-class families to start consuming more bread than tortillas (SourceMex 2004).

Although Hacienda BC may not have had much success selling bagged tortillas in supermarkets, they have been successful distributing tortillas to restaurants and small tortillerias. One of their most successful operations has been selling their tortillas to the maquila sector. Every day thousands of tortillas are eaten in the lunchrooms of the maquila industry. Many of these factories provide free lunch for their employees, so even though these employees are not buying Hacienda BC's products in the store, they are eating them for lunch daily. TortiMX hopes that this familiarization process will change the Mexican palate. The operations manager at Hacienda BC says, "People are eating our product in the maquilas, and they are getting to know us and like us. We are changing their mind about tortillas. We are proving that our tortillas are just as good as the ones from the street." At the same time that TortiMX struggles with its tortilla-manufacturing operations, tortillas are increasing in popularity in the United States.

Tortillas Beat the Bagel: The Growth of Tortilla Popularity in the United States

Tortilla production is one of the fastest growing sectors of the U.S. baking industry. According to the Tortilla Industry Association (TIA): "Tortilla's popularity has reached record heights, making this staple literally the best thing since sliced bread. Having cornered 32 percent of the sales for the U.S. bread industry, tortillas trail white bread sales by only two percent— making them the second most popular bread type in America with sales that far surpass those of whole wheat bread, bagels and rolls" (TIA 2003a, 1). However, there seems to be inconsistencies in the TIA's report; the 2002 Economic Census reports that tortillas are only about 3 percent of sales for the U.S. bread industry. However, industry leaders claim that the census does not include sales from small independent businesses and restaurants or items such as frozen foods that contain tortillas. The TIA states that tortilla manufacturing is a US$5 billion industry (TIA 2003a). Regardless of the inconsistencies in data, any casual observer or consumer of tortillas has witnessed the dramatic increase in popularity of the product in the United States. According to the 2002 Economic Census (United States Census Bureau, 2002), there are 297 tortilla-manufacturing establishments in the United States, and 66 of them are in California. This is up from 235 establishments in 1997, with 58 establishments in California. According to the 1997 Economic Census, these 58 businesses employ 4,258 workers.[4] The average industry wage for tortilla production workers in 1997 was

$8.62 an hour (United States Census Bureau 1997). Twenty-five percent of all tortilla-manufacturing plants are located in California.

The popularity of tortillas can be attributed to various factors. First is the increasing population of Latina/os in the United States, particularly in the Southwest. Second is the fact that American tastes are changing, and people in the United States are willing to try ethnic foods. Finally, the tortilla industry has made a conscious attempt to deracialize its own product. Latina/os (particularly Mexicans and Central Americans) and lovers of Mexican food will frequently eat tortillas and can be counted on as loyal clients. However, in order to become one of the most popular bread products in the United States, the tortilla industry had to find a way to diversify its usage.

One of the main methods used by the industry to diversify its product's use was to find creative ways to promote the product as more than simply ethnic food. This was done with the invention of "wraps." Wraps, unlike tortillas, are not seen as an ethnic food. They come in different colors and flavors (i.e., green/spinach), they are larger, and they can be filled with anything. TortiUS, for example, produces wraps in three different colors in the same factory that produces its tortillas. Many people are surprised to discover that wraps are essentially large tortillas with food coloring or "natural" flavors (which can cover a multitude of unspecified ingredients). The industry is constantly looking for new ways to change the tortilla. For example, at the Fifteenth Annual Convention and Trade Exposition of the Tortilla Industry Association in 2004, there was a seminar called The Tortilla Reincarnate: A Culinary Arts Demonstration (TIA 2004). The description of the seminar is as follows:

> The session will describe a culinary approach to product development in manufacturing. Classic culinary arts will be reviewed, with an emphasis on how food scientists can develop such skills. We will make a plain tortilla and a tortilla with a twist using the global pantry concept. We will then morph a tortilla—starting with tortilla dough, we will make a non-tortilla and blend ethnic influences. Finally, the non-tortilla will be given a function, and a well rounded meal will be built around it. The session concludes with a wine social." (TIA 2004).

This session description illustrates how the industry is trying to deracialize its product by creating a "non-tortilla" to which ethnic and nonethnic ingredients can be added. In essence it creates a product that is devoid of cultural connotation.

Because of the growing Latina/o population in the United States and the continuous marketing of the tortilla as a versatile product, Tortimundo (through its subsidiary) expanded operations from Mexico to the United States.

TortiUS in the Southwest

By the mid-twentieth century, Don Enrique Hernandez, president and founder of Tortimundo and its future subsidiaries TortiUS and TortiMX (tortilla manufacturing), Agrimaiz (corn and wheat mills), and Tech (tortilla machinery), had built a small empire in corn flour production in Mexico. In the 1970s he realized that corn production was not enough and that his company should expand operations to produce tortillas in the United States for the growing Latina/o population.

Hernandez chose California as the site for TortiUS's first factory, which was built in the 1970s. A senior executive at TortiUS said, "It was a natural choice, given California's huge agricultural territory (ability to grow corn), its proximity to Mexico, and a large Latino population." In the 1970s, What began as a small operation grew into an empire. Today, one state in the region is home to two of the largest tortilla plants in the world, with smaller factories in various cities, and two corn and wheat flour mills, all subsidiaries of Tortimundo. In the early 1980s, TortiUS was already one of the largest competitors in the market when it began acquiring smaller tortillerias in California. By the late 1980s, TortiUS had also acquired its largest competitor, Sonora Tortillas. In fact, TortiUS is called the "evil empire" by many small tortilla businesses across the country because the company puts them out of business.[5]

Eventually, Enrique Hernandez decided to consolidate all of his acquisitions, and he built TortiUS's first megafactory, with 250,000 square feet and dozens of assembly lines. This factory (where I conducted most of my research) produces corn and wheat flour tortillas. The California factory supplies tortillas to well-known fast-food chains, supermarkets, military bases, school districts, hospitals, and Indian reservations. Two years later he built a smaller factory in another city (mainly for small-scale distribution). Next he built another megafactory, with 350,000 square feet, dozens of tortilla assembly lines, and several chip and tostada lines. TortiUS's second megafactory was subsidized to the tune of $400,000 by the local redevelopment agency.[6]

TortiUS's California plants are the corporation's flagship factories. TortiUS invests enormous resources in maintaining them in excellent condition. As a result of innovations in technology and corn flour, TortiUS has produced an inexpensive and versatile product for both the Latina/o and American markets. It is able to cater to both of these markets by creating different tortilla brands, both produced in the same manufacturing facility. One brand, considered most authentic by Latina/os, I call Tortimex, and the other, geared to the American palate, is called Hacienda Tortillas. Workers laugh at the fact that the public gets fooled by these simple tricks. Felipe Gonzalez told me:

> We have a family friend who is very picky about his tortillas. He comes over and says I would never buy any tortillas from Hacienda; they are not real tortillas like those from Mexico. I ask him what tortillas he buys, and he said I buy the authentic tortillas the brand called Tortimex. I laugh and say, "Yes, you are right; those are much better tortillas," even though I know that these are the very tortillas that I produce on a daily basis. I don't tell him this information, because he is proud of finding an "authentic" tortilla, and why ruin it for him.

This confusion among consumers demonstrates that TortiUS has been very successful in marketing its tortillas to diverse groups. This marketing strategy is one of the most important reasons that TortiUS is successful in the U.S. market.

Conclusion

In this chapter I have described the history of the corn and tortilla industry in Mexico and the United States and the conditions under which Tortimundo grew into a transnational corporation. The corporation's success in Mexico can be largely attributed to neoliberal state policies that privatized the corn and tortilla markets, making it easier for a few large corporations to become central players in the industry. While Tortimundo expanded to the United States in the mid-1970s, it was not until vast profits were made in the early 1990s (through privatization of the corn and tortilla industries) that Tortimundo was able to expand on a global scale. In the United States, the company was able to take advantage of a large Latina/o population. Furthermore, U.S. industry growth and support from the TIA led to marketing innovations such as the wrap, which further increased the growth of the tortilla industry. The quickly growing popularity of tortillas in the U.S. market facilitated further expansion and profits for Tortimundo. Chapter 3 discusses the role of the state in the United States and Mexico as well as between the two nations. It is imperative to understand the complex role of the state in order to understand its impact in the labor process of Hacienda CA and Hacienda BC (Chapters 4 and 5).

3

A TALE OF TWO COUNTRIES

Immigration Policy and Globalization in the United States and Mexico

When you say "America" you refer to the territory stretching between the icecaps of the two poles. So to hell with your barriers and frontier guards!

DIEGO RIVERA, San Francisco 1931

In Chapter 1, I discussed the importance of including the state in any analysis of the labor process. In this chapter, I illustrate how the state is a central player in promoting and producing policies that have facilitated a rise in despotic labor control practices. In the United States, the new uses of despotism are most prevalent in immigrant communities and workplaces, where U.S. immigration policies and laws have shaped the labor market by creating pools of cheap immigrant labor in which workers have few rights. In other words, U.S. immigration policy works as a hidden labor policy. In Mexico, on the other hand, despotism is most prevalent in border regions and in the maquila industry. Here despotism is connected to U.S. border policy, such as the militarization of the U.S.-Mexico border, free trade policy, such as the North American Free Trade Agreement (NAFTA), and the relationship between the state and labor relations. This chapter presents the macro-level processes that impact the day-to-day lives of workers. These state policies help produce systems that allow managers to effectively maintain coercive control on the shop floor.

U.S. Immigration Policy in a Historical Perspective

On December 8, 2005, James Sensenbrenner (R-WI) introduced the Border Protection, Anti-Terrorism, and Illegal Immigration Act (HR4437), otherwise know as the Sensenbrenner bill, to the U.S. House of Representatives. On December 16, 2005, the House approved HR 4437 by a vote of 239 to 182 (National Immigration Law Center, 2005). The bill did not make it through the Senate and thus did not become law. Nevertheless, the passage of the Sensenbrenner bill in the House sent shock waves throughout immigrant communities. It also helped fuel protests by millions of immigrants across the United States in March and April 2006 and was a catalyst for the May 1, 2006, economic strike (El Gran Paro Americano), the first such strike the United States had seen in decades.

The bill, touted as immigration reform legislation, would have been one of the harshest immigration measures in the history of U.S. immigration policy. Among the most severe provisions of the bill was the proposal to extend the U.S.-Mexico fence, which currently exists mostly at main border checkpoints, to encompass the entire length of the 1,952-mile border.[1] The U.S.-Mexico border has been porous since the Mexican-American War, especially during times of labor shortages in the United States. However, in the last fifteen years, the border has become increasingly militarized. The proposal for extending the border fence would drastically increase the militarization of the border and severely impact migrants who have been displaced by economic globalization.

Another central feature of the bill was to institutionalize the criminalization of immigrants. The bill had several elements designed to accomplish this purpose. First, the bill elevates the unlawful presence of immigrants in the United States from a civil violation of immigration law to a criminal violation, which could result in imprisonment and/or a fine. Furthermore, violation of immigration law, no matter how minor, would be considered an aggravated felony. This classification would have had a massively punitive effect because it would have made immigrants who are charged with a felony ineligible for lawful status in the future (including asylum) (National Immigration Law Center 2005).

In addition to making the unlawful presence of immigrants a crime, the bill proposed the expansion of the definition of *alien smuggling* to include anyone who assists undocumented immigrants in the United States.

Assistance to undocumented immigrants would be a crime punishable by up to five years' imprisonment (National Immigration Law Center 2005). This means that service providers such as social workers, doctors, lawyers, and non-profit and other service organizations, could be deemed criminals under the new classification. This proposal would not only affect service providers, it would affect anyone who has routine contact with undocumented immigrants, including, for example, someone who hires an undocumented domestic worker or nanny.

Finally, the bill proposed to establish an instant verification program. Under the 1986 Immigration Reform and Control Act, employers are not allowed to hire undocumented immigrants. Enforcement of this law has been very weak and has served to penalize immigrant workers much more than their employers. With an instant verification program, employers and those who refer workers to employers (such as temporary worker agencies) would have to report a worker's Social Security number to the Employment Eligibility Verification System (EEVS) within three days of employment. The EEVS would respond to the employer within three days, stating whether the Social Security number provided matches the administration's records. One of the biggest problems with this system is that it includes no safeguards for errors in the EEVS system.[2] Because employers under this system would be required to fire workers if EEVS reported no matching number for them, the unjust dismissal of thousands of workers could result. Furthermore, workers would not be able to file class action lawsuits against the government to seek redress (National Immigration Law Center 2005).

While this bill is disturbing in the post-civil rights era, it is not unprecedented. Such immigration policy has shaped the United States since its inception. As Aristide Zolberg (2006, 1) aptly puts it, the United States is "a nation by design." By this he means that immigration policy has been a fundamental tool of nation building. Immigration policy was particularly important for building the kind of nation that the founding fathers were striving to achieve, that is, "a politically integrated *white* republic" (Zolberg 2006, 2).[3] Eventually, capitalists recognized the importance of immigrants, both as a source of cheap labor during industrialization and as a mechanism for dividing the working class. As Zolberg (2006, 5) points out, the United States was transformed from an "'Anglo-American' nation into a unique 'nation of immigrants.'" However, with migration of immigrants from non-European countries, especially China, this rhetoric of a "nation of immigrants" posed some serious challenges to nation formation in the United States. How was the United States going to deal with unwanted immigrants under the rubric of "a nation of immigrants"? One way to control unwanted immigration was to racialize immigration policy.

Omi and Winant's (1994) concept of a "racial state" is useful for understanding how and why immigration policy became racialized. Furthermore, the concept allows us to understand how the control of labor flow is connected to exploitation. According to Omi and Winant (1994, 82), the U.S. state is "inherently racial," composed of institutions, policies, and social relations that are all racialized. Immigration policy is therefore not race neutral, as it is often perceived to be, but rather part of lawmakers' efforts to control the racial complexion of the country and the meaning that race takes on both domestically and internationally.

The year 1882 marked the first immigration act that placed race and ethnic barriers on immigration. As a result of pressure from white workers, particularly in the West, Congress passed the Chinese Exclusion Act of 1882, which denied Chinese immigrants entry into the United States for ten years (Glenn 2002). This was followed by other anti-Asian immigration laws. The period from 1924 to 1965 marked the most restrictionist era in U.S. immigration history. However, even during this time period, restriction was focused unequally on various ethnic/racial groups. For example, the Immigration Act of 1924 cut off almost all immigration from Asia and instituted national quotas restricting immigration from eastern and southern Europe, Africa, and the Middle East. However, Latin America was largely excluded from the quota system due to the demand for Mexican agricultural labor.[4]

However, while Europeans and Asians faced restricted entry into the United States, during World War II labor shortages brought the introduction of the Bracero Program (1942–1964), which was instituted by the U.S and Mexican governments to bring Mexican workers to labor temporarily as guest workers in agriculture. Thousands of Mexicans entered the United States as a result of this program. At the end of World War II, when their labor was no longer needed, they were repatriated to border cities in Mexico, even though many of the Bracero Program workers had U.S.-born children. Repatriation to the border created a crisis of unemployment in the border cities of Mexico, ultimately giving the impetus for the maquiladora program (Barrera 1979; Almaguer 1994; Glenn 2002; Cowie 1999).

In 1965 immigration policy took a dramatic turn. The Immigration Act of 1965 marked the end of the nationality-based quota system instituted in the 1920s. The elimination of national origin quotas demonstrated a new era of racial liberalism. As a result of victories in the civil rights movement of the time, national origins quotas were now seen as a step backward. Immigration policy was no longer to be determined by ethnic/racial desirability, but rather access was granted through a formal process that would be equal for all. However, despite its seemingly progressive character, the Immigration Act of 1965 nonetheless continued restrictionist immigration policy. As Ngai (2004, 227) argues, "The Immigration Act of 1965 did not 'open' immigration, for it continued and, indeed, extended the reach of numerical restrictions, a policy that would reproduce the problem of illegal immigration, especially from Mexico, to the present day."

Two of the act's most conservative measures were a numerical ceiling on immigration and quotas imposed on Western Hemisphere immigration, which disproportionately affected Mexico and Canada. In fact, Ngai (2004, 261) argues that "the imposition of a 20,000 annual quota on Mexico recast Mexican migration as 'illegal.' When one considers that in the early 1960s 'legal' Mexican migration comprised some 200,000 braceros and 35,000 regular admissions for permanent residency, the transfer of migration to 'illegal' form should have surprised no one." While the Immigration Act of 1965 was a watershed victory for eastern and southern Europeans who had been restricted from entry in 1924, the act was more complicated in terms of other migration. The act opened the door for immigration from Asia and Africa, while simultaneously restricting immigration from Latin America (Mexico in particular) and the Caribbean (Ngai 2004).

From Schizophrenic to Restrictionist

Immigration policy in the 1980s was simultaneously restrictionist and schizophrenic.[5] The United States recognized the importance of immigrants to the secondary labor market, particularly in the service sector, labor-intensive manufacturing, and construction. By the same token, there was tremendous nativism and fear of an "alien invasion." By the 1990s, the United States once again situated itself firmly in the restrictionist camp.

In this section we visit policies in the 1980s and 1990s that set the stage for contemporary immigration policy. While a full discussion of the history of all U.S. immigration policies is outside the scope of this book, I would like to focus on some recent policies that illustrate the role of the state in the labor process.

Immigration Reform and Control Act 1986   The Immigration Reform and Control Act (IRCA) of 1986 illustrates the schizophrenic nature of the period. The law simultaneously granted amnesty to undocumented immigrants and imposed employer sanctions that would have dramatic repercussions for undocumented immigrants in the United States. The amnesty provision of IRCA legalized nearly three million undocumented immigrants, mostly from Mexico and Central America, who had lived in the United States continuously since before 1982. While the amnesty provision of the act represented a significant victory for the immigrants' rights movement, the employer sanction provision marked a step backward. Employer sanctions designate penalties for employers who knowingly hire undocumented immigrants. All employees hired after November 6, 1986, must fill out and sign an Employment Eligibility Verification Form (I-9). While this law seems to punish employers for hiring undocumented immigrants, it actually has a much greater impact on undocumented immigrants seeking employment.[6] There have been very few cases in which employers have been sanctioned for violating the law. Many employers are able to escape sanctions by claiming that they had "reasonable" evidence that the person they were employing was eligible for employment.

The effect of employer sanctions is that it allows employers to be more coercive with undocumented workers than they were previously. Instead of deterring the hiring of undocumented immigrants (the intended purpose), employer sanctions actually created an incentive for employers to seek undocumented workers whom they could exploit (National Immigration Law Center 2007a). Because they are not supposed to hire "illegal aliens," employers often use their hiring practices as an excuse to underpay workers, pay them in cash, and force them to work in unbearable conditions while having little or no fear that the employer will be reported to the Immigration and Naturalization Services (INS). Employers themselves have actually called or threatened to call the INS to report their employees (Calavita 1992; Chavez 1968). Employers can get away with this easily because they can say that they did not know their employees were undocumented; therefore, the employer can escape fines. If employer sanctions were to be repealed, undocumented immigrants would actually be less vulnerable and employers less likely to specifically seek them out (National Immigration Law Center 2007a). The biggest benefit of this kind of schizophrenic policy is that employers get the workers that they want—workers with few rights. Undocumented workers are therefore the ideal workers because they are both cheap and have few rights.

Operation Gatekeeper   Operation Gatekeeper (California), Operation Hold the Line (Texas), and Operation Safeguard (Arizona) are some of the most restrictive policies passed in the mid-1990s and illustrate how immigration policy became progressively more punitive. All three initiatives were intended to deter illegal immigration from Mexico.

Gatekeeper was touted as an INS initiative to "restore integrity and safety to the San Diego Border crossing" (INS 1998). The initiative increased the number of border patrol agents from 980 (in 1994) to 2,264 (in 1998). In addition to increased numbers of agents, the initiative increased fencing around the border from six miles to forty-two miles, lighting from one mile to six miles, number of infrared scopes from twelve to fifty-nine, underground sensors from 448 to 1,214, and added many other computer systems (INS 1998). This policy did not, in fact, stop immigration; it only made it harder for people to cross the border at relatively safe places and forced them to cross in more dangerous places, such as the Arizona desert (Nevins 2002). Furthermore, the policy broke up families, as few families were willing to take such risks by crossing a dangerous border together.

Since the implementation of Operation Gatekeeper there have been over two hundred deaths at the San Diego border crossing alone. If we look at the length of the border from San Diego, California, to Brownsville, Texas, there were 1,889 deaths between 1998 and 2003 (California Rural Legal Assistance Foundation 2003). As a result of the increased risks in crossing the border, policies such as Gatekeeper, Hold the Line, and Safeguard make the potential for deportation a much more serious threat to immigrants who already risked their lives to cross over to the United States. This creates a chilling effect on immigrant resistance to state policy.

Proposition 187   In 1994, the same year that Operation Gatekeeper was implemented, Californians voted to adopt Proposition 187. This proposition sought to deny undocumented immigrants and their children the right to an education, medical care, and social services (Ono and Sloop 2002). A large social movement made up of immigrant advocacy groups, unions, and community members emerged both during the build-up to the election and after the election. Hundreds of immigrants participated in door-to-door canvassing, as well as a mass march of over 100,000 people in downtown Los Angeles, to defeat the proposition. Pressure by these groups was also constant during the legal battles that ensued following the election (Ono and Sloop 2002). However, the measure was passed by a majority of Californians. Still, despite the proposition's popularity, the State Supreme Court ruled most of its provisions unconstitutional (American Civil Liberties Union 1997).

Illegal Immigration Reform and Immigrant Responsibility Act 1996   In addition to border enforcement programs such as Operation Gatekeeper and nativist, anti-immigrant legislation, the 1990s saw the criminalization of immigrants. The Illegal Immigration Reform and Immigrant Responsibility Act (IIRIRA), passed during the Clinton administration, played a crucial role in this increased criminalization of both undocumented and legal residents. According to Parenti (1999, 143), the law contains "three significant changes: the number of crimes that could lead to deportation was expanded, the laws became retroactive, and 'aggravated felons' could no longer contest their deportation in any way." These changes in the law are significant for a number of reasons. For instance, the law allows expedited deportations, and legal residents with a felony record can also be deported. This category includes people who might have once overstayed their visas, a very common phenomenon in immigrant communities.

In addition to the criminal provisions of the law, the IIRIRA also "requires the conducting of employment authorization verification pilot programs" (INS 1998). Furthermore, Title V of the IIRIRA "contains amendments to the welfare bill, the Social Security Act, and the INA which are directed at limiting aliens' access to public benefits. Proof of citizenship is required to receive public benefits and verification of immigration status is required for Social Security and higher-educational assistance. A transition period (until April 1, 1997) is established for aliens who are currently receiving food stamps" (INS 1997).

The three components of the law, criminalization, employment verification, and restrictions on public benefits, all create a system in which both undocumented and documented immigrants are further driven into the shadows of society. Immigrants cannot work, they are not eligible for public benefits, and now they can be deported for felonies they committed thirty years ago.

While the amnesty legislation under the IRCA 1986 provision was a victory for the immigrant rights movement, employer sanctions, Operation Gatekeeper, and the IIRIRA have seriously restricted the rights of immigrant workers. These policies have particularly benefited the capitalist class, because, while they have not restricted actual immigration in the United States, they have fostered the formation of a class of workers with few citizenship rights and protections. As a result, most of these immigrants work in the low-wage service sector, labor-intensive manufacturing, and construction, where unscrupulous employers have used these policies to maintain labor control. Still, immigrants in the 1980s and 1990s participated in social movements to fight nativism and joined unions at unprecedented levels. Resistance to these kinds of policies and workplace oppression will be discussed in Chapter 6.

Post-9/11 Immigration Policy

Immigration reform was at the top of George Bush's campaign agenda in 2000. After he took office in January 2001, immigration reform remained one of his top priorities. In the months after Bush took office, he held several meetings with President Vicente Fox of Mexico to discuss immigration reform. However, after the events of September 11, 2001, immigration reform was taken off the table. Furthermore, emerging discussions of immigration policy shifted toward border enforcement and antiterrorism. The INS was quickly subsumed under the Department of Homeland Security after the passage of the USA PATRIOT Act and became Immigration and Customs Enforcement (ICE). Prior to 9/11 the INS budget was divided into two categories: providing services and processing applications (higher budget) and enforcement (much lower budget). After ICE was formed, the budget for services and processing applications was reduced to be substantially below the budget for enforcement. These changes have resulted in greater backlogs for processing immigration applications and a greater expenditure on militarizing the border.

In addition to shifts in agency bureaucracies as a result of the Patriot Act, the rights of immigrants were further restricted by the Supreme Court decision *Hoffman v. National Labor Relations Board* and the Social Security No-Match letters. After 9/11, the criminalization of immigrants became much more visible to the public, the media, and in immigration policy. "Americans" became much more aware of immigrants. Fear about terrorism quickly turned into hysteria regarding "illegals" crossing the border. The policies below are examples of the heightened criminalization of immigrants.

Hoffman v. National Labor Relations Board   Six months after 9/11, the Supreme Court ruled in *Hoffman Plastics Compounds, Inc. v. National Labor Relations Board (NLRB)* that "the NLRB had overstepped its authority in its judgment by awarding back pay to José Castro (an undocumented immigrant)," (Robin 2003, 4). The Court argued that providing back pay to undocumented workers conflicted with U.S. Immigration law (Immigration Reform and Control Act of 1986). Therefore, undocumented workers who were fired for protected activity under the NLRA, such as union organizing, were not entitled to back wages "for years of work not performed, for wages that could not lawfully have been earned, and for a job obtained in the first instance by *criminal fraud*" (*Hoffman Plastics, Inc v. NLRB* 2002).[7]

This case began when José Castro, an employee of Hoffman Plastics, and several co-workers were fired for their union activities. The NLRB subsequently ruled that Hoffman Plastics had violated the NLRA and therefore ordered back wages (for years not worked due to being fired) to the fired employees. When Castro testified at the NLRB and disclosed his documentation status, the NLRB ruled that he was entitled to back wages regardless of immigration status. Hoffman Plastics appealed this decision, and the Supreme Court reversed the NLRB ruling (Robin 2003). This is a significant decision given that all workers are supposed to be protected under the NLRA, Fair Labor Standards Act (FLSA), and other federal statutes regardless of immigration status.

Fortunately for workers, the Court ruled only on the NLRA. Workers are still protected under the FLSA, regardless of immigration status, and can file for back wages on hours actually worked. However, it is not clear how the Supreme Court would rule if faced with a case addressing the

FLSA. Regardless, the *Hoffman* decision has some serious implications for union organizing. The Supreme Court ruling that undocumented workers are not protected if they are fired for organizing a union could create a chilling effect on both a union's willingness to take on an organizing drive in a heavily immigrant industry and an immigrant's willingness to participate in an organizing drive. Unions had been able to state that U.S. labor law would protect workers from getting fired if they organized in their workplace. This claim is no longer true for undocumented immigrant workers. This change not only has consequences for the labor movement and its ability to bring immigrant workers into its ranks, but it also serves the larger purpose of maintaining a low-wage, racialized labor force for large and small companies alike. Many lawyers and immigrant advocates believe that the Hoffman decision will not decrease the employment of undocumented immigrants, as the Court supposedly intended, but rather, "employers will seek undocumented workers. The Court held that there is no financial penalty for violating the NLRA when employing illegal aliens. From an employer's standpoint, hiring illegal aliens is beneficial.... If by chance the workers want to organize a union, the employer need not worry, it can just fire all of the union supporters with little to no repercussions" (Robin 2003, 10).

Social Security No-Match Letters   The second program that has seriously impacted immigrant workers, especially in the post-9/11 environment, is the Social Security No-Match program. This program began in 1997, but it grew significantly after 9/11. Between 2000 and 2002, the number of Social Security No-Match letters sent from the administration to employers rose from about 50,000 to over 900,000.

Beginning in 1997, the Social Security Administration (SSA) began sending No-Match letters to employers whose workers' Social Security numbers did not match those in the SSA's system. While the administration claims not to be targeting immigrant workers, these letters have had huge repercussions on these very workers. All No-Match letters issued state "it is not a basis, in and of itself, for [an employer] to take adverse action against an employee, such as laying off, suspending, firing, or discriminating against an individual who appears on the list."[8] But despite its apparently innocuous intentions, the SSA's No-Match letter has become a significant and often insurmountable obstacle to job security for immigrant workers in diverse industries.

Immigrant advocacy groups and unions suspect that thousands of workers have been fired as a result of this policy. In fact, a recent study by the Center for Urban Economic Development at the University of Illinois at Chicago showed that a full 53.6 percent of employers who received No-Match letters responded by firing their employees (Mehta, Theodore, and Hincapié 2003). In addition, the report indicated that 25 percent of workers fired as a result of No-Match letters reported they were fired as retaliation for complaining about working conditions. Twenty-one percent reported that they were fired for union activity. Organizers believe that scores of workers have been threatened, harassed, and disciplined, particularly during organizing drives, by employers using the letter as a pretext. Moreover, many immigrants quit their jobs when faced with the No-Match letter because they are afraid of the potential for deportation. Furthermore, many immigrants have no faith that existing institutions will preserve their legal rights, a distrust seemingly justified by these statistics.

In March of 2003, the SSA issued a Spanish version of the No-Match letter, but they forgot to include the Spanish qualifier "no" in the letter's wording. The letter read "employers *can* retaliate," instead of *cannot*. These constant "errors" on behalf of the administration wreak havoc in the workplace and in immigrant communities. In 2004 the number of letters issued by the SSA dropped to 130,000, but this drop was not comforting to immigrant workers given the administration's new pilot program of instant verification.

Under this new program, employers need only call the SSA to instantly verify whether an employee has a valid Social Security number. This could result in an even greater number of firings if employers are forced to use instant verification on existing employees. While No-Match letters often negatively affect individual employers, they benefit employers *as a class* because this policy produces a legitimate fear that maintains workers in jobs with low wages and poor working conditions.

Immigration Reform Is Reintroduced

Bush's Temporary Worker Program   Two and a half years after 9/11, President Bush reintroduced discussion of immigration by proposing a temporary worker program. Under the program current undocumented workers would submit an application and pay a registration fee. Foreign workers could also apply if they have a job offer from an employer in the United States.

Workers would be able to have temporary legal status for three years, renewable once (Alonso-Zaldivar 2004). According to Bush, workers in the program "will now be protected by labor laws, with the right to change jobs, earn fair wages, and enjoy the same working conditions that the law requires for American workers" (Bush 2004). While the proposed temporary worker program is a small step toward opening discussions for legalization, it is a program rife with problems. One of the most significant faults with the program is that it would give employers too much power. If a worker stops working for a particular employer, he or she would have to find another sponsoring employer or leave the United States. Furthermore, workers could renew their temporary status only once. After six years, workers would be required to return to their home countries. This program, remarkably similar to the Bracero Program, essentially creates cheap labor for employers in the United States. While workers would theoretically be protected under U.S. labor law, it is difficult to see how they would use those rights given their dependence on a single employer.

The Comprehensive Immigration Reform Act of 2006   After the Sensenbrenner bill passed the House of Representatives in December 2005, the Senate quickly began working on a compromise bill. Senators Kennedy and McCain put together a compromise bill, as did Senators Spector, Hagel, and Martínez. In April 2006, these bills merged into the Senate Compromise Bill (2611), which became known as the Comprehensive Immigration Reform Act of 2006 when it passed the Senate on May 25.

Unlike Bush's broad temporary worker program, this immigration reform bill creates a limited legalization program for people in four categories: people who came to the United States before April 2001, those who came between April 2001 and January 2004, those who have worked in agriculture at least two years, and finally immigrants who came as children and have been living in the United States all their lives. In addition, the bill includes a guest-worker program that creates 200,000 nonimmigrant visas annually. Participants in the guest-worker program would be allowed to work in the United States for three years, with the possibility of extending their stay for another three years (National Immigration Project 2006). The bill also includes some of the same harsh measures that were introduced in the Sensenbrenner bill. For example, the compromise bill would require employers to participate in an electronic verification system to verify employment eligibility and limits the documents that can be used to prove work authorization. The bill also includes border enforcement provisions, such as building new fencing along the border and increasing border patrols, and it authorizes the presence of the National Guard at the U.S.-Mexico border. Other harsh measures include the following: failure to file a change of address form with the Department of Homeland Security would result in jail time; illegal entry would be a misdemeanor crime; immigration violators would be added to the National Crime Information Database; noncitizen smuggling would be redefined to include minor acts of assistance to an undocumented person (with exceptions for religious and humanitarian service organizations); local law enforcement would enforce federal immigration law; and English would become the official U.S. language (immigrants would have no rights to government services or materials in any other language).

While the Senate's compromise bill proposed would allow a limited legalization program, it would also further the criminalization of immigrants and the militarization of the border. The bill would have a devastating impact on those immigrants not eligible for legalization.[9] On the other hand, the bill would be a victory for employers as a class. The guest-worker program would ensure that immigrants are tied to *one* employer while in the United States. Although there are provisions within the guest-worker program to protect the labor rights of these workers, the effect of being completely dependent on one employer would create a chilling effect on union organizing or even complaining about working conditions due to the threat of being fired. Furthermore, the bill's harsh provisions experienced by workers who are not eligible for legalization would make them even more vulnerable and easily exploited than they are. Because employer sanctions have not worked, employers could easily take advantage of the bill's harsh provisions by threatening workers with deportation, hiring them at lower wages, and forcing them to work longer hours—in short, in sweatshop conditions. Workers not eligible for legalization have little choice but to accept the employer's conditions. The compromise bill failed to pass the House in 2006, due to opposition from both sides of the political spectrum. It therefore did not become law.

Secure Borders, Economic Opportunity and Immigration Reform Act of 2007
The Secure Borders, Economic Opportunity and Immigration Reform Act was introduced in the Senate in May 2007, by Senators Reid, Kennedy,

Leahy, Menendez, and Salazar. This bill, supported by President Bush, was another attempt to pass bipartisan immigration reform legislation. The bill contains provisions similar to the bill introduced in 2006. It includes one-time provisions such as a path to legal status for undocumented immigrants, the DREAM Act, and backlog reduction. However, it also proposes permanent changes to U.S. immigration law that are generally punitive (National Immigration Law Center 2007b). Some of the same flawed policies in the 2006 immigration proposal are reintroduced in this bill. This includes an employment verification system, a poorly conceived guest-worker program, and the continued militarization of the border. The bill introduces other stringent requirements for a legal stay in the United States, such as continuous full employment. Furthermore, the bill would also set limits on family reunification.

The Secure Borders, Economic Opportunity and Immigration Reform Act failed in the Senate (June 2007). While President Bush spent significant energy in pushing the Republican Party to support the bill, Senate Republicans and Democrats could not reach a compromise. In the end, the vote in the Senate to close discussion and move to a final vote on the bill failed 53 to 46 (Green 2007). It is unlikely that a comprehensive immigration reform proposal will pass Congress during the Bush administration. There is no doubt that immigration will continue to be an important issue on the national agenda, particularly during the 2008 presidential election.

Racialized and Gendered State Policies and Employer Coercion

The policies discussed above create a state-sanctioned system of cheap, racialized labor (Glenn 2002; Maher 2002). They force many immigrant workers to labor under sweatshop conditions in the secondary and informal labor markets (Hondagneu-Sotelo 1994; Bonacich and Appelbaum 2000). Moreover, the militarization of the border, as well as employer sanctions, have made the costs of return migration much greater with the result that fewer migrants will return to their home countries for fear that they will be unable to return to the United States (Massey et al. 2002).

These policies push immigrants into the shadows of American society, denying them both social and political citizenship. While these polices are theoretically race-neutral, they are applied differently to immigrants of color, especially Mexicans and Central Americans. For example, Operation Gatekeeper is not targeted at illegal Canadian, Ukranian, or Polish immigrants. Immigration policy, while theoretically not targeted toward specific immigrants, is nevertheless a racialized policy of the state.

The state policies elaborated above are also gendered. Bonacich and Appelbaum (2000) cite the Immigration Reform and Control Act of 1986 as an explanation for the increase of male workers in the garment industry. They argue that before employer sanctions, undocumented male workers were often able to find better paying manufacturing jobs in large factories and nonimmigrant industries. However, when employer sanctions became policy, larger manufacturing plants and nonimmigrant industries were more likely to enforce the requirement for legal documents. Thus employer sanctions were, at least in part, responsible for driving male workers to the underground and informal economy of the garment industry (thereby causing some displacement of immigrant women). Bonacich and Appelbaum (2000, 152–153) point out that "on average women comprised 46% of the workers in factories.... Some Korean contractors reported a preference for male workers who were less likely to miss work because of child care and other domestic responsibilities." I elaborate on their analysis by demonstrating that this phenomenon exists not only in the garment industry but also in other immigrant industries, such as food manufacturing. This is particularly the case in the California Tortilla industry (see Chapter 4).

Immigration policy has become a key factor in how employers maintain control of their shop floors. The shift in capital-labor relations, the lack of unionization in immigrant industries, and racialized and gendered state policies have created a labor system in the United States in which many employers no longer need to create a labor regime governed by hegemony. Instead they can opt for despotism. These processes will be further elaborated in Chapter 4.

Labor Policy in a Quasi-Colonized State

In the United States the role of the state in the labor process, particularly in immigration policy, is remarkably clear. The role of the state in Mexico is more complex because of Mexico's position in the world economy. While the United States is a superpower and deals with very little external evaluation from either other countries or supranational institutions such as the World Bank, Mexico does not have such an advantage. Throughout history the Mexican state has had to fight for its sovereignty. The contemporary period is no exception. The role of the Mexican state in the labor process is therefore complicated by its relationships with the United States and other countries, supranational institutions, and its own internal politics. While the trajectory of the Mexican state is more complicated, and perhaps less obviously interventionist, the result is similar to the role of the state in the United States. In Mexico employers also benefit from state policy that gives them the tools and opportunities for maintaining coercive shop-floor environments.

I divide the state policies that shape the labor process in Mexico into three categories: Mexico's relationship with supranational institutions, such as the General Agreement on Trade and Tariffs (GATT), The World Bank, World Trade Organization (WTO), and NAFTA; U.S. policies that impact the border region, particularly the labor market; and Mexican state policies.

The Historical Relationship between the United States and Mexico

The United States and Mexico have had a long and complicated history. It can almost be characterized as a colonial relationship (Almaguer 1994). Mexico has always struggled both to maintain its sovereignty and to allow foreign capital into its territory. It swings between periods of economic and working-class nationalism and attracting foreign investment (Caulfield 1998). Cowie (1999) convincingly shows this shift in the Mexico-U.S. relationship through his historical analysis of Ciudad Juárez. Because Ciudad Juárez is so far away from Mexico City, it is extremely expensive to ship Mexican goods to this border town. Expensive shipments were not only a problem for Juárez but also for all cities in Northern Mexico that share a border with the United States. The lack of access to resources for border cities resulted in their increased dependence on the United States. The Mexican government became concerned that border towns would be dominated by the United States, thus in 1885 it set up a tariff-free zone along the length of the Mexican border. According to Cowie (1999, 104), the government designed the free-trade provision to allow European goods to enter free of tariff in order to compete with U.S.-made products. Local and federal officials hoped this strategy would keep Mexicans from migrating across the border to live, where goods were cheaper and jobs more readily available. Business leaders on the U.S. side reacted vehemently.... The *Lone Star* complained that under the rules of the zona libre, "foreign wines and liquors, China ware, imported groceries, and indeed all articles of necessity and luxury can now be purchased on the other side much cheaper than here. If this continues it will not be long before we will see our merchant tailors with their cutters and workmen [on the Mexican side of the border] turning out custom made clothing from ten to fifty percent cheaper than the same could be bought for on this side."

As a result of an inordinate amount of U.S. pressure, the tariff-free provision was eliminated in 1905.

In the 1940s, Mexico implemented the import substitution model of development. Under this model, Mexico would protect its national industries and encourage their growth through high tariffs, restrictions on foreign investment, and direct import controls. "By protecting fledgling national industries from international markets, leaders in the developing world hoped to break their countries' reliance on foreign-made goods, which had locked them into a cycle of exporting unprocessed commodities in exchange for foreign manufactured goods" (Cowie 1999, 109). On the one hand, nationalist-oriented industrialization gave unions power, nationalized industry, and increased the gross domestic product by an average of 6 percent between 1940 and 1965. On the other hand, the import substitution model created increased inequality, inflated exchange rates, and never really reached the border cities (Middlebrook 1991; Cowie 1999).

The year 1964 marked the end of the Bracero Program. This created massive unemployment in border cities as thousands of braceros were repatriated. As a way to solve its high unemployment rate, the National Border Program created the Border Industrialization Project and invited transnational corporations into the border cities where they would be able to access cheap labor. And so the maquila project was born.[10]

Since the 1980s, Mexico has pursued a neoliberal development strategy (Caulfield 1998; De la Garza 2003a, 2003b; Bensusán and Cook 2003). In order to receive funds from the International Monetary Fund (IMF) and the World Bank, Mexico has adopted a structural adjustment program.

This program involved the mass privatization of national industries, cuts in social spending, and a loosening of labor law in the border zone. According to Caulfield (1998, 122), "The appointments of businessmen as state officials have become commonplace...the new set of conditions represent a decline in the relative autonomy of the state and are reflected in the private sector's growing capacity to shape state policy."

I would also argue that the private-sector Mexican elites are an increasing force in what Robinson (2004), Sklair (2001), and Salas-Poras (1996) call the transnational capitalist class. In my view this is not an indication of the state losing power. On the contrary, it clearly shows the ways in which Mexican elites have become state actors and how the state is acting in the interest of the capitalist class.

Supranational Institutions and Mexican Sovereignty

It is impossible to discuss the role of the state in the labor process without first discussing the relationship between Mexico and supranational institutions such as the GATT, the World Bank, and the IMF. In the late 1970s, a group of Mexican industrialists called the Grupo Monterrey launched the Center for Economic Studies in the tradition of the Chicago School of Economics led by Milton Friedman. The purpose of this center was to promote neoliberal economic policies. Part of the program was intended to save Mexico from an economic crisis by negotiating a three-year debt repayment plan with the IMF. This program "called for cutting the state's deficit, freezing wages, easing government price controls, and the promotion of exports to pay the deficit" (Caulfield 1998, 125). The full scale of the plan was not implemented due to Mexico's oil boom, which shielded the country for a period of six years. After the oil bust, the result of world oil prices falling, Mexico was forced to negotiate a structural adjustment plan. This included the privatization of national industries and the full implementation of an export-led development model. "By 1986 Mexico had become the largest single recipient of World Bank funding" (Caulfield 1998, 126).

In 1986 Mexico joined the GATT, which further opened the Mexican market to foreign investors. GATT "removed many of the remaining protections for domestic industries" (Hathaway 2000, 113). According to Caulfield (1998, 128), "The state abandoned its long-time argument that agreements of international organizations should never [supersede] national sovereignty....In many cases, Mexican GATT membership supersedes national laws that govern working conditions and child labor. Indeed, Article XX of GATT bans slavery, but says nothing about child labor, sweatshop conditions or minimum safety standards." The maquila industry,[11] while originally designed by Mexican individuals trying to resolve the crisis of unemployment in northern border cities, was rapidly taken over by American transnational corporations.[12] It was then held up by the international community as a model for export-led development. The maquila industry has enjoyed enormous success because "Mexican policy makers have employed effective deunionization and favorable concessions to foreign capital at the expense of Mexican workers" (Caulfield 1998, 128). This trend continued with the passage of NAFTA in 1994. NAFTA increased the number of maquilas around the border, but it also extended the benefits once available only in the border zone to the whole of Mexico. It opened up the border for both U.S. and Mexican corporations, though many Mexican corporations argue that it has really been more beneficial to U.S. corporations. One clear example of this benefit is the U.S.-imposed restriction of Mexican trucks crossing the U.S. border, a position that the International Brotherhood of Teamsters supported. A trade panel found that the United States was in violation of NAFTA because it allowed Mexican trucks to operate only within designated commercial zones (most of which are limited to twenty miles inside the U.S. border). While the United States agreed to comply with NAFTA, it has not yet opened its border to Mexican trucks. Meanwhile, U.S. trucks cross the border into Mexico with no restrictions.

NAFTA has made it difficult for some Mexican corporations, particularly those in industries such as apparel and electronics, to compete with U.S. corporations. This is a result of several factors: (a) the Mexican government is often more willing to turn a blind eye to the violations of U.S. corporations; (b) U.S. corporations are sometimes more efficient than their Mexican counterparts; (c) many Mexican consumers prefer U.S.-made products; and (d) U.S. corporations often receive hidden subsidies from the U.S. government that allow them to compete more effectively. Mexican corporations are responding to these challenges by pushing for labor law reform that would permit more "flexible arrangements, increase productivity, and quality control" (Caulfield 1998, 132).

Mexican President Vicente Fox's party (National Action Party, or PAN) responded to these pressures by proposing labor laws that would make it nearly impossible for workers to strike, change unions, or join independent unions (Alexander and La Botz 2003). President Felipe Calderón, elected in 2006, plans to continue to push for these same labor law reforms. These reforms will further erode the protections that Mexican workers once had under the Mexican constitution, one of the most progressive in the world (on paper). These protections included a minimum wage, an eight-hour workday, paid vacation and sick days, annual bonuses, maternity leave, and other progressive provisions.

The relationship between Mexico and these supranational institutions has played a critical role in shaping the labor process in Mexico. However, it is important to clarify that neoliberalism in Mexico is not exclusively the result of Mexico's relationship with supranational institutions. Mexico's own capitalist class has pushed many neoliberal policies and reforms. The result has been a neoliberal development model that seeks to attract foreign capital. This has resulted in decreased wages and working conditions for Mexican workers, deunionization, and ever-decreasing constitutional protection (Torriente 1997; Caulfield 1998; Cowie 1999; Hathaway 2000). While the relationship between Mexico and these supranational institutions is critical to the supply of cheap labor for transnational corporations, U.S. immigration policy is an equally important force in shaping the Mexican labor process.

U.S. Policy Impact on Mexico

As discussed previously, Mexico historically has had a complicated relationship with the United States. The struggle for Mexico has always been to balance foreign investment with the protection of national sovereignty. U.S. immigration policy has also had a critical impact in shaping the Mexican labor market and its overall economy. During the 1940s, U.S. immigration policy encouraged the migration of male workers through the infamous Bracero Program. The Bracero Program played an important role in alleviating U.S. labor shortages and Mexican unemployment. While the IRCA of 1986 created a feminization of migration through its family reunification provisions, which allowed immigrants' relatives to migrate to the United States (Hondagneu Sotelo 1994), we still see a larger percentage of male migration. According to Instituto Nacional de Estadística Geografía e Informática (INEGI 2003a), 75 percent of Mexicans migrating to the United States each year are men. INEGI (2003b) also documents that 1.1 percent of men living in Baja California immigrated to the United States between 1995 and 2000, while only 0.7 percent of women did so. These figures do not specifically identify undocumented migration, but they do give us a sense of migration overall.

I would argue that higher rates of male migration can be at least partially attributed to the militarization of the border. Families who have traveled to border cities to cross the U.S.-Mexico border discover that the risks of crossing are too great. As a result, men cross the border, leaving their families behind in new cities with no familial networks. Their female partners are then forced to join the local labor market. Many of these women turn to the maquila industry as a source of employment. State policy then reproduces this notion of a labor market full of docile, ready-made (Sklair 1993; Salzinger 2003) women to be used at the whim of transnational corporations. The recent decline of the maquila industry in Mexico as a whole, but particularly in the border region, has forced women to look for more stable employment in Mexican national industries (discussed in Chapter 4).

After September 11, 2001, the United States began a campaign to pressure the Mexican government to better enforce its border with the United States and Guatemala. This pressure resulted in the U.S.-Mexico Border Partnership Action Plan in 2002 (Bensinger 2004). The plan attempts to reduce corruption of Mexican border enforcement officials, as well as increase their enforcement of the Mexican side of the border. Mexican border officials will thus serve as reinforcement for the U.S. Border Patrol. The result is even greater restrictions on the mobility of labor, making it more difficult for migrants to cross at safer border-crossing areas. This is yet another policy that pushes men to cross alone without their families.

The U.S. policies discussed above serve as illustrations of how the United States continually and systematically erodes Mexican sovereignty. One can say the United States is operating as a transnational state[13] within a particular region based on its ability to shape border labor markets and economic policy. Next we turn to Mexican state policies and their impact on the labor process.

A Constitution Forgotten?

Article 123 of the Mexican constitution established the rights of workers in Mexico. The constitution was written in 1917, during the Mexican

Revolution (1910–1920), to promote the welfare of workers. Protections under the Mexican constitution include the ability of workers to organize unions, receive minimum wages, establish seniority, earn bonuses, get paid vacations and days of rest (Sunday), participate in profit sharing, receive housing subsidies, work an eight-hour day, have the right to strike, receive equal pay for equal work, and have protection against sex discrimination (La Botz 1992; Torriente 1997). While it was a very progressive constitution when first written, subsequent adjustments significantly weakened it. Goldfrank (2003) argues that the Mexican constitution was never truly robust because the strength of the revolution did not come from the peasantry but rather from elite liberal reformers. Additionally, in the late 1920s and early 1930s, the Calles presidency established federal labor law in Mexico. While this federal law included Article 123, it also established the Boards of Conciliation and Arbitration (BCAs). These boards give an enormous amount of power to the state, which historically has represented the Mexican elite (Alexander and La Botz 2003; Bensusán and Cook 2003). While there is significant variation among the BCAs in different states, in Baja California they are particularly noted for being repressive. This makes the enforcement of labor provisions all the more challenging.

There are several reasons that the labor provisions of the constitution are not enforced. First, these provisions are not attractive to foreign capital investment. Second, Mexican industries, which must abide by the provisions, are not able to compete with foreign investors. Third, Mexico has a long history of entrenched union corruption and state involvement in labor relations. The first two reasons for lack of enforcement have already been discussed. The third reason is discussed next.

Entrenched union corruption exists in Mexico mainly for two reasons. First, Mexican state policies have had direct influence in Mexican labor law and labor relations since the 1930s, and the Mexican constitution has been continuously eroded. Labor issues were more systematically addressed in Mexican federal labor law; however, this same law granted unprecedented powers to the state. Under federal labor law, the government now had a role in deciding labor-management and intraunion conflicts as well as "discretionary authority to interpret the constitutional protections for labor through its control of the tripartite labor boards and tribunals" (Bensusán 2000; Bensusán and Cook 2003).

The state's role in labor relations created a symbiotic relationship between the major labor union, the Confederación de Trabajadores Mexicanos (CTM), and the political party in power, the Institutional Revolutionary Party (PRI). The PRI granted the CTM state access and resources, and the CTM turned out votes for the PRI (Middlebrook 1995; Bensusán and Cook 2003). In effect, the CTM became known as a *charro* union. Charro unions are those unions that are more concerned with keeping in line with government policies than protecting the rights of workers (La Botz 1992; Torriente 1997; Caulfield 1998; Hathaway 2000). Unions in Mexico have been able to maintain control of workers and maintain "labor peace" through protection contracts and exclusion clauses in collective-bargaining agreements (Bensusán and Cook 2003). In the case of protection contracts, these unions essentially strike a deal with employers without any input from workers. Often workers do not even know they have a union. Exclusion clauses force employers to fire workers who have been expelled from the union. Unions are able to maintain labor discipline by threatening to expel anyone who is not loyal to the union or considered a troublemaker (Bensusán and Cook 2003). In the end, despite a progressive constitution, workers lost rights because of the relationship between state and union in Mexican industrial relations. After the political transition in 2000, when the PAN was elected after 70 years of PRI rule, some had hopes for labor law reform and labor revitalization. However, the neoliberal economic policies of the PAN have essentially ensured the status quo (Bensusán and Cook 2003).

Second, U.S. anti-communist policies also helped shape entrenched Mexican unions. The United States has long involved itself in changing the early anarcho-syndicalist and communist tendencies of the Mexican labor movement. In the early twenties, the Wobblies (Industrial Workers of the World; IWW) were actively organizing Mexican industries in Mexico as well as Mexican workers in the United States. At this time the Mexican labor movement consisted of many anarcho-syndicalists. During the same period, the American Federation of Labor (AFL) became very concerned with the communist tendencies of the Mexican labor movement. The AFL played a critical role in pressuring and working directly with the Mexican government (which was in dire need of foreign capital) to establish the CTM, which was much more in line with the position of the AFL and Mexican elites.

Throughout the course of Mexican labor history, the United States government and the AFL helped establish other charro unions, such as the Confederación Revolucionario de Obreros y Campesinos and the Confederación Regional de Obreros Mexicanos.[14] Caulfield (1998, 37) argues that "the extension of AFL style unionism into Mexico meant higher wages and democratic rights for the nation's workers; at the same time it insulated them from radical or revolutionary theories, ensuring the hegemony of U.S. interests." In fact, the U.S. labor movement financed an intensive anti-communist propaganda campaign by providing the CTM and other charro unions with money for publications and the distribution of literature. Furthermore, CTM leaders were invited to leadership development programs at the American Cultural Institute, where they studied industrial relations and were taught strategies they could use to break radical unions in Mexico. They also received United States Information Service grants to travel to Washington, D.C., for additional training on breaking unions.

This discussion of unions in Mexico sets the context for the rampant violations and nonenforcement of Mexican constitutional labor protections and federal labor law. State nonintervention does not mean the government is not prosecuting a self-conscious policy. The state and official state unions often turn a blind eye to violations of labor law both by transnational and Mexican corporations. This cannot be separated from the role the United States played in promoting the charro-style system of Mexican unionism. However, the fact that the state is seemingly noninterventionist is in itself a strategic state policy. Today, with the need to attract foreign capital, the constitutional labor provisions have been further eroded. The maquila sector, in particular, has seen the violation of many provisions of the constitution, particularly regarding the formation of independent unions.

Conclusion

Transnational corporations benefit from the restriction of labor mobility and the creation of cheap labor pools. I have argued that in the United States racialized state policies are critical to shaping the labor process by giving employers tools of coercion. In the past, the state has acted as a buffer between capital and labor, thereby giving workers alternatives and forcing employers to construct hegemonic labor regimes. Today, employers of immigrant workers, particularly those who are undocumented, can construct despotic labor regimes using state policy. Therefore, on the U.S. side of the border, we see what I call an *immigration regime,* where employers can use workers' racialized status to engage in superexploitation. The immigration regime serves to limit workers' movement into the primary labor market, where they could enjoy upward mobility through higher wages and better working conditions.

U.S. state policies also impact the labor process in Mexico. The extreme militarization of the border and the criminalization of immigrants create a system whereby men more commonly take the risks of crossing the border while leaving their families behind in border cities with few or no familial networks. Women are thus forced into the labor market and serve as a supply of cheap, vulnerable labor for the maquila industry and Mexican national industries operating on the border. The process of globalization, which involves the neoliberal export-processing development model and Mexico's relationship with supranational organizations such as the GATT, NAFTA, World Bank, and WTO, has forced Mexico to loosen its constitutional provisions protecting the rights of workers. Mexican state nonintervention is, in fact, a strategic policy, as the state, like the charro unions closely allied with it, turns a blind eye to violations of labor law by both Mexican and transnational corporations alike. This feeds these corporations with a pool of cheap, female labor.

This does not mean that workers do not have agency against transnational capital. Workers engage in resistance every day. In Mexico, workers have taken enormous risks in contesting charro union leadership and have had some success in forming independent unions (Hathaway 2000). In the United States, immigrant workers are joining the ranks of labor in greater numbers than ever before (Milkman 2000). The point is that the shift in capital-labor relations, marked by a neoliberal state, has profound implications for the labor process in the United States and Mexico. The exploitation of workers by transnational corporations cannot be studied without an analysis of the state.

4

Hacienda CA

Immigration Regime

The factory is surrounded by video cameras inside and out. Workers have to check in with an armed security guard, and there are signs that say "the company has the right to search all employees." My initial feeling is that it is a very rigid environment.

Field Notes—January 31, 2002

Hacienda CA is an enormous yet nondescript factory located in the middle of a predominantly working-class Latina/o neighborhood. It is in a particularly industrial part of the neighborhood and is surrounded by residential areas. Outside the factory there are two silos taller than a five-story building: one silo contains water and the other, oil. These silos feed water and oil to the tortilla production machines inside the factory. Attached to the main factory is a warehouse with dozens of trucks parked next to it for the distribution of tortillas.

Upon entering Hacienda CA for the first time, I was struck by three things: the large modern space with new machines, the cleanliness and brightness of the factory, and the smell of warm corn tortillas wafting through the air. Having been in other food-processing factories in California (including smaller tortillerias) that were dingy and dark, I was impressed by the general condition of the factory. However, soon after my initial impressions, a shift change occurred, and I began to get a sense of the less than idyllic factory environment.

As workers arrive at the stark white factory trimmed with blue, they encounter heavy surveillance. Security cameras and guards are present both inside and outside the factory. The high level of security is the first indication that work at Hacienda CA is highly regimented. In a lockstep fashion, workers walk directly to their lockers, remove any jewelry they are wearing, and put on mandatory hairnets and earplugs. Additionally, workers in quality control have to put on lab coats, and those in the warehouse must put on back support braces. After workers don their gear, they walk to their jobs on the shop floor.

In this chapter, I argue that while wages and benefits and health and safety at Hacienda CA are relatively good (explained later in this chapter and in Chapter 6), the factory environment is highly regimented, and hegemonic and despotic control operate side by side. The factory regime at Hacienda CA is characterized by what I call an *immigration regime*. The immigration regime represents broad societal politics, which include state policies, labor market conditions, and the anti-immigrant climate (which is racialized). These societal politics have profound impacts on the shop floor of Hacienda CA because managers effectively use the immigration regime as a method of labor control. We see that the immigration regime operates as both a labor market regime, because of immigrant workers' vulnerable position in the labor market, and as a factory regime, because of how workers are divided on the shop floor. In other words, there is a dynamic interaction between the state, labor market, and shop-floor.

Under the immigration regime, labor control is carried out in mainly three ways: divide and conquer strategies, coerced worker commitment, and the threat of offshore production. Managers use workers' racial status and immigration standing to pit documented and undocumented men against each other. Managerial control on the shop floor is more hegemonic for documented workers and more despotic for undocumented workers. State policies and restrictions on immigration allow managers to treat undocumented workers as second-class citizens. Managers also construct the work at the factory as "men's work." This serves to divide men and women in the factory. Furthermore, both managers and documented workers feminize the work of undocumented men who work alongside women on the production line; this leads to further marginalization of undocumented men in the factory.

The status of undocumented workers allows managers to maintain a relatively stable workforce through what Steven McKay (2006) calls "alienative commitment." Undocumented workers in the factory "consent" to their working conditions because they understand the high risks of losing their jobs (labor market vulnerability), or even worse, deportation. Wells (1996, 178) also found these concerns in her study of undocumented workers in California agriculture: "[M]ore than any other factor, it is workers' consciousness of their limited options and dispensability in the labor market that elicits their commitment to strawberry jobs [and] their engagement in their own recruitment and control." Because of these factors, managers can maintain a two-tier work regime in which documented workers are managed through hegemonic control, while undocumented workers are managed though coercion. This two-tier structure allows managers to maintain a stable workforce and ensure worker commitment.

Managers also use the threat of offshore production to enforce shop-floor control. They tell workers that they are lucky to have a job because the company could move to Mexico. Most workers do not realize that Hacienda already has factories in Mexico. In reality, Hacienda CA could never move U.S. production to Mexico because the product is too perishable. Nonetheless, telling workers that the corporation will move off-shore is a useful and effective threat.

Because Hacienda CA is nonunion and has a split hegemonic-despotic labor control strategy, it is markedly different from the case of Allied, the hegemonic factory discussed in Burawoy's *The Politics of Production*. Unlike Allied, Hacienda CA has no collective bargaining or grievance machinery that "restrained management from its authoritarian impulses" (Burawoy 1985, 10). What has happened to the hegemonic consent-driven factory? It is not clear to me that hegemonic regimes were ever prevalent in nonunion, low wage, immigrant industries. As Burawoy (1976, 1985) aptly points out, undocumented immigrant workers in the California agriculture industry were managed by despotic control, while citizens were managed with hegemonic control. I argue that this not only applies to the agriculture industry, but the argument can be extended to most low-wage immigrant industries in the United States. Therefore, the idea of a consent-driven factory really only applies to a certain population, namely unionized primary sector workers who are U.S. citizens. That being said, the swift rise of neoliberalism in the United States has all but destroyed completely hegemonic regimes in both union and nonunionized industries today. What we are seeing now is either the rise of despotism in factories or the combination of hegemony and despotism that we see at Tortimundo. This has particularly affected immigrant industries where the reserve army of cheap immigrant labor is large and the rights of undocumented workers are continuously shrinking. Hacienda CA takes advantage of these structural conditions to enforce coercion on the shop floor.

Inside the Factory

Hacienda has two factories in the city where this research took place, the largest two that the firm owns in the United States. Combined, these two factories employ over one thousand workers.[1] The main Hacienda CA factory employs 499 hourly workers, of whom 372 (75 percent) are men and 127 (25 percent) are women. All of the workers are Latina/os. Managers suspect that half of the workers in the factory are undocumented.[2] The vast majority of them are Mexican (72 percent), followed by Guatemalans (10 percent), Salvadorans (10 percent), and other Central Americans (8 percent). Most employees are full-time workers. However, 20 percent of the work is divided between part-time and temporary workers. The production workers are not represented by a union, but the truck drivers who deliver Tortimex products won a union organizing campaign in the 1990s and are represented by the International Brotherhood of Teamsters.

About a third of the workforce at Hacienda used to work at one of the smaller tortillerias that Hacienda acquired and were able continue working by accepting a job at Hacienda CA. Hacienda CA offered these workers jobs because transferring of employees was part of the acquisitions negotiation and settlement and because the workers were already trained for their jobs. Directly after acquiring these small companies, Hacienda CA operated in each of these smaller factory facilities until enough capital was accumulated to build the enormous Hacienda CA factory. After building the new factory, all operations were centralized there. Essentially, the goal of buying out these small tortillerias was to eliminate competition. Jobs at these smaller family-owned tortillerias had largely been based on workers' hometown networks. Workers at Sonora Tortillas were all recruited from Sonora Mexico, where the owner of the tortilleria was born. Workers at Lupitas Tortillas were predominantly from Michoacan. The main reason for network hiring in these small tortillerias was that they exclusively operated in ethnic enclave economies that relied on trust relationships. Therefore, it was very important to these businesses that they find employees that had some relationship to other workers in the factory or employees who were from the owners' hometowns (Waldinger 1999; Kwong 1999). However, Hacienda CA currently minimizes hiring by networks because it produces too many problems with favoritism on the shop floor. Instead, they rely on newspaper ads and unemployed workers walking up to the factory to put their names on an employment waiting list.

The Hacienda CA megafactory operates the plants twenty-four hours a day, seven days a week, 365 days a year. According to Alejandro, a manager,[3] the company doesn't give workers any paid holidays because tortilla production does not slow down during the holidays. In fact, demand increases. I reacted with surprise to his comment, and Alejandro hastened to clarify that the company does treat its employees very well. As an example he mentioned that Hacienda CA shuts down for half a day every summer to host a company family picnic.

Despite a regimented environment, for many workers Hacienda represents the most stable and best-paid job they have had while in the United Stares. All of the workers that I interviewed had previously worked in garment, gardening, day labor, and food manufacturing, and they reported receiving lower wages and few or no benefits. The average wage for a full-time production worker at Hacienda CA is $8.79 per hour. Full-time workers also receive paid vacation (two weeks for one to five years of employment, three weeks for six to twelve years), health benefits (although workers pay 25 percent of the cost of health insurance in addition to deductibles), sick days, and a pension plan.[4] The pension plan is extremely limited, as Hacienda contributes only 1 percent of wages earned to the plan. Health benefits and the pension plan can be directly attributed to the union contract obtained by the Hacienda truck drivers. After Hacienda lost its antiunion campaign, the consultants it hired recommended that Hacienda raise wages, provide a health plan, and reorganize its lower level managerial structure.[5] These benefits created better working conditions in the factory. The health insurance is appreciated by workers even though many cannot afford it. In other words, the company's antiunion tactics have helped improve working conditions and decrease the likelihood of unionization.

On the Shop Floor

There are six departments at Hacienda CA: maintenance, quality control, warehouse, production (includes assembly line and machine operators), measuring room (where workers premeasure the ingredients), and trucking. There is a gendered division of labor in the factory, although it is not rigidly enforced. Women work almost exclusively on the line; however, there are a few who work in quality control and the measuring room. Men also work on the line but dominate other jobs such as warehouse worker, truck driving, and machine operation. The one exception is the nightshift, where mostly undocumented men occupy nearly all job titles. All in all, the gender breakdown on the actual assembly line during day shifts is 50 percent women and 50 percent men, but the factory as a whole employs 75 percent men.

The production machines and lines occupy the heart of the CA plant. By standing in the center of the factory, one can see the warehouse, the measuring room, and maintenance and quality control departments. The production machines are all stainless steel and are maintained in spotless condition. The twelve corn tortilla production lines and thirteen flour lines churn out 18,400 pounds of corn tortillas and 13,000 pounds of flour tortillas a day. These machines generate a tremendous amount of heat and noise. In fact, the noise level in the center of the factory is so high that it is nearly impossible to hear people talking a foot away.

Despite the foot traffic and the production of a food product, the shop floor is impeccably clean. In fact, the factory is so clean that I would describe it as a hypersanitized environment. This level of sanitation is maintained so that the company does not get surprised by frequent and random inspections by the Food and Drug Administration (FDA). Maintaining a clean and healthy environment also allows Hacienda CA to maintain its prized ISO 9000 status, which opens up many markets for the company's products.[6] Furthermore, Hacienda CA receives a certificate from the ISO that provides a guarantee to businesses that Hacienda CA will produce a consistently good-quality product, made under strict regulations.

In order to maintain quality at the level of industry standards, Hacienda CA must be the model of efficiency. This it is. Workers look like they are part of a well-oiled machine as they repeat a cycle over and over during the course of the day. First, machine operators feed the giant stainless steel machines with ingredients for a particular kind of tortilla. Oil and flour are dispensed from an elaborate tubing system on the ceiling of the factory that is connected to silos on the outside. Other dry ingredients, such as preservatives and salt, come from the measuring room. For flour tortillas, operators program nearby machines to achieve the temperature, size, and coloration desired for each type of tortilla. Everything in the tortilla-making process is controlled. Customers can order tortillas in a particular size, shape, and color (including the number of burn marks). The same operator puts the dry ingredients into a large vat and then goes to another machine that dispenses the oil and water. The dough is mechanically mixed in the vat and is transferred to a machine that forms pieces of dough into small balls (depending on what kind of tortilla). The balls are transferred from the machine to a special conveyor belt. They then go through a heated (350° F) tortilla presser that makes the tortilla flat and cooks the center. Next, the tortillas go into a 400° F oven for twenty-six seconds; this finishes the cooking process and gives the tortillas their coloration. After the oven, the conveyor belt carries the tortillas through a cooling system for one minute. When the tortillas have been cooled, workers on the line pick out defective tortillas and throw them away. Others stack the tortillas into piles, preparing them for the bagging machine that places them in bags and seals them (except for packages that contain more than fifty tortillas, which are manually bagged). The bagged tortillas continue on the conveyor belt to the machine that stamps their expiration date and then to a turntable. Once on the turntable, the bags are placed into crates, which are hauled to the warehouse.

The pace of work in the factory is intense. Tortillas come down the line at very fast rates, and workers are constantly rushing to make sure they do not fall behind. Omnipresent surveillance, particularly in the production and warehouse sections of the factory, makes workers aware that they are being constantly monitored, and they work faster in order to make sure that managers know that they are keeping up with (and sometimes ahead of) production. Six security cameras surround the production area. There is also one security camera in each of the other departments, with the exception of the warehouse; it has seven security cameras because sales transactions with small restaurants often take place there. On any given day, $50,000 in cash passes through the warehouse, so management feels the need for extra security. There are also security cameras in the locker and lunch rooms and in each senior manager's office.

The Immigration Regime

Up to this point, we have witnessed the highly automated and mechanical aspects of tortilla manufacturing as well as the heavy monitoring of workers. Next, different managerial strategies for enforcing shop-floor control are explored.

Managerial Organization and Strategy

Managerial organization functions on three levels at Tortimundo. First, on the transnational level, second, at the subsidiary level (TortiUS, TortiMX), and finally, at the factory level (Hacienda CA and Hacienda BC).

Senior management officials at Tortimundo are all Mexican men. They are directors of large divisions such as Tortimundo in the United States, Tortimundo in Central America, and Tortimundo in Europe. Several are related to the president of the company. Like Don Enrique, these executives can be considered part of the transnational capitalist class (TCC). Their interests are completely allied with those of Don Enrique. These executives have tight relationships with elites around the world.

At the U.S. subsidiary level, vice presidents for the company are mostly Mexican, but there are also a few Euro-American men. Roberto Echeverría, a senior executive for Hacienda in the United States, is a Mexican man who received his formal education in the United States. He is in charge of planning, giving the company direction, coming up with new proposals, and the overseeing of all the manufacturing plants in the United States. His connection with the factory level is remote. His headquarters are in a different state. At most he visits the various factories four times a year. In his view, TortiUS is a family. He repeatedly mentions that being a Mexican company in the United States is very difficult because laws and policies favor the United States over Mexican corporations.

At the factory level, Hacienda CA has a complex managerial structure. A regional operations manager oversees operations in California. He spends several of his work days per week at the two city factories. The operations manager at the Hacienda CA plant oversees all departments and ensures that target goals for the plant are being met. He reports to the regional operations manager. The production manager oversees all aspects of production and reports to the operations manager, but he does not interfere in other departments, such as quality control, warehouse, etc. There are also lead managers at each of Hacienda's departments who report to the operations manager, except for the warehouse manager, who reports to production as well as operations. Below this top leadership structure are supervisors and line leaders.

There are four supervisors in the production department and three in the warehouse. They are responsible for supervising line leaders, handling worker complaints (or referring them to personnel), and discipline on the shop floor. Discipline includes writing people up for being late or not coming to work. The twelve line leaders at Hacienda CA are paid roughly two dollars more per hour than production workers. They are responsible for reporting absenteeism, tardiness, and "bad" behavior on the line. They also have the power to grant workers permission to use the restroom and permission to take lunch and other breaks.[7]

All members of the management structure at Hacienda CA are Latina/o. The top managerial staff are all men. None of the managers for the Hacienda CA plant has a direct familial connection with the Hernandez family (the owners of Tortimundo). There are two women supervisors and three women line leaders. The production manager at Hacienda CA has worked for the company for thirty years. He started as a temporary worker in Mexico, cooking Nixtamal. Later, he came to California and started working his way up the ladder until he became one of the plant managers.[8] While this level of upward mobility is unusual in the factory, the story is commonly repeated among workers who have similar aspirations. Most other top managers have college degrees from Mexico and started working at Hacienda as managers. Managers at Hacienda are all immigrants who have been in the United States between five and thirty-five years.

Leadership at Hacienda is hierarchical and authoritarian. The department managers and operations managers have meetings once a month, where they make plans. These meetings are where production goals are set, as well as policies on hiring, firing, and discipline. Managers in each department have weekly meetings with the supervisors in their departments. Additionally, the production manager also meets with line leaders. When I asked the production manager why they do not use a team model of management to get more worker input, he responded, "We can't trust people with no education to be making decisions for this company.

They just have no concept of how difficult and complicated it is to manufacture food. Besides, they only work here because they have few or no alternatives, so we have all the input we need." Team models are often hegemonic ways of enforcing shop-floor control (Parker and Slaughter 1988; Appelbaum and Batt 1994; Smith 1997; Vallas 2003). Workers are placed in teams where they have some decision-making ability. The small amount of power in the team often gives workers the sense that they and their ideas are important to the production process. The effect of this is increased worker loyalty to the company.

I followed up by asking a manager why supervisors and line leaders are not given more leadership, and he responded, "These people show great potential to go somewhere in this company, but they are too close to the workers still. They don't have a managerial mentality, and they are too sympathetic." This kind of mentality is not exclusive to Hacienda CA; it is common in many manufacturing industries and has been well-documented in industrial relations literature (Burawoy 1979). Nevertheless, workers do not feel that supervisors and line leaders are sympathetic. Workers often have many more problems with lower management than upper management at Hacienda CA. María says, "they [line leaders] think they own the whole company. They think that if they punish us they will get promoted." María and other workers think that supervisors and line leaders are more likely to be punitive than managers in the factory. This is not necessarily true. Managers at the next level can also be very punitive. However, workers have more direct contact with supervisors and line leaders and so often perceive them as especially punitive.

In addition to the despotic-hegemonic approach to labor control and the division of workers on the shop floor, there is also a different mechanism of labor control that exists between all workers and the different levels of management in the corporation. Managerial strategies for labor control use the complicated relationship between the factory, subsidiary, and transnational corporation as an advantage. I've already mentioned that at the subsidiary level, managers do not have frequent interaction with workers in the factory. This allows the subsidiary managers to play a "good cop" role with workers. At the factory level, however, managers and supervisors are responsible for efficiency and meeting production goals. Their relationship with workers is different and much more disciplinary. In other words they play the role of "bad cop." This bifurcated strategy of labor control is

useful because it allows the subsidiary to escape blame for coercive strategies used on the shop floor. The effect on workers is that they tend to view
the subsidiary with admiration and loyalty while seeing managers on the
shop floor as "bad apples."

Because vice presidents at the subsidiary level are disconnected from the
day-to-day rhythm of the factory, they are more likely to value workers'
contributions in the abstract. Roberto, one of the senior executives, spoke
at length about the role of workers in making U.S. Hacienda a successful
corporation. Roberto explained that his peers ask him why he associates
with the workers. Roberto always replies that employees "should be valued
for what they contribute, not what they earn." He is sympathetic to immigrant workers trying to make a better living in the United States. "We
know it's hard for them, and we try to make the workplace a second home
for them while they get the skills to take better jobs." Roberto expressed
concern regarding the hostile U.S. climate for Latina/o immigrant workers. For example, Roberto extensively described how Hacienda is unlike
other corporations because it has kept its "Mexican ways." He says, "Here
at Hacienda, we are like a family, we appreciate the workers' handiwork
(*mano de obra*), we have soccer teams that they can join, and yearly family picnics. We also try to give workers incentives such as employee of the
month. We all have an immigrant experience, and that is why the company
and its workers bond so well. We all want to make it in the inhospitable
climate of the U.S."

Upper management at the subsidiary level is effective at producing
ideas about their "ideal worker," a hard-working, but vulnerable Mexican
immigrant. He does not mention any particular worker by name. In other
words, Roberto is expressing his closeness to an abstract, generic Mexican
immigrant worker. Because Roberto and other high-level managers have
very little interaction with the day-to-day routine of the shop floor, they
are effective at promoting the idea that Hacienda in the United States is
looking out for the best interest of its Latina/o workers laboring in a hostile
U.S. climate. This approach is vastly different from the labor control strategy of factory level managers who have relationships with real workers.

Managers and supervisors at the factory level share a strict disciplinary
approach to running the Hacienda CA factory. Efraín explained that he
had to work hard to get where he was. He started out at the very bottom
and rose to the top. He argues that many immigrant workers today lack

initiative and drive. Efraín says, "All they can think about is going back to Mexico. They need to focus on their work and stop dreaming." Efraín states that he deserves to be in a managerial position because he perceives himself as a harder worker than new immigrants working at the factory today. Efraín articulates that it is particularly important to run an efficient operation if the California factories want to continue to be flagships for the corporation. He says, "Our factory runs twenty-four hours a day, seven days a week. Employees need to be on time and ready to work. They can socialize on their days off." When Efraín began working in the tortilla industry, before Hacienda bought out the small tortilleria where he began, factories did not operate around the clock. Efraín never had to work all night as do workers in the factory today. This is not to say that he did not work hard to achieve his goals, but his comparison between his own hard work and the supposed laziness of immigrant workers today lacks credibility. Furthermore, Efraín is reinforcing a general stereotype that Mexican people are lazy. This serves as a justification for him to be a disciplinarian, to drive workers harder, and, as manager, to distance himself from the workers. Efraín says that his strict style produces good production results. He hopes to be rewarded with continued movement up the corporate ladder.

Alejandro, one of several regional managers, oversees all Hacienda factories in the Southwest. He argues that he sees the difference in factories that are run in a strict manner and those that are more lenient: "The factories that are run in a strict fashion are more productive. That's the bottom line." I asked him what he thinks of Roberto's vision. Alejandro responded that he really respects Roberto's leadership, "However, Roberto does not have to deal with workers on a daily basis. He does not have to deal with lateness, incompetence, and shift changes. We have to work around these issues, so we have a harder line. That doesn't mean that we don't respect the workers." Managers and supervisors at the shop-floor level are far less interested in worker loyalty and more interested in meeting production goals. Their model for enforcing labor control is strict discipline.

As stated previously, the top executives at Tortimundo and Hacienda are part of the transnational capitalist class. Their interests are tied to those of the corporation. Middle managers at Hacienda CA constitute a different class, but their interests are still tied to those of the corporation. In other words, they are two different, but complementary interests, shaped by class ideologies. Middle managers are constantly looking up, aspiring to enter the realm of the TCC. As a result, they use their power in coercive ways. As has been evidenced in many factory studies, while the executives in the TCC are seemingly magnanimous, the middle managers and supervisors at the bottom rule by the stick.

It is important to emphasize that the different managerial discourses and rhetoric between the subsidiary and the shop-floor managers do not represent competing strategies. Ultimately, all managers, whether upper management or lower management, have the same goal: to make the company the most profitable possible and to move up the managerial hierarchy. These two distinct but compatible strategies serve a very important role. Workers' complaints and frustrations are maintained and dealt with on a factory level. As a result, while workers are often frustrated and angry at managers on the shop floor, they can still identify with the corporation as a whole. Most workers that I spoke to believed that they were being exploited by "bad" managers on the shop floor, but that the company that they worked for was essentially good. Mario illustrates this point when he says, "Well, we have some bad managers, but that doesn't mean the company as a whole is rotten." Lower-level managers have to do the dirty work of firing, disciplining, and speeding up the work. Upper management can come in a couple of times a year, praise workers for contributing to the company, and host family picnics. Exploitation by the transnational corporation is therefore obscured from workers on the shop floor.

Workers also identify with upper management and the corporation because the company is a Mexican transnational that has had a lot of success in the United States. Production workers see that the highest positions in the company are occupied by people like them, Mexicanos. They see that upper management at the company has achieved the so-called American dream, which many of them also hope to achieve. Fabian comments, "maybe someday I can be like them [upper management], move up in the company and be respected." High-level managers have achieved things that workers want, such as good wages and citizenship rights.[9]

This difference between upper subsidiary-level management and lower plant-level management is important to the process of racialization. Racialization deals not only with racial difference but also racial sameness. In this case, managers at TortiUS, both at the subsidiary and factory levels, have an advantage because they are Mexican and effective at producing ethnic solidarity. At the subsidiary level managers produce ethnic solidarity by evoking the Mexican family, especially gendered notions of protecting the workers. On the shop-floor level, managers and supervisors act like the head of the household, the disciplinarian who will straighten out problem family members. Ethnic solidarity makes it difficult for workers to be fully dismissive of managers. Even though workers resent plant-level management because of mistreatment, they still respect the fact that these managers have advanced in the company. It would be easier to react and organize against Anglo managers because there would be no ethnic solidarity.

Working Conditions, Control, and Discipline

Hacienda CA has a regimented environment. This environment is part of the factory-level managerial strategy of labor control. As a result, there are strict disciplinary policies in the factory that are designed to constantly remind workers that managers set the rules and have the power over their work. For example, workers who are over five minutes late are either sent home for the day with no pay or suspended for two days, depending on their history of tardiness. Ramón commented, "Even though the managers are Mexican, they act like gringos with the clock. We can't be even a second late." Ramón is commenting on cultural differences between Mexicans and white Americans. His assumption is that nothing runs on time in Latin America and that everything runs on time in the United States. As a result, it is strange to him that Mexican managers "act like gringos." Indeed, even though this is a Mexican corporation, it is run on a U.S. model of business, where efficiency—as a tool of control and power—is at a premium.

Rules and practices regarding health and safety reflect this strict supervisory style. For instance, if a worker is injured on the job, he or she must see the company doctor first. If the doctor deems the worker healthy, the worker must return to work immediately. Evaricio was hurt pulling the cap off a silo a couple of years ago. The injury resulted in a lot of bleeding and headaches. The company doctor gave him permission to rest for two days. Evaricio said "I told them that my headaches were unbearable, and I asked them for an extended leave. They said that if I didn't report to work the next day that I would be out of a job." Evaricio did not feel well enough to go back to work so soon after his accident, but he knew that managers were serious when they told him that he would be out of a job if he did not return. As a result he returned to work the next day. Fortunately, Evaricio did not get worse, but he felt dizzy for several days after going back to work. His injury could have caused another serious accident on the shop floor. This is the way that management communicates who has power, even over something as personal as health.

Workers are also prohibited from eating the defective tortillas that come off the line. Defective tortillas are those that either have a hole in them or have too many burn marks on them. According to managers, this rule exists because there is a sanitation code specifying that workers cannot eat food products off the assembly line. However, there is no rule that the company cannot give these defective tortillas to workers once they are no longer on the production line. Instead of giving tortillas to workers, the tortillas are thrown in the trash. This indicates management's unwillingness to bend the rules. In this example, managers are not only controlling the production of work on the shop floor, they are also controlling behavior. The most common ways in which managers and supervisors find out about workers eating defective tortillas are through security cameras, reporting by other workers, and reporting by line leaders. According to both managers and workers, the first time a worker is caught eating a defective tortilla he is given a warning. The second time, up to an hour's pay is docked from his salary.

In addition to strict discipline, managers find other ways to enforce labor control on the shop floor. There is a general lack of communication and trust among workers. Security cameras as well as the noise level in the factory ensure that workers communicate only on issues strictly related to production. In fact, workers in this factory do not really build any friendships. I asked Ricardo (a warehouse worker) if he could recommend some of his friends to me; his response was: "I have no friends in the factory. I don't have time to make friends, and we have to work too hard. Besides I don't trust anyone in the factory. I mean how do I know that they won't tell the boss?" This is a very common sentiment expressed, among undocumented workers particularly.

There is especially little interaction and trust between men and women in the factory. This is partially explained by the fact that management takes the issue of sexual harassment very seriously. There are signs all over the factory in English and Spanish that say "Sexual Harassment Is Against the Law." Sexual harassment is of serious concern to managers for several reasons. First, managers feel that sexual harassment creates a work environment that is not conducive to productivity. Efficiency is especially important to Hacienda CA because of the large number of orders that this factory receives from fast-food chains and local restaurants. Second, because the factory is staffed predominantly by men, managers are concerned that women workers could sue Hacienda CA if they do not maintain a strong position on sexual harassment. A manager told me of one instance in which a male worker made a pass at a woman worker, and her husband beat him later that evening after work. The male worker was fired by Hacienda CA for inappropriate behavior. There are a significant number of single men in the factory, and they fear this happening to them, so they avoid women at all cost.

There are several other explanations for the lack of friendship and solidarity among workers. The noisy factory environment is not conducive to building relationships. As a result there is very little communication in the production room and especially on the assembly line. Communication between workers in the warehouse is also very difficult because workers are often on forklifts that make a lot of noise as they move boxes. Even when workers are in parts of the factory where there is little noise, such as the lunchroom or locker room, there is little time for building relationships. Those rooms are also monitored by security cameras with audio systems, limiting what workers feel that they can say aloud. They are particularly careful about saying anything that managers could use against them. Second, workers' sensitive immigration status and the differential treatment received by documented and undocumented workers also lead to mistrust.

Immigration Policy on the Shop Floor

The working conditions at Hacienda CA are intensive. As discussed above, this intensity is not simply a result of a fast production cycle but also because of the way shop-floor control is enacted. A principal mechanism of control occurs through management's constant use of immigration status as a coercive tool. Immigration status plays a critical role in the way wages, working conditions, and rights are determined in the factory. Ramón, a worker who has been with the company for over five years, said, "I have been working the late night shift for five years. Every time I want to switch to another shift, they tell me that I have to keep working from 10 P.M. to 6 A.M. or else I will lose my job. The manager tells me that the INS is less likely to raid in the evening and that they are putting me in this shift for my own protection."[10] Ramón's situation illustrates how managers use immigration status to prevent workers from being able to change shifts. On the one hand, managers tell Ramón that he will lose his job if he keeps complaining about this issue, and on the other they are saying that they are only protecting him from the INS. Managers skillfully use both paternalism and threats to keep workers such as Ramón in the evening shift. This is not unlike the story I heard from other workers in the factory. Guillermo, another worker, said that his immigration status has prevented him from getting promotions. "I have been with this company for fifteen years, and I am still a line worker. I started earning the minimum wage, and now I only earn $8.50. I have seen other workers who have their 'mica' (green card) become line supervisors in less than three years."

The marginalized status of undocumented workers in the factory affects them not only in economic ways. One worker explained how this status demoralized workers and undermined their sense of self worth. Rosalina said, "On many occasions I have needed to use the restroom and have been denied the ability to go and relieve myself. This is humiliating." Rosalina's account reflects numerous stories that workers communicated to me. Most workers, especially undocumented workers, felt that they received very little respect on the job and that their dignity was constantly undermined. I witnessed many examples of this kind of abuse from line supervisors (who are all legal residents). Line supervisors would often allow the few documented workers on the line to go to the restroom, while denying these rights to undocumented workers. When I went back to do follow-up interviews, I asked where Rosalina was. Ernesto told me she had been fired for complaining to the production manager about the unfair supervisor who would not give her bathroom breaks. The fact that Ernesto, who works in another part of the factory, knows about this story when there is little communication between workers in production and warehouse, suggests that the story was widely circulated. These are the kinds of lessons from management that give workers pause when considering contesting their working conditions.

Managers at Hacienda CA not only use immigration status, they also use immigration policies against undocumented workers in the factory.

In 2001, Hacienda CA started using Social Security No-Match letters to demote undocumented workers. Fabian said, "The [managers] moved me to packaging, and lowered my wage to the minimum. They said that they were doing me a favor letting me work. I was a liability to the company." However, when I spoke to the managers about this letter, they were not seriously concerned about its ramifications for the company. One manager said, "We know we sometimes put the company at risk when we hire workers with questionable status, but they need jobs and we benefit from their labor. In the end, to be profitable you have to take risks. We are willing to take this risk because it gives us an edge in a very competitive market." Ricardo, a production worker, told me that the company re-uses the No-Match letter they received once from the administration, year after year. He says, "They showed me the letter one time and demoted me. The next year they showed me the same letter. I was very concerned because I had just fixed my status, so I called the Social Security Administration to correct the information on the letter. The Social Security office told me that they had not sent out the letter to the company that particular year. This is how I knew that they [managers] were manipulating us." Workers also told me that uncooperative workers got fired as a result of the No-Match letter.

Managers have also used *Hoffman v. NLRB* (2002) to enforce shop-floor control. This decision states that undocumented workers are not entitled to back wages for wages lost due to activities protected under the National Labor Relations Act (NLRA).[11] The case involved an undocumented immigrant who tried to organize a union at Hoffman Plastics. He was fired because of his union activity (a violation under the NLRA). Under normal circumstances the remedy for this violation of the law would be to be paid back wages for the time that he was unemployed as a result of being fired for protected activity. This is no longer the case. Undocumented immigrants are no longer eligible to receive back wages for the time they were unemployed, because of their immigration status. Several months after the *Hoffman* decision, Hacienda CA held a captive audience meeting in which the company gave a presentation on the negative role of unions in the workplace. According to managers, the *Hoffman* decision itself prompted the meeting. At the meeting, Hernán, a manager, said, "You see, this country does not want you; the laws will not protect you. We are the only ones that can protect you. This is the difference between a Mexican company and an

American one." This quote illustrates the level of paternalism with which many ethnic entrepreneurs operate. Managers provide an important example demonstrating how U.S. law treats undocumented immigrants as disposable. The company presents itself as providing immigrant workers a service by holding a meeting where they explain a new law. Furthermore, managers make explicit that only a Mexican company will be able to protect workers against harsh U.S. law. In other words, managers are trying to distinguish Hacienda CA from factories that are not owed by Mexicans. The idea that your ethnic group inherently has your best interests at heart is an idea that is used by many ethnic entrepreneurs to maintain shop-floor control of their co-ethnics (Kwong 1999; Chun 2001). By the same token, managers use restrictive U.S. immigration law to enforce coercion on the shop floor. By informing workers about new laws, managers in fact create significant fear on the shop floor. Fear also serves the purpose of controlling documented workers by making explicit that they will never be treated as well in an "American" (white) corporation as they are at Hacienda. These practices also make clear that to maintain their privileged position in the factory, documented workers must not make any trouble.

State policy that can be directly used on the shop floor, such as Social Security No-Match letters and *Hoffman v. NLRB,* plays a critical role in enforcing a coercive factory regime for undocumented workers at Hacienda CA. However, these are not the only state policies from which management benefits. The increased militarization of the border, particularly through Operation Gatekeeper, also shapes the regime at Hacienda CA. Workers who once were able to cross the border relatively freely now have to take more serious risks (Massey et al. 2002). These risks include possible death by crossing the Arizona desert. The numbers of deaths in 2003 alone were over 150 (Carroll and González 2003). There have also been increased incidents of harassment and abuse by Border Patrol. In the past several years there has been an increase in the number of vigilante groups along the border. The most famous of these is the Minutemen Project—civilians who patrol the border and harass migrants in the name of homeland security. All of these conditions make crossing the border a much more dangerous endeavor than previously. These restrictions come at the same time that neoliberal policies are driving hundreds of thousands of people out of the Mexican countryside and pushing them to seek employment across the border in the United States. Thus, crossing the border has become more difficult at precisely the same time when workers are most desperate to cross. Mario explains the difficulties of heightened border security. "I was deported once [ten years ago] and I was afraid, but I managed to come back with few problems. Today I am terrified of being deported. I don't think I would make it back. I am always hearing stories from my family of people dying. I can't risk making too much trouble, because I can't risk being sent back." Herman, another packager, said, "Life is very hard, and I am alone, but what can I do? If I take a trip to Mexico, maybe I will not make it back to the U.S." These stories illustrate the reality of increased risk of deportation in the last several years. In fact, even workers who have been deported in the past fear being deported in 2008 because it is much more difficult to re-enter the United States. Furthermore, crossing the border costs more money than it did ten years ago. Coyotes[12] (people who are hired by immigrants to assist them in crossing the border into the United States) have always charged a significant amount of money for helping people cross the border, but in recent years it has increased to exorbitant amounts. The increased risks of deportation because of the militarization of the border and other policies are yet another restriction on workers' options. In the past workers felt more comfortable moving between the United States and Mexico. Now, many of them feel trapped in the United States. Massey et al (2002) calculate that the rate of return migration to Mexico for undocumented migrants within a year after entering the United States dropped from 45 percent in the 1980s to roughly 25 percent in 2000. Moreover, workers at Hacienda CA believe they are better off working for a Mexican company that understands their situation, so resisting managerial control on the shop floor becomes even more difficult. Furthermore, the increased immigration of Mexicans as a result of neoliberal policies, which have displaced workers, affects the labor market conditions for immigrants already in the United States. Therefore, workers at Hacienda CA have to endure more job competition and fewer mobility opportunities in the industry.

However, despite increased risks of deportation, it is not deportation itself that is the biggest problem. As De Genova (2005, 8) writes, "It is deportability and not deportation as such, that has rendered Mexican labor to be a distinctly disposable commodity.... 'Illegality' provides an apparatus for producing and sustaining the tractability of Mexican migrants as labor." Corporations (including Tortimundo) would lose if there were mass deportations of undocumented immigrants. However, some deportations are necessary for the idea of deportation to be a credible threat. Corporations benefit from this credible threat, because even though they know that undocumented immigrants as a class are not disposable, they perceive that individual undocumented immigrants are. As Mike Davis (1999, 27) argues, "La Línea [the border]...has never been intended to stop labor from migrating *al otro lado* [to the other side]. On the contrary, it functions like a dam, creating a reservoir of labor-power on the Mexican side of the border that can be tapped on demand." In concrete terms, at Hacienda CA this means that undocumented workers are paid less, subject to humiliation, and given the worst shifts in the factory.

The Effects of Welfare Reform

Immigration policies are not the only ones that affect workers and shop-floor politics. The continuing erosion of the welfare state (see Chapter 3) has also had a significant impact on immigrants. While citizens and long-standing residents have access to an ever-shrinking social safety net, undocumented workers, and even many legal immigrants, are denied access to welfare, Supplemental Security Income, food stamps, and other programs.[13] Jesús, a production worker, said, "I wanted to quit work for a while, go on welfare, and look for a better life. When I went to the social worker, she said that I was not eligible. I have been a legal resident in this country for three years. Every year I pay taxes. I was not eligible, can you believe that?"

Part of the problem with welfare reform is that it severely limits the alternatives of immigrant workers, creating a pool of displaced workers, much as the neoliberal policies in Mexico do. As discussed in Chapter 3, under the 1996 Personal Responsibility and Work Opportunity Reconciliation Act (PRWORA), "Legal immigrants are ineligible unless they are (1) veterans, (2) refugees, or (3) have worked in the U.S. for ten years or more" (Reese and Ramirez 2002, 3). Jesús has only been working in the United States for seven years, so he is ineligible for benefits. This puts Jesús in a difficult situation. On the one hand he is a legal permanent resident, and this gives him the ability to quit his job and find another without having to worry about proving his immigration status. However, Jesús doesn't speak English very well, nor does he have an advanced degree. Therefore, the jobs available to him in the California labor market pay either similar wages (without the benefits he currently receives) or even lower wages. Jesús wants to learn English and a skilled trade so that he could get a higher-paying job in construction. However, because he does not have access to the welfare system, and unemployment benefits are too low, Jesús feels that he is forced to stay at Hacienda CA. Jesús's insecure position is dictated by state policy and labor market opportunities; however, it has ramifications for the factory regime, as well. Managers at Hacienda CA are well aware of the lack of alternatives, even for documented workers, in the California labor market.[14] This gives them the ability to create a shop-floor regime whereby they make the documented workers feel like they have a decent deal in this factory compared with undocumented workers and documented workers outside this factory who make lower wages or equivalent wages with no benefits. This lack of alternatives also helps keep turnover down and maintain stability.

Enriqueta, a production worker, is a U.S. citizen, but she can't imagine quitting because of the changes due to welfare reforms. Before getting her job at Hacienda CA, she spent four years on welfare. She told me the following story. "I went to the manager to complain about the line supervisor who had yelled at me. I told him that if he didn't do something about the way I was being treated, I would quit. He said, 'Don't be so dramatic.' You probably won't find work, and you can only get welfare for one more year before you are permanently kicked out of the system. Do you really want to risk that?' The sad thing is that he is right. I need to save that last year I have for really bad times."

As part of PRWORA, the total number of years a person can be on welfare over his or her lifetime is five. Enriqueta is in a serious position. As she said in her statement, she cannot just quit her job because she does not know if she will find another one. And if she does not, then she has to go on welfare. But at age 40, using her last year of welfare is risky. This is another example of how a weak social safety net impacts immigrant workers' alternatives. The weak social safety net has increased workers' reliance on the labor market and decreased the buffer between employers and workers. In other words, workers have less bargaining power. Burawoy (1985) argues that the dependence of workers on the sale of their labor power is one key factor that allows employers to maintain a coercive regime. This is most certainly the case for the undocumented workers at the Hacienda CA plant, but even documented workers have limited possibilities.

The quotes above reflect how managers can use the weak social safety net in the United States to retain control on the shop floor. While the work at Hacienda CA is considered unskilled and workers can learn how to do it relatively quickly, high turnover is bad for productivity. Ultimately, managers want to create a sense that workers are disposable (especially undocumented workers) while at the same time ensuring a stable work force. By treating documented workers relatively well, compared with their labor market opportunities, they are able to ensure stability. Undocumented workers have even fewer alternatives than documented workers and often choose to remain employed at Hacienda CA rather than risk quitting and not obtaining other employment with the same wages and benefits.

Offshore Production

Managers at Hacienda CA also use the threat of moving offshore to impose control on the shop floor. At several of the worker–management meetings I attended, managers told workers that they were lucky to have a well-paid manufacturing job in California. Efraín, a manager, said, "Manufacturing is a dying industry in the U.S. Many companies are moving to Mexico and other places where labor is cheaper and profits are higher. We stay here because we care about the community. Consider yourselves fortunate." In my interview with several Hacienda CA truck drivers, they said that during their contract campaign management frequently said they were going to be forced to shut down the plant and move it across the border where labor is cheaper. The drivers knew the company was trying to dissuade them from striking. However, they found it surprising when I told them that Hacienda already had a factory in Mexico. In fact, most workers that I interviewed had no knowledge of the other factory.

It is clear that managers at Hacienda use the threat of moving offshore as a method of maintaining and enforcing shop-floor control. Ironically, Tortimundo and its subsidiary TortiUS depend on the border for its survival. The corporation's profits rest on its ability to effectively market Mexican food and Mexican culture to the United States. This would be more difficult if there were no border.

Racialization and Gender at the Point of Production

Managers successfully use ideas about race and gender to produce divisions and discourses in order to help them implement the immigration regime in the factory. This is distinct, but related, process from using the specific state policies discussed above, because workers' own subjectivities are invoked in this practice. Unlike Burawoy (1979, 1985), who relies primarily on economic factors in his discussion of shop-floor control, I argue that workers themselves produce and reproduce discourses and divisions around racialization and gender at the point of production that sometimes mirror managers' ideas and sometimes reflect workers' independent concerns about how to organize relations of power on the shop floor. It is the relationship between managerial strategies and workers' subjectivities on the shop floor that makes the immigration regime at Hacienda CA so effective.

The factory regime at Hacienda CA can be considered racialized for several reasons. First, Hacienda's workers labor in a racialized industry. When immigrants are concentrated in particular industries, these jobs are seen as immigrant jobs (Hossfeld 1988; Cornelius 1998). Employers construct and reproduce the notion that immigrants are particularly well suited for these occupations (Maher 2002), and as a result, these industries become racialized. This idea certainly applies to the tortilla industry, where employers claim that only Latina/os are willing to work in such a difficult occupation. Managers at TortiUS also like to make the claim that while blacks and whites like to eat tortillas, tortillas do not "belong" to them culturally, another reason they do not want to work in this industry. Another example of racialization is the wage differential in the baked goods versus tortilla production industries. According to the Current Population Survey 2000 data (Bureau of Labor Statistics 2001), white native-born production workers in the baked goods industry in California earn on average $14.46 per hour. Their native-born Hispanic counterparts average $10.34 per hour. Average wages in tortilla manufacturing (a classification that falls under the baked goods industry), which is composed of predominantly foreign-born workers, are $8.62 per hour.[15]

Second, racialized and exclusionary state policies such as those discussed above and in Chapter 3 deny Latina/o immigrant workers, and especially undocumented workers, civil, social, and political citizenship rights. While these policies seem to be race-neutral because they impact all immigrants regardless of racial or ethnic background, they are in fact heavily racialized. We see evidence of this in a number of ways. For example, compare the militarized U.S.-Mexico border with the less controlled U.S.-Canada border.[16]

This difference can, at least in part, be attributed to white Americans' concern about the "brown invasion," as witnessed in the most recent immigration reform debate. Furthermore, some of the most vicious anti-immigrant legislation has come at a time when white, European migration is at an all time low, while migration from Latin America, Asia, and the Caribbean is high.

The denial of these rights is particularly important to employers such as Tortimundo for several reasons. In this era of capitalist restructuring, employers claim that they cannot pay fair wages and benefits because of global competition. Immigration has historically remained the best option for cheap labor. Restrictions on immigration do not completely prevent immigrants from migrating, which Tortimundo knows. Restrictions instead act as a method of social control. This denial of citizenship rights forces immigrants to fear their neighbors, law enforcement, and employers. Employers benefit from both the hostile social climate and the element of social control. Employers have a greater capacity to be coercive as restrictions on immigrant rights increase, as we see at Hacienda CA. For example, employers might withhold pay from workers, force them to work overtime without pay, or threaten to report workers to Immigration and Customs Enforcement for deportation if they complain about working conditions. As a result, many workers do not access the social agencies that could be used to protect their rights, such as the Department of Labor and the Occupational Health and Safety Administration. This is not to say that immigrant workers do not stand up for their rights. Some do. We have witnessed this kind of resistance in recent immigrant worker organizing campaigns and most notably in the 2006 May Day marches, where millions of immigrants came out against Sensenbrenner bill, the proposed anti-immigrant legislation. However, one important aspect of these policies is that they make it much more difficult for undocumented immigrant workers to fight back.

Finally, managers, supervisors, and line leaders at Hacienda CA use the racialized status of Latina/o immigrants to create a caste system of labor on the shop floor, which they use as part of their immigration regime. By pitting documented and undocumented workers against each other, management at the factory is denying rights within the workplace to a group of workers who have limited social, political, and economic rights in the broader society. As Maher (2002, 27) explains, "This opposition between citizens and aliens is...about the extent to which a person is imagined to have legitimate claims to rights." Ultimately, undocumented workers are not imagined to have legitimate claims to rights. Latina/os (Mexicans in particular), once constructed as "white" (Barrera 1979; Almaguer 1994; Glenn 2002), are now commonly racialized as non-white and "illegal" (Ngai 2004; De Genova 2005). Maher (2002) gives the example of a speech by Pat Buchanan in San Diego where he cites the following story as evidence for the marginalization of whites. "My daughter had split her eyebrow open in an accident and my wife and I rushed her to our local hospital. Although our community is not more than 8 percent Hispanic, a third or more of the emergency room clearly were recent arrivals from south of the border...they were speaking only Spanish. I watched illegal alien after illegal alien go ahead of us. Illegal aliens to the front of the line, American citizens to the rear" (McGrath in Buchanan 2000; Maher 2002, 30).

This account illustrates common assumptions in the United States. First, Buchanan assumes that because the patients in the hospital were speaking Spanish and looked "Hispanic," they were automatically "recent arrivals from south of the border." He does not entertain the possibility that the Latina/o patients were born and raised in the United States and grew up speaking Spanish and English. Second, by saying "illegal aliens to the front of the line, American citizens to the rear," he is assuming that the Latina/os in the room are "illegal." Once again, there is an alternate explanation that Buchanan does not consider. According to Buchanan, looking Hispanic and speaking Spanish automatically make you an illegal. It is easy to dismiss Buchanan as a right wing ideologue. However, his quote resonates with many in the United States. It fuels the paranoia that immigrants, particularly Mexican immigrants, are taking away jobs from deserving U.S. citizens and draining social services. If we substitute white Canadians for the Latina/os in the hospital, Buchanan would most certainly not have made the same claims, because he most likely would not have been able to differentiate between white Canadians and white Americans.

I argue that if all Mexican workers are constructed as illegal, then Mexican managers can use that racialized status to enforce shop-floor control. Unique to the situation at Hacienda is that both managers and workers are of the same ethnicity, so there is no clear "racial" basis to the process of racialization. In the context of a Mexican firm with predominantly Mexican workers, race is produced on the shop floor by treating Latina/os differently (more favorably) if they are documented, thereby bolstering the notion of the inherent inferiority of undocumented Latina/os. In my interviews with supervisors and documented workers, many of them characterized undocumented workers as dirty, uneducated, whiny, fearful, and "indios."[17] Calling the undocumented workers dirty was particularly interesting given that everyone in the factory wears a clean white uniform with white shoes. Nobody is actually dirty in the factory, but the idea that undocumented workers are dirty is part of the way that documented racialize and stigmatize undocumented.

Eugenio, a documented worker, told me in private, "We have no choice but to dislike the undocumented workers. Because they are treated poorly, we are treated relatively well. If they were not the scapegoat, the managers would pick another group. We have all been in their shoes and treated badly. They need to pay their dues. In the future they will be like us. They will take advantage of someone else." Documented workers thus clearly understand that they have a vested interest in separating themselves from undocumented workers. As a result of their legal status, they gain access to higher wages, better shifts, and access to rights, such as using the restroom. Documented workers in the factory are significantly more privileged than their undocumented counterparts and clearly work to maintain that privilege. This privileged status is a result of the hegemonic managerial control strategy for documented workers in the factory. Documented workers especially have a vested interest in this privilege, because the way they are treated at Hacienda CA is different from how they may be treated in a non-Mexican-owned workplace where they might be racialized as illegal, regardless of their actual status. In short, one could argue that documented workers at Hacienda CA are treated as though they are on their way to being "white."

As we have seen, undocumented workers are treated as "non-white" at Hacienda CA. They are stigmatized and have to endure the poorest working conditions and lowest wages. What makes the situation even more complicated is that workers' immigration status is the subject of rumors spread by management. These rumors are used as tools of control to spread fear and to divide and rule. As a result of the inaccuracy of rumors, some documented workers get treated as undocumented workers and vice versa.

Hacienda is certainly not the only employer that racializes its workforce despite sharing the same ethnicity. This kind of racialization can also be seen in William Julius Wilson's book *When Work Disappears*. In his study, African American managers held negative stereotypes of inner city African American workers that were similar to those held by white managers. Black managers often discriminated in their hiring practices as a result of these stereotypes (Wilson 1996). In other words, black managers used the racialized status of black workers, drawing on stereotypes of laziness to discriminate in hiring practices. These black managers simultaneously relied upon racialized stereotypes about other workers' "inherent" hard-working ethic to hire them into a particular workplace. This same sentiment was expressed to me by one of the senior executives at TortiUS. According to Roberto, they hire predominantly Latina/o immigrants because no other ethnic group wants to labor in such difficult working conditions. Implicit in this notion is the idea that only Latino (specifically younger male) workers are capable of and willing to work hard. This is of course not true, but it is the kind of racialized rhetoric that employers use in their hiring practices. On a similar note, Waldinger and Lichter (2003) argue that "the availability of the immigrants facilitates the activation of employers' preferences, which lead them to seek out workers from the group they perceive least likely to give trouble." While the majority of employers in Waldinger and Lichter's study are Euro-Americans, this idea can be extended to all employers, including minority employers. Employers view immigrants, Latina/o immigrants in particular, as least likely to make trouble because of their vulnerable situation as undocumented workers. They assume that these workers will be more submissive and controllable than black and other workers.

The factory regime at Hacienda CA is also gendered. First and foremost, work at Hacienda CA is constructed by both managers and male workers as men's work. Second, undocumented men, who are most likely to work and interact with women, are often perceived by managers and co-workers to be less than "real men."

In one of my first interviews with a vice president at TortiUS, I asked whether he considered tortilla making to be women's work, given its history. He responded, "Tortilla making used to be women's work, back in the days when it wasn't so mechanized. Today it is a very different process. It is much more mechanized, and as a result it is much more suited for men." This is a striking admission because 75 percent of Hacienda CA workers are male. This is a marked contrast with workers at the Hacienda BC factory, who are 72 percent female (see Chapter 5). In this example, the vice president is clearly equating a mechanized work environment with men's work. However, as Milkman (1987) argues, these kinds of statements and representations about work are simply another way to rationalize gender segregation in hiring. There is nothing about the reality of the work that makes a job inherently men's work or women's work. Nonetheless, in the United States managers from the subsidiary as well as the factory argued that tortilla making is hard labor that is more suitable for men.

Much of Hacienda's recruitment information also emphasizes the heavy nature of the work: "We are looking for strong people who can work with machines." Not all the men in the factory work as machine operators, so what does "working with machines" mean in this context? Managers stated that this included all machines in the factory, including the conveyor belts that move tortillas from raw masa to the final stages of packaging. In their view even standing on the assembly line packaging tortillas was working with machinery. Managers were very careful to distinguish tortilla manufacturing from tortilla making. In their view the manufacturing process is men's work, while artisanal tortilla making remains women's work. Distinguishing these two kinds of work has the effect of promoting one as a modern process and the other as a traditional process. TortiUS is interested in bringing tortillas into the twenty-first century. This means not only modernizing the product but also modernizing the production process.

I asked a manager if it wasn't more cost effective for them to hire women, since women tend to earn less than men. He responded that it was not cheaper because women quit their jobs frequently, and this high turnover was not good for the company. I also asked one of the vice presidents in the United States why they hire so many men. He responded, "Tortilla manufacturing is very difficult work, hard work. There are many machines. We find that many women quit fast because they just cannot take the pace of the work. I constantly have problems with my staff not wanting to hire women. I tell them that it doesn't matter what they think, we cannot discriminate. But the women keep leaving."

One of the vice presidents of TortiUS and a manager at Hacienda CA claim that they have a problem with the quick turnover of women. However, Hacienda CA has never really made an effort to hire many women. Male employees have been in the majority since the day the factory opened.

In fact, the men that I interviewed didn't really understand why women work in this kind of a factory since in their minds it was clearly men's work. Ramón said, "Any decent husband would not permit his wife to work in a factory with so many men. Hey! At least the women aren't driving trucks yet. That would be something else." Ramón and other men in the factory think that it is inappropriate for women to work in a factory with so many men. Ramón commented, "There are a lot of men in the factory, because this is men's work. If women want to work, they should go work in a field that is more appropriate for women. For example, my wife works in a garment factory." These examples from Ramón illustrate that men in the factory are trying to hold on to their masculinity by also constructing the work as men's work. A component of this masculinity is the preserving of the moral purity of women. Women workers in the factory are viewed as less than "pure" because they work with a lot of men.

Managers are effective at telling the story that tortilla manufacturing requires hard work and muscle and that women are not suitable for the job, which is why there is a high turnover of women. Male workers on the shop floor can effectively tell the story that women have no place in a factory that employs so many men and that requires such hard labor.

However, the women I interviewed (some of whom had been in the factory for over ten years) had a very different perspective. Women workers expressed an indifference toward working with men. Eliza said, "The men don't bother me. Every place [company] I have ever worked has treated me like a man anyway. They expect you to produce like a man; they don't care about your gender." Contrary to Ramón's gender analysis about the suitability of women in a male-dominated workplace, Eliza and other women point out that they feel masculinized in *all* workplaces. She argues that women workers are forced to produce with the same intensity associated with men's work regardless of what kind of factory it is. In other words, she does not feel that she gets special treatment for being a woman in any workplace whether it is traditionally women's work or not. According to women I interviewed, very few women leave the factory because of the difficult work. Rosa said, "In all my years here [at Hacienda], I have only seen a handful of women leave because the work was too difficult. In my opinion, the managers just do not like to hire women. They feel more comfortable ordering the men around." More often women leave in order to get jobs that are more flexible, such as domestic work. Only occasionally do they leave because either they or their husbands feel uncomfortable that they work in a predominantly male environment.

While managers and documented workers at Hacienda CA construct tortilla manufacturing as men's work, they also simultaneously feminize undocumented men. For example, I mentioned previously that women workers in the day shifts work almost exclusively on the assembly line; however, there are not enough women workers employed in the factory to fill all the assembly line needs, so men also have to work on the assembly line. According to the workers I interviewed, men who work on the assembly line during the day shifts fall into three categories: undocumented men, newly promoted undocumented men (those who recently worked the night shift), and documented men who normally do another job, but are being disciplined for bad behavior by having to work on the assembly line as punishment. Ricardo comments "It's so humiliating to have to work on the line. Other workers make fun of us for being like women." The reason Ricardo feels that working on the line is humiliating is because he feels that working where most of the women work diminishes his masculinity. Undocumented men in particular are feminized because they have to work on the line permanently and not as discipline or punishment for a few days. This creates the sense among documented workers that undocumented men are not "real" men, because if they were, they would be earning more money, working better shifts, and doing jobs in the factory that did not require them working with women. For example, Oscar commented, "They [men] look like girls making tortillas. It's so ridiculous." Because the factory is a predominantly male, women workers are viewed as especially vulnerable. In a similar way, undocumented men's vulnerable immigration status is seen as a weakness and is therefore feminized. Interestingly, undocumented men working the night shift are not feminized for doing assembly line work. In fact, managers, who need to fill night shift jobs, promote all jobs in the night shift as especially masculine.

The factory regime at Hacienda CA illustrates how racialization and gender are produced at the point of production by both managers and workers. Racialization and gender are central features of maintaining the division of workers and enforcement of shop-floor control.

Conclusion

In the past thirty years of manufacturing tortillas, Tortimundo has become the giant of the industry. The company was particularly successful in acquiring small, family-owned businesses and turning them into the Hacienda CA factories. Labor control in the factory is enforced and maintained by taking advantage of workers' immigration status, gender, and racialized position in the U.S. labor market. The state plays a critical role in producing the immigration regime that exists at Hacienda CA. Anti-immigrant laws and policies, as well as the increasing erosion of the social compact, have reduced workers' rights to minimum standards. The conditions under neoliberalism have most detrimentally impacted immigrant workers, particularly undocumented workers.

While managers use the immigration regime to divide workers and enforce shop-floor control, workers themselves reproduce raced and gendered notions at the point of production. The erosion of worker protection standards and the racialized status of Latina/o immigrants in the United States allows managers to maintain a two-tier regime of hegemony rule for documented workers and despotic rule for undocumented workers. As a result of successfully dividing workers and creating an environment of fear, Hacienda managers are able to enforce an immigration regime on the shop floor.

5

Hacienda BC

Gender Regime

The walls of the human resources office are full of black and white
photographs of indigenous women from the early twentieth century
making tortillas by hand in the home. The women have a tired, but satisfied
look on their faces. While very few of them are smiling, many of them
look like they are almost presenting their tortillas to the camera. I asked the
Human Resources manager about these pictures; he said it was a tribute to
the long history of women in the tortilla industry.

Field Notes—July 24, 2002

The first time I visited the Hacienda BC (Mexico) factory, I was convinced that I was going to find a classic maquiladora, a modern sweatshop of the sort that I had read about in books and seen in documentaries. I imagined slave wages, abuse, and terrible working conditions.

To my surprise, the factory environment was much more relaxed and cordial than I had expected. In the morning, dozens of Hacienda workers get off the bus already wearing their crisp white uniforms. They walk down a dirt street for two blocks until they reach the factory. Workers casually stroll into the factory. They drop their purses and bags in their lockers and proceed to the shop floor, where attendance is taken at 6 A.M. Unlike Hacienda CA, the BC factory is not surrounded by security cameras. Nor are there any internal cameras monitoring workers' every move on the shop floor. There is one security guard who walks around the outside of the factory during the evening shift from 2 P.M. to 10 P.M. The lack of monitoring by security cameras creates a very different work climate from that at Hacienda CA.

It took six weeks of fieldwork at the Hacienda BC factory before I really gained a concrete sense of factory operations. I was presented with a relatively clean factory, workers and managers who seemingly got along, wages that were not too far below the maquiladora average, and relatively lax disciplinary policies. This was a very different operation from that of the Hacienda CA factory, where adverse working conditions were immediately visible. However, after a month of fieldwork, I began noticing that the conditions on the shop floor were not as benign as I had originally thought. Managers and supervisors used their positions of power to sexually harass women on the shop floor, there were serious divisions between women in the factory, and women's economic situations were dire.

In this chapter, I argue that while the factory is much less regimented than Hacienda CA, it nevertheless operates through coercive control. Unlike the Hacienda CA plant, where managers' control is exerted through an immigration regime, Hacienda BC is governed by what I am calling a *gender regime*. The gender regime has three main features. First, work at Hacienda BC is feminized, largely because of the Baja California labor market, which is shaped by state policies and employer preferences for hiring women. Second, women and men experience differential treatment. Men work in higher-wage job titles and have more independence and control over their working conditions. Women, on the other hand, work exclusively in production, earn lower wages, and compete for job stability. Finally, the regime is both sexualized and racialized. It is sexualized because women workers in the plant work in a sexually charged environment in which male managers make sexual advances such as kissing, hugging, pinching bottoms, forcing women on dates, and rubbing up against them in exchange for job stability. The regime is also racialized because male managers pit lighter- and darker-skinned women against each other, with lighter-skinned and younger women getting more attention from management than older and darker-skinned women. This creates a divisive situation on the shop floor because many women feel compelled to compete with each other and outdo one another both in playing flirtatious games and in productivity.

Unlike the immigration regime at Hacienda CA, where hegemony and despotism operate side by side and there is a workforce that is roughly equal parts undocumented and documented, the gender regime at Hacienda BC is predominantly coercive, despite good conditions for men. Mainly this is due to the disproportionate number of women in the factory who work in production. Managerial control is largely focused in the production area of the factory where most women work, and thus the primary characteristic of the overall regime is coercive.

Managers discipline women who directly or indirectly challenge their advances. They also differentially promote women who are lighter-skinned. These forms of overt coercion are possible due to the lack of alternatives for women in the Baja California labor market. Women workers themselves participate in the managerial strategy of divide and conquer because competing on productivity and playing flirtatious games for promotion leads to both perceived and real job stability and higher wages. The gender regime at Hacienda BC is possible in large part because of two interrelated phenomena: neoliberal state policies and Mexican labor law. As in Hacienda CA, at this factory we also witness the intersection and dynamic interaction between labor market conditions and the factory regime.

Globalization, in particular, free-trade policies such as the North American Free Trade Agreement (NAFTA), has led to the displacement and migration of a significant number of workers who now are employed at Hacienda BC. These families migrated from the interior of Mexico to Mexican border states and, in some instances, to the United States. When workers and their families reached the border, they were confronted with a heavily militarized situation. Families made strategic decisions to allow men to migrate while leaving women and children behind in Baja California with few or no familial networks. Women were forced to find jobs in the local labor market. The main opportunities for them in this labor market were in the booming, yet unstable, maquiladora industry. Many women chose to work at Hacienda BC because the factory represented a stable work environment. It isn't that there is something inherent in single women and mothers that makes them vulnerable. Rather, it is the combination of the militarization of the U.S. border and the instability of the maquiladora industry, due to competition from other countries, that creates this vulnerability. In fact, of the 140 production workers at Hacienda BC, 72 percent of them are women and only 28 percent men. This is a marked contrast to Hacienda CA, where 75 percent of the workers are men.

These economic conditions fit well with managers' gendered notions that women are better suited for assembly line work. Work at Hacienda BC is constructed as women's work, and recruitment is targeted at women. Managers know about women's vulnerable situation in the labor market and take advantage of it to assert their own power. As a result, women workers are constantly harassed and hypersexualized by managers and supervisors at Hacienda BC. Managers know they can get away with it, because the women need stable employment. While at Hacienda CA I saw managers use immigration policies and the racialization of undocumented workers to divide workers by immigration status; at Hacienda BC, managers use skin color to divide women workers on the shop floor.

Managers can get away with sexual harassment because labor laws are not enforced and, more fundamentally, because of the structural conditions under which labor law in Mexico was developed (Middlebrook 1995; Bensusán 2000). Managers at Hacienda BC can sexually harass women on the shop floor because they know that it will be of little consequence. Even if women workers filed complaints against the company, such complaints are likely to go nowhere. Therefore, Hacienda BC can maintain a gender regime fueled by coerciveness.

Inside Hacienda BC

Hacienda BC is located near border-crossing areas in Baja California. The large white factory with blue trim is in the center of a lower-middle class neighborhood that is surrounded by small maquiladoras. The neighborhood attracts a significant amount of pollution from the airport, from factories, and from the traffic along the very busy highway that cuts through it. The Hacienda BC factory is about half the size of the Hacienda CA facility. It operates only six days a week on two shifts compared with the twenty-four hours a day, seven days a week production at the California factory.[1]

The factory is a relatively clean, but it looks dingy compared with the shiny, bright environment at the California plant, even though both factories opened in the mid-1990s. Hacienda BC's bathrooms are clean and well equipped. There are no rodents anywhere in the factory. The locker and lunchrooms are also kept neat. As one of the managers takes me on a tour of the factory, he tells me that the building was originally constructed to be a warehouse and was not intended to be a factory. The company has had to make numerous adjustments to make it work. As a result, the factory has poor ventilation, and it is extremely hot.

While Tortimundo manufactures the tortilla machines for both plants, those at Hacienda BC are slightly older and less-expensive models. In the factory there are numerous infractions of what would be considered health and safety standards in the United States. First, many of the machines do not have side covers, and open flames are in plain view. This contributes to both the heat in the factory and numerous minor burn injuries that workers have reported. Second, there is spilled oil from the fried-product machines on the floor. This oil, infrequently cleaned up, traps small insects in cracks in the flooring. Workers wear hairnets, but no back braces or earplugs. Unlike Hacienda CA, Hacienda BC is not required to provide workers' compensation insurance. Therefore, it has less incentive to provide safety equipment.

Workers at Hacienda BC are all Mexican. According to managers, over 90 percent of the workers come from somewhere other than Baja California. Workers I interviewed tended to be either from Guerrero or Jalisco, states located in southwest Mexico, far from the U.S.-Mexico border region. The high flow of migrants from other places in Mexico has effects on the organization of labor in the factory. Several managers at Hacienda BC pointed out that they liked hiring workers who migrated from the interior because they are less likely to know their rights and they have fewer family ties near the border. The lack of many social networks creates a high level of dependence on job stability. One manager said, "We like hiring women from the interior because they know less, so they complain less."

It is important to emphasize that managers are not just interested in women workers, but rather specifically single women or single mothers with few familial networks in the area. In fact, Hacienda BC's labor recruitment strategy is completely geared toward women. Job advertisements read: "Looking for women, stable work, well paid." The fact that managers felt that they could state their intentions in such a bold manner indicates that they have utmost confidence in their ability to recruit and retain women workers.

The division of labor at Hacienda BC is quite different from that of the California plant, where the division of labor was complex. In Hacienda

CA both men and women worked on the assembly line, but only men worked in the warehouse and trucking. Hacienda BC follows a more rigid division of labor. Women exclusively work in production and men mostly work in trucking and warehouse. Machine operation is dominated by men, but there are a few women who work with machines. This gendered division of labor in the factory is mainly due to the fact that women are considered better at assembly line work by managers, who are all men. I asked the production manager at Hacienda BC why they hire more women than men. He responded, "Haven't you read all of the studies that prove that women are better suited for assembly line work? Women are more patient. They can stand around and do this work for hours. Men are impatient. They constantly have to do something different. Women are simply better for the job. Besides, producing tortillas has been in the hands of women for centuries. The process has changed, but women are still responsible for feeding the family." This statement reflects the quintessential argument about the "ideal" woman worker.

Many scholars who have written about maquiladoras have found similar statements from managers in these maquilas who are looking for the docile and dexterous woman. Salzinger (2003) argues that this "trope of productive femininity" has become central to transnational production. My findings at Tortimundo illustrate that both Mexican and U.S. transnationals readily use the concept of productive femininity to justify their gendered work environments. This trope is particularly strong at Hacienda BC because women's suitability for assembly line work becomes conflated with the traditional home production of tortillas by women. Historically, however, not all women produced tortillas. For example, in Mexico women of Spanish heritage or upper-class standing never had tortilla making "in their blood," nor was it their job to produce them. However, producing tortillas was and is definitely part of being a "good woman" among indigenous and poor women. Therefore, tortilla making is differentiated by class and race/ethnicity. Rather than take it as given, managers at Hacienda BC try to create the image that tortilla making is a process that belongs to all women. In this way they actively justify employing both poor and middle-class women in the factory. As we will see later, this is intricately connected with skin color politics on the shop floor.

Many of the women workers themselves tend to agree with this gendered analysis of production, but they have a different take on it. Rosa

Marta said, "I see it as women's work. Tortilla making is a tradition that women have in their blood. It doesn't make a difference if now we are doing it in a factory as well as in our homes." Women commented that they thought managers were correct in their assumptions about women and assembly line work. Rosa Marta said "Look at garments. Women produced clothing in the home, and now they are producing it in the factory. Tortillas are the same thing. We have the skill and patience for this work. Now we are finally getting paid for doing it." While there is no disagreement between women and managers that tortilla making is women's work, there is a clear distinction in their vision. Male managers use the idea that women are better suited for assembly line work because of some innate capabilities (nimble fingers, docility, etc). Women workers think it is women's work because they have been producing tortillas in the home for years without getting paid for their work, and now they are paid.

Managers at Hacienda BC engage in more network hiring than those at Hacienda CA, but they prefer not to use this mechanism because they think it produces too many unproductive tensions on the shop floor.[2] They are particularly concerned about family members of workers migrating to Baja California and getting jobs at the factory. Managers argue that this would cause familial disputes to enter the realm of production and would thus lower productivity. According to Enrique, a supervisor, "The last thing we need is workers fighting over family problems in the workplace. We need workers to be efficient, and fighting reduces efficiency." Furthermore, Ernesto, a manager, stated, "Then family members would create excuses for other family members who did not come to work. We don't need the hassle." Most workers I interviewed heard about the job through flyers and advertisements in local newspapers. A few workers heard about the positions available from former co-workers in the maquiladora industry.

For many workers, Hacienda BC offers a more stable and better paid employment opportunity than other jobs they have had in the area. Most of the women I interviewed were former garment and electronics maquila workers. They left the maquilas because of seven-day work weeks and the instability of the industry in bad economic times. At the Baja California plant, production workers earn an average of MX$86 pesos per day, which translates to about US$9.39 per day or $1.17 per hour.[3] Workers in the overall maquiladora sector earn roughly $1.37 per hour[4] (Secretaría del Trabajo y Previsión Social 2003b), and factory workers in the food industry of the maquiladora sector earn only $0.91 per hour (Secretaría del Trabajoy Previsión Social 2003c). While Hacienda BC's wages are lower than wages in the maquiladora sector overall, they are higher than average wages in the food industry of that sector. Women that I interviewed valued stability over higher wages, particularly because of their status as single women and mothers without family in the area. Hacienda BC provides the stable jobs that these women are seeking.

Workers at Hacienda BC also receive paid vacation and meager health insurance benefits. The Mexican government requires that companies pay for health insurance. As a result, Hacienda BC offers only basic benefits. The production manager says, "I wish we didn't have to pay any health benefits. After all we already have a doctor in house, but the law requires it." Workers are not required to pay any of the health care costs, but they have very poor coverage. According to Marta, "we can go and see a doctor, but that's about it. We have to pay for any medicine the doctor gives us. Forget about getting seriously ill. That's when it becomes a big problem."

Similar to Hacienda CA, Hacienda BC's company doctor also routinely underestimates the amount of time a worker should have off for a particular injury. Eva, a production worker, said, "I burned my hand on the tostada machine. It was very painful. I could barely move my fingers. The doctor told me I could have one day off. I told them that I did not think that was enough time. The supervisor told me I could find another job if I didn't think he was being reasonable. I was afraid I would lose my job, so I went back to work the next day. I didn't even take the day that I was given off." While injuries on the job are not pervasive, Eva's statement indicates that workers are pressured to return to work immediately after an injury. This kind of labor control mechanism contributes to a flow of production with little interruption, and it intimidates workers so that they won't demand basic rights on the shop floor.

Another benefit that workers receive by working at Hacienda BC is a six-day work week. According to several workers, many of the local maquiladoras require them to work seven days a week. The maquiladoras can force this schedule because they are in a border zone where government officials turn a blind eye to violations of labor law, which specifies a six-day work week. Because so many women are single mothers, the one day off a week is very important to them. While the wages at Hacienda BC are lower than the average maquila wage of nearly $11 per day, this is compensated for by job stability in the factory. Several workers I spoke to took pay cuts when they shifted from working in the maquiladora to Hacienda BC. Rosa said, "I am making less here than in the maquila, but I know that the factory is not going to close and move to another country." Additionally, some of the workers I interviewed were making well below the $11 average in maquilas, so leaving the maquila to work at Hacienda BC resulted in higher wages.

On the Shop Floor

Workers at the Hacienda BC plant are divided into three departments: warehouse, trucking, and production. The production department is the largest part of the factory. There are two flour and two corn tortilla lines and four fried-product lines. While half as productive as the California factory in terms of output per person hour, and slightly more labor intensive, Hacienda BC nevertheless churns out about 9,000 pounds of corn tortillas, 6,500 pounds of flour tortillas, and 7,000 pounds of fried products (mainly tostadas and chips) per day. Each worker produces about 124 pounds of flour tortillas per hour. The production process for tortillas is very similar to that described in Chapter 4. Both the California and Baja California factories have the same number of workers on the production line for standard corn and flour tortillas. However, the machines are slightly different in terms of quality, and the pace is slower at Hacienda BC. Nevertheless, workers are making the same movements in both factories.

Fried products are the only products that Hacienda BC exports to the United States, even though fried products are also produced at Hacienda CA. Exportation is possible because these products have a longer shelf life than fresh tortillas, and therefore border wait times are not as serious. As

TABLE 1. Flour tortilla manufacturing productivity

	Hacienda CA	Hacienda BC
Pounds per hour	13,000	992.1
Production lines	12	2
Pounds per hour per line	1,083.33	496.05
Persons per line	3.58	4
Pounds per person per hour	302.6071	124.0125

Data from company records.

discussed in other chapters, it is not feasible for Tortimundo to have all of its production in Mexico because of turnaround time involved in border crossings and lengthy border inspections. According to managers, it is much cheaper to produce fried products at Hacienda BC because it is so labor intensive compared with tortilla production. The production of regular tortillas requires only about four people on the assembly line, but for fried products there are fifteen. Fried products are labor intensive because they are fragile. Workers have to be extremely careful about how they package tostadas and chips so as to reduce breakage and therefore waste. It is cheaper to produce fried products in Mexico because wages are much lower than in the United States. However, not all fried products are produced in Mexico, as the Hacienda BC factory does not have the capacity to produce fried products for all of California. Furthermore, border wait times and transportation costs remain important factors in the calculation.

Gender Regime

So far, we have discussed the differences in workforce and factory work environment between the Hacienda CA and Hacienda BC factories. The differences in managerial style, the use of race and gender at the point of production, and the impact of state polices and labor market conditions are all evident on the shop floor.

Managerial Organization and Strategy

There are both similarities and differences with respect to managerial organization and strategy when comparing the Hacienda CA and Hacienda BC factories. The organization between the subsidiary and the local factory is essentially the same in both the United States and Mexico. However, managerial strategy both at the local and subsidiary level is very different in Mexico.

Francisco Gutiérrez, a senior executive for TortiMX, views his job in terms similar to that of Roberto, a senior executive at TortiUS. However, in addition to planning and managing all of Hacienda Mexico's manufacturing facilities, Francisco believes that he also has to convince the Mexican people of the quality of the product. He expresses defensiveness when pressed to discuss the success of the U.S. versus Mexican factories. "Roberto has it a little easier than me, because Americans and Latinos love tortillas and they are used to eating supermarket tortillas. In Mexico people love tortillas, but they are used to making them at home or buying them fresh from a corner tortilleria. It's my job to make sure we produce a tortilla that rivals the fresh ones." Francisco dreams of the day when the Mexican tortilla manufacturing factories produce as much as the U.S. ones. He is envious of the fact that Roberto does not need to spend time convincing the U.S. population of the quality of the product and can focus his efforts at building and coordinating factories. Much like Roberto, Francisco has very little interaction with workers in the tortilla industry. His office is located in a different state from the factory. He travels to observe the factory only four times a year. Therefore his relationship with workers is on a very different level from that of the shop-floor managers and supervisors.

Factory level managerial organization at Hacienda BC is much looser than at Hacienda CA. There is no regional operations manager. There is, however, a plant operations manager who regularly reports to corporate offices in another state. He is in charge of generating reports and overseeing all aspects of production and quality control. Under him is a production manager who oversees the daily operation of the factory; he reports to the operations manager once a week. The warehouse manager is in charge of sales and overseeing the truck drivers.

In addition to this top leadership structure there are supervisors and line leaders. Supervisors (all men) report to each of their department heads. Line leaders are not formally managers. They occupy an interesting position between workers and managers. Line leaders (mostly women) are workers who lead the assembly line on a given day. The position is usually determined by who gets to work first rather than by a promotion system. This is significant, because unlike at Hacienda CA, line leaders have less control and authority over workers on the line. Because it is not a promotion system, workers tend to identify more with their fellow line workers than with managers and supervisors. In contrast to Hacienda CA, it is managers and supervisors in the production department, rather than line leaders, who handle complaints. The line leader position gives these workers significant power, however. While there is no monetary compensation for this job, line leaders control the speed of the line and can therefore slow it down or speed it up when they deem it necessary.

All of the managers are men, and some of them have an affiliation with Don Enrique Hernandez. Tortimundo engages in network hiring when recruiting executives and managers. For example, the operations manager is the son of a close family friend, the production manager went to school with one of Don Enrique's sons, and the warehouse manager is an in-law. All of these managers have college educations. Two of them graduated from universities in the United States.

As in Hacienda CA, leadership at the Baja California plant is quite hierarchical. The operations manager meets with the production and warehouse managers weekly. Production and warehouse managers meet with the supervisors weekly. Once a month they all meet with Don Enrique's son, who holds an executive position in the corporation, to coordinate the national effort. Once a year production and operations managers from Tortimundo's operations in the United States and Mexico get together in a week-long retreat.

While organizationally the subsidiary and factories are similar to that of TortiUS, the managerial strategy is different. If you will recall, managers at TortiUS (the subsidiary level) used the rhetoric of the Mexican family to show the importance of Mexican workers to the company. Workers related well to executives at the subsidiary level because they had very little interaction with these managers, and the interactions they had were positive. At the factory level, managers were disciplinarians, and the factory regime was regimented. Workers generally had negative experiences with managers on the shop floor. At TortiMX, the divisions are not as stark. In general, there is much less interaction between workers and executives in TortiMX than there is in TortiUS. There are no company picnics or soccer teams, for example. Interactions between workers and executives occur only when executives visit the shop floor. Visits to the factory are not social occasions, and so workers do not relate to executives on a social level. This reflects the typical distinction between U.S. and Mexican corporate cultures.

Instead of relying on the "family" and social events to maintain worker loyalty, executives at TortiMX use nationalism to ensure support from workers. For example, Francisco says, "Many of my workers previously worked in garment and electronics maquiladoras. They always complained that those factories were very unstable and that they did not like their gringo and Asian bosses. My workers are proud to work for a 100 percent Mexican company. We pay them good wages and give them a stable job.

This creates loyalty to the company. Since we want to build and expand in the future, loyalty is important." In other words, part of what makes this company attractive for workers is that it is a Mexican corporation. Many workers have had bad experiences working with Asian and U.S. managers in maquiladoras in Baja California. TortiMX strives to clearly differentiate itself from the negative impression workers have of Asian and U.S. managers. They do this by appealing to nationalist sentiment. They are a Mexican corporation competing with U.S. corporations that have unfair advantages. Using this strategy does not mean that workers do not perceive that they are being exploited, but in some sense many workers would rather be exploited by "their own" than by foreign companies. For example, María points out, "I prefer to work for a Mexican company, because we at least we know that the money being generated by a Mexican company is benefiting Mexico." While it is true that some of the profits generated by this corporation are being reinvested in Mexico, it is also important to remember that this is a transnational corporation. Profits also allow the corporation to expand globally.

Shop-floor managers at Hacienda BC also have a different managerial strategy from that of the Hacienda CA managers. Unlike the Hacienda CA managers, both Rafael and Felipe—two managers at Hacienda BC— are more relaxed in their managerial approach. The Hacienda BC factory is essentially the antithesis of the Hacienda CA factory in terms of regimentation. This creates a very different shop-floor environment.

Workers appear to be more relaxed and cordial. They talk, take frequent bathroom breaks, and eat defective tortillas off the line. The production manager's office overlooks the shop floor, but workers do not appear to be intimidated by this. The manager routinely comes down from his office to observe production, but workers do not speed up or stop talking when he does. Disciplinary policies at Hacienda BC are also very different from those at the California plant. Workers routinely get to the factory ten to fifteen minutes late, something that would be grounds for dismissal at Hacienda CA. When I questioned Felipe about worker tardiness, he asks me, "What can I do? It's part of our culture. How can I expect the workers to be here on time when I know that the busses run late? Many also have children to take care of. It's impossible to demand punctuality." The managers do tend to be stricter when it comes to not showing up to work. Workers who do not have an excused absence and do not call in sick are docked pay. Nevertheless, they do not believe in excessively strict disciplinary procedures. This is in part due to the fact that Hacienda BC has lower production levels than Hacienda CA. They also have fewer workers to manage.

Both Felipe and Rafael ground their explanation of their managerial style in cultural issues. For example, Felipe said, "Mexicans are always late; it's part of our culture." Rafael said that he does not feel that he can be strict with women: "You just can't be rough with women. The last thing I want is for them to get emotional during working hours." While managers at Hacienda BC are less focused on disciplinary action in the factory, they are no less coercive than their California counterparts. Coercion simply manifests itself in different ways. Managers at Hacienda BC do not have to enforce strict discipline and divide documented and undocumented workers to maintain labor control. Instead, they use women's vulnerable position in the labor market and sexual harassment to enforce the same kind of control. And by treating dark- and light-skinned women workers differently they effectively divide workers.

Gender and Race at the Point of Production

Working conditions at Hacienda BC are also intense, but less so than at Hacienda CA. Tortillas come down the line at a rapid rate, and workers simultaneously stack, bag, and pack them into boxes. The fried-products line moves a little more slowly, because workers have to handle the tostadas with care so that they do not break. While at first glace the factory environment seems much more casual and cordial than the one at Hacienda CA, upon deeper investigation it becomes apparent that coercion is a central feature of factory organization at Hacienda BC. I witnessed managers and supervisors routinely walking around the shop floor, where they would often stand behind the women, hug them, tickle them, and kiss them on the cheek. Many of the women workers looked uncomfortable during these actions. Some sighed, others would try to wrestle out of managers' arms, and yet others seemed to shrink as managers passed by. Oftentimes women workers' faces appeared angry, upset, or simply annoyed. Nevertheless, all the women I interviewed felt it necessary to tolerate managerial harassment and try not to show too many negative facial expressions for fear of losing their jobs. Joaquina, a production worker, said, "It's part of the work culture. If we want to keep our jobs we have to go along with it. I don't like it. It makes me feel demoralized, but what can I do." Many women feel like they are constantly performing a balancing act. They need to attract enough attention from managers in order to stay in the manager's favor (and therefore keep their jobs), while at the same time try to avoid being harassed too much. The need to attract attention from managers creates a situation on the shop floor where many women feel compelled to outdo one another in playing flirtatious games. Women in the factory are very creative, as it is extremely difficult to flirt in a white uniform, white tennis shoes, and a hairnet.

Flirtatious behavior comes in the form of expression through makeup and body language. Managers who walk around the shop floor would notice and comment on even the smallest details, such as a new lipstick color or eye shadow. I routinely overheard managers making comments to women about their beautiful makeup. Women regularly change their appearance by applying different color shadows, eye liners, and lipstick. There is a lot of talk in the factory between women about the latest trends in makeup. Women workers who are friends often share magazines during lunch to look at and discuss these trends. According to Rosa Marta, women are particularly interested in these trends to "see what new colors exist, that managers in the factory will like." I asked her if women also read these magazines to impress their boyfriends or other men in their lives. She said "not really, not for that. It's really to impress the managers when we come to work."

Another way women are able to express and differentiate themselves is through the use of body language. The most common forms of body language were smiling, winking, placing one hand on the waist, giggling, and pouting. Most women made it clear that they do not like to engage in these flirtatious tactics, but they feel that managers expect it and that this expectation is connected to long-term job stability. However, on a couple of occasions women did admit that they enjoyed flirting. One woman even stated that she would like to date one of the supervisors. Some women were quite skilled at using body language and makeup, while others were quite obviously straining themselves by fidgeting, wincing, and hunching, while at the same time, trying to attract attention.

There are a couple of interesting and contradictory points to be made about women and sexuality in the factory. On the one hand the factory and women's uniforms are sanitized (plain white uniform, hairnet, and tennis shoes). On the other hand women are hypersexualized by managers. In order to strike the balance between the sanitized and the sexualized, women use their sexuality in smart and creative ways (Freeman 2000). Makeup and body language allow women to express themselves, since the uniform they are forced to wear detracts from individual beauty. Salzinger (2003) also found this kind of "produced" sexuality in one of the factories she studied.

The appearance of women and the use of makeup to flirt with managers and supervisors is also racialized. From my observations on the shop floor and interviews with women, managers pay significantly more attention to the lighter-skinned women than the darker-skinned women. This creates competition between women workers. Those who have darker skin think that lighter-skinned women have it easy and that their job stability is certain because they have the attention of managers. Georgina (who has dark skin) commented, "the güeritas [light skin/white] girls don't have to worry about keeping their jobs, because managers are constantly giving them attention." Lighter-skinned women, on the other hand, complain more about sexual harassment and never being left alone by managers. Carla says, "I'm tired of being bothered by supervisors as though I was their property." Women are caught in multiple oppressions (skin color, poverty, and gender) that intersect at the point of production. Because these women are poor, job security is essential. If they are lighter-skinned, they believe that they have more job security because they are given more attention, but they also have to endure more sexual harassment. If they are darker-skinned, they face less sexual harassment, but they believe that they have less job security.

Notions of beauty are wrapped up in lighter skin and eye color. The common assumption shared by managers and these women is that lighter-skinned women need less makeup because they have "natural" beauty, while darker-skinned women need more makeup because they need to play on their "good" features. On several separate occasions a supervisor told two different light-skinned women "You shouldn't put on so much makeup. Women with your complexion don't need it, because you are already beautiful." Darker-women internalize these notions as a result of the work environment. Georgina told me "I never wore makeup before working here. But, I'm not a güera, so I need to use makeup to highlight my features."

While I was able to access company data on the number of people fired and those who left in 2001–2002, I was not able to access the names of those fired. From my own observations it is not clear to me that darker-skinned women are in fact fired more often than lighter-skinned women. However, it is a generalized perception among workers. What I was able to observe during my time in the factory is that darker- and lighter-skinned women are differentially promoted. For example, Carmen, who is considered light, was promoted to be an assistant machine operator, even though she has only been an employee for five years, has a spotty attendance record, arrives late, and is no more productive than other women in the factory. Georgina, who is considered to be dark-skinned, has been at the factory for nearly ten years and has never been promoted. The perception of both discriminatory firing and differential promotions serve the purpose of managerial control. I asked the production manager how he thinks women respond to his advances. He said, "It doesn't matter. In Baja California we have a very unique situation. There are many single women, and many single mothers. These women need a stable job, and since they do not have husbands, they do whatever we want. They do whatever is necessary to keep their jobs." This indicates that management at the factory feels a general disregard for how women perceive them. They are very confident they can behave any way they want because of women's vulnerable position in the local labor market.

Women emphasized that sexual harassment happens not only as part of the work day. Managers and supervisors also harass women after hours. Women reported that managers tried to set up dates with them as they were leaving work, and one woman even said that a supervisor called her at home. Most women I spoke to felt that they could stand up to sexual harassment outside of the workplace more firmly than inside the workplace because they could more easily avoid managers or use their children as an excuse. However, several women reported feeling forced to go out with a manager. Lupe said, "One time a supervisor told me that I had to go to dinner with him. I told him that I could not, that I had to go home and feed my children. He said that if I didn't he would have to let me go. I was terrified of losing my job, so I went." I asked her why she did not try to find other work. She commented, "Despite the advances, this is a good job, a stable job. Before coming here I worked in a garment maquila. There I was not paid for over three weeks. The working conditions were terrible, and I was screamed at. I cannot afford to wait three weeks for my paycheck. Here at least I have friends. The women have similar experiences and so we bond." Lupe's statement highlights several issues. First, Lupe emphasizes the value of job stability and a steady paycheck. Many women suggested that dealing with sexual harassment was something they were willing to live with in order to be able to take care of their families in a consistent way. Second, Lupe also illustrates the importance of having a community of friends in the factory. Women workers often ride the bus together to and from work. They are very collegial, both on the line and during breaks and lunch. Women who live close to each other sometimes share child care and cooking responsibilities. Often women get together on their days off and talk while their kids are playing. The friendships between certain women in the factory are very strong, although not across the board.

There is also a significant amount of friction and competition between women. Supervisors at Hacienda BC are particularly adept at dividing women and increasing competition between them. I asked Oscar, a supervisor, if he thought women competed with each other for his attention. He responded, "Yes. A little competition is always a good motivator. We feel it keeps productivity levels up. We try to be fair when we are giving women compliments so that they all feel good about themselves. But you know women, they can never get enough." I asked Oscar what he means when he said women can never get enough. His response indicated that he genuinely felt that women loved receiving his attention and constantly were demanding more of it. In particular, he perceived flirting and makeup as evidence of demand. However, as we saw from the women's perspective, many of them want attention only because they feel that they need it in order to maintain their job security. Another interesting point about Oscar's statement is that he directly links the competition between women to production. On some level this indicates that managers and supervisors are well aware that sexual harassment is productive in this workplace.

Because of the structure of competition on the shop floor, some women did not feel a common bond with certain other women. Gloria said, "Sure, we all have some common experiences. But the younger, lighter-skinned women get more attention. This is difficult for the rest of us, because we are forced to work harder while those women have it easier on the line." Gloria and other women very clearly pointed out that "community" is often complicated by skin color. In other words, the factory is not one big happy family of women. It is especially important to remember that workers are not a homogeneous, undifferentiated group (Sabel 1982; Fernandes 1997), because managers and supervisors play on these differences.

It is often difficult to figure out what constitutes *lighter* and *darker*. While there are clear examples of either very dark- or very fair-skinned workers, most women in the factory were somewhere in the middle. This middle territory is very complicated. At first, I was very perplexed by women workers' self-identification as being light or dark. The issue was never that clear to me. In this middle range of skin color, I interviewed women who I perceived to be "lighter" but who identified as "dark" and "darker" women who identified as "light." What emerged from my field notes was that the identity of being dark and light skinned is complicated by class status and education.[5]

All the women workers' economic situation was poor, but this had not necessarily always been the case. Carmen, for instance, finished high school and has parents who are teachers. Carmen left Jalisco because her husband wanted to first look for opportunities in Baja California and then cross the border into the United States. Her husband found a job as a low-level engineer at a maquiladora. For a couple of years he had a steady job and a middle-class income. In 1998 the maquiladora he was working for moved to China, and he was laid off. Because the border was particularly difficult to cross at that time, they decided that Carmen would stay in Baja California and find a job and her husband would cross the border. Carmen worked in an electronics maquiladora for a year before finding the position at Hacienda BC. Even though Carmen has darker skin, she identifies as light, and the managers identify her as white. When I asked Carmen why she identified as light, pointing out that Marisol (who is lighter than Carmen) identifies as dark, Carmen had a very simple answer: "Well, it's because I have an education. Marisol only finished elementary school. I finished high school." When I asked the supervisor the same question, he said "Carmen comes from a good family, she speaks proper Spanish. Marisol comes from a poor family." When the supervisor uses "good family" as a class term, he is referring to the fact that Carmen comes from a middle-class background.

Unlike at Hacienda CA, the ties and interaction between women and men are strong at Hacienda BC. At the California factory men and women had very little communication and very little interaction, in part due to the division of labor. Hacienda BC is completely different, despite their more rigid gender division of labor. Men and women workers constantly joke and talk with one another. In some cases women workers are better friends with the men in the factory than with other women. This is a direct result of the competition between women. Gloria said, "The men are less complicated than the women in the factory. We don't need to compete with them [men]." Men are generally outside of the production process, because they tend to work mostly in the warehouse and trucking. Therefore, women are not engaging in direct competition with them. In general, the better communication between all workers in the factory can be partially attributed to the lack of security, the smaller size of the factory, and machines that are less noisy than those at Hacienda CA.

There is substantial interaction between women and men during lunch and on the way to and from work. Furthermore, women in the factory often ask their male colleagues for advice regarding harassment from managers and supervisors. Rosa says, "I ask the men about how to respond to managers' advances all the time. They have a different perspective." Men offer insight on what managers might want from women. Often they tell their women colleagues what they have overheard being said about them by managers and supervisors. Gloria says, "Antonio tells us when the managers say negative things about us [women]." Male workers also give women advice on makeup. For example, they talk to women about what kind of makeup they like to see their wives and girlfriends wearing. Women in the factory assume that male managers and workers will have similar taste, and so the ideas of men workers are really important to them. Despite the deep friendships between men and women in the factory, only a few of these relationships have turned romantic. Many of the men are married, and a good number of the single women (whose partners are in the United States) feel loyalty to their relationships. Nevertheless, unlike at Hacienda CA, there are romantic interactions between men and women in the factory.

I asked the warehouse manager if men ever felt left out or marginalized at Hacienda BC, given that so much attention was focused on women workers. He said, "The men in the factory are proud of their work. They are not tortilla makers, and they understand this. They also understand that the work they do is critical to the entire operation, and without them there would be no tortillas." Antonio, one of the machine operators said, "Yes, managers and supervisors do give the women more attention. They have a lot of fun with them. The men do not feel left out. We don't care. In fact it's better for us, because they [the managers] just let us get our own work done." Men in the factory do not see themselves as controlled or subject to the arbitrary authority of managers. They do not have to worry about seeking attention because they are not competing with each other for job stability, as they are in different job titles. The lack of competition between women and men on the shop floor points to the functioning of the internal labor market at Hacienda BC. At this factory, the internal labor market for men is clear. They move from lower-paying jobs to higher-paying jobs and managerial positions based on job openings, seniority, and performance (Doeringer and Piore 1971). Women, on the other hand, have nearly no prospects for mobility within the factory. There is essentially no internal labor market that operates for their job titles because nearly all women work on the assembly line. At Hacienda BC we see how labor control for women workers is despotic, while control for male workers is hegemonic. Essentially, men are left alone and have upward mobility. It is in their best interest not to become involved in disputes between women and managers. However, as discussed previously, given the number of women who work in the factory, especially on the line, the overall character of the regime is coercive.

It is surprising that there is no resentment between men and women in the factory, because men earn more money. I conducted a wage comparison for workers in the factory. Male machine operators and warehouse workers, all men, earn a full $2 more per day than the line workers, who are all women. Even female machine operators doing exactly the same work as men make a dollar less per day than their male counterparts. I asked the production manager about this difference. He said, "Well yes, the men do earn more. Their job requires more hard labor or technical expertise with machines. Besides, many of them have families to support." I responded by saying "don't the single mothers also have families to support?" He said, "sure, but they do not have to support very many people, only themselves and their small children." Despite the fact that most women in the factory are single mothers, managers insist on the notion of the male breadwinner as the primary explanation for why men earn more money.

The Paradox of Gender

How can tortilla work simultaneously be men's work at Hacienda CA and women's work at Hacienda BC? Neither managers' justifications or workers' predictions really explain this difference, so how can we explain this anomaly? One possible explanation could be the differences in technology and product lines between the U.S. and Mexican factories. At the Baja California factory, the machines are older models than those at Hacienda CA. Hacienda BC produces labor-intensive fried products, Hacienda CA does not produce fried products, but they do produce labor-intensive low-calorie tortillas (which require the same number of workers on the line as fried products). If we simply look at the production of corn and flour tortillas in each factory (the products that both factories produce the most), the product line differences essentially balance out. The same proportions of workers in each factory work in the more labor-intensive assembly. However, differences in technology at each factory still remain a viable explanation. The larger factory and newer machines at Hacienda CA do make it a more capital-intensive factory. One could argue that there are enough differences in technology in the factory to justify the different division of labor. Using this argument, men are hired in California because it is more capital intensive; labor-saving costs are not as important in this kind of factory, and managers can afford to pay for the cost of a male workforce. Women are hired in Hacienda BC because the work is more labor intensive; managers need to keep labor costs down, which is done by hiring women, who are traditionally cheaper to hire than male workers (Cohn 1985, 2000). While this argument works to explain why Hacienda BC hires more women, it does not fully explain why more men are hired at Hacienda CA, especially since men and women earn essentially the same wage in that factory. Therefore, why wouldn't the factory hire equal numbers of men and women? There must be other reasons, in addition to that of technology, that explain why Hacienda CA hires more men than women.

I argue that the labor market plays a significant role in why men dominate the workforce at Hacienda CA. Managers at Hacienda CA need the night shift to be fully operational. In fact, the night shift is one of the most important shifts for the factory, as this is the time period where they produce the most tortillas for restaurants and fast-food chains for delivery the next morning. Because women are unwilling to work late at night, managers needed to employ men for this shift period. Currently, only about 5 percent of women in the factory work the 10 P.M. to 6 A.M. shift; most women work either from 6 A.M. to 2 P.M. (the preferred shift) or 2 P.M. to 10 P.M. Of course, the night shift (10 P.M to 6 A.M) is not a popular shift for any of the workers in the factory. Managers compensate for this by forcing undocumented workers and new production employees to work this shift. Documented workers who start out in the night shift are usually able to move into a day shift within a year of working at Hacienda CA, but undocumented workers do not have the benefits of this mobility. In fact, unlike in many unionized factories in the primary labor market, there is no bureaucratized internal labor market at Hacienda CA (Doeringer and Piore 1971). What exists is a very informal internal labor market primarily structured through favoritism and immigration status. The fact that women are unwilling to work the night shift largely explains why this shift is so male dominated, but what explains why the day shifts are also predominantly male at Hacienda CA? This can be explained by two main factors.

First, managers need to construct tortilla manufacturing as men's work in order to successfully recruit men into the factory. If men were to see a tortilla factory full of women, they would be less likely to take the job because they would view it as a "female" occupation. Of course, some jobs in the factory, such as warehouse work, are already exclusively male, and therefore men do not need a lot of convincing to do these jobs. However, assembly line work during the day is a mixed (men and women) occupation. In order to successfully recruit men to the factory, managers need to limit the number of women and construct the work as men's work. The factory cannot openly discriminate against women, so this partially explains why 25 percent of the workforce is female.

Recall that managers justify constructing work at Hacienda CA as men's work because the work entails using machines and doing a lot of lifting. When I confronted the operations manager at Hacienda BC with this puzzle, he said, "Really? I don't know, [shrugs]. It's a strange thing. Maybe they haven't read the literature." It was very common for managers at Hacienda BC to rely on this "literature" on women workers as a source of expertise. Whenever they could not answer my questions, they pulled out the expertise in the literature as an explanation. The manager's statement that the Hacienda CA managers have not read the literature indicated to me that he either did not want to answer my question or was avoiding it altogether. Managers often naturalize gender and then do not feel any need to account for it. Nonetheless, I was perplexed by his response, especially because managers at each location see each other for business at least once a year. Surely they know about each other's production strategies.

Second, as previously mentioned, immigrant men at Hacienda CA are not necessarily more expensive labor than immigrant women. This phenomenon was also found in Bonacich and Appelbaum's (2000) study of the Los Angeles garment industry. Immigrant male production workers (the majority of whom are undocumented) were only making an average of five cents more per hour than their immigrant female counterparts. Managers did allude to the flexibility of men over women, which is beneficial to managers in the long run. Once again, this rhetoric of flexibility is a gendered justification for job discrimination in the factory (Milkman 1987). Given the option of hiring men over women for essentially the same wage, managers choose men because of their gendered notions of flexibility and familial responsibilities.

At Hacienda BC, the opposite is true. Women earn substantially lower wages than do men in the factory because women work on the assembly line; their labor is considered unskilled (and labor intensive). Women's vulnerable position in the local labor market, particularly because of the instability of the maquila industry, their having few or no familial networks in the area, and the difficulty of crossing the border into the United States due to harsh immigration policy—all make them a much more attractive (and cheaper) option. Furthermore, Hacienda BC does not have a graveyard shift as does Hacienda CA, so they have no need to recruit workers (men in particular) to work through the night. Managers are able to construct the work as women's work by recalling the long history of women in tortilla making and the recent trope of women being more suited for assembly line work.

Ultimately, managers at Hacienda CA and Hacienda BC have to do what best advances their interests (and profit) in their respective factories. This means hiring more men at Hacienda CA, and constructing the work as men's work, and hiring more women at Hacienda BC, and constructing the work as women's work.

Gender, Racialization, and Productivity   If we understand managerial control to be fundamentally about profit, we might ask, how is a gender regime that is characterized by hiring more women than men productive? In other words, how do these managerial tactics lead to more profit? The most obvious answer is that the cost of production is lowered by hiring more women. Women in the factory earn a full $2 less per day than men. This is the primary reason that Hacienda BC hires more women in its factory and the primary way in which production costs are reduced.

The fact that women earn far less than men explains why more women are hired in the factory. But how do we explain why the sexualized and racialized environment is productive? Women workers believe that gaining the attention of managers will more effectively provide them with job stability. If a woman is noticed more favorably by managers, they will be less likely to punish or fire her. Dark-skinned women workers feel that they need to work harder to gain managerial attention. One way they accomplish this is by producing more tortillas. Georgina, who is considered dark, told me that many of the darker-skinned women participate in using makeup and flirting to gain favor, but feel that is not enough; they feel they have to be more productive than lighter-skinned women. She says, "I try to be the first one at work so that I can be a line leader and speed up the line so that I can tell the manager that my line was more productive than the other lines." Georgina speeds up the line to gain the attention of managers. According to her, managers respond quite favorably. She says, "they see me as a very hard worker." Darker-skinned women on the tostada line stated that they also increased their own productivity to gain the attention of managers. Gloria said, "we developed a technique to handle the fragile tostadas faster." The tostada line is very labor intensive because of the fragile nature of the product. As Gloria describes it, some women workers on the line have developed ways of working quickly while handling the product with care. These dynamics became quite visible in my own observations of the shop floor. When lighter-skinned women feel that darker-skinned women were getting too much attention because of their productivity, they also ramp up their own productivity by either becoming line leaders, bagging tortillas at a faster rate, or finding other work such as sweeping or cleaning bathrooms during down time. Thus women workers consistently work against their class interests in order to retain the attention of managers.

I was able to gain access to productivity data for the months I was in the factory. Despite observations of spurts of increased productivity and comments by women about increased productivity, the statistics showed relatively consistent production levels. Even when women sped up the line or bagged at a faster rate for some amount of time, productivity numbers did not substantially increase, although there was a slight increase. That being said, I think that it is a mistake to look at productivity numbers only. Women workers whose job it is to work on the line, but who clean bathrooms and sweep the factory during down time, are being "productive" even though this kind of productivity is not recorded. In a very concrete sense they are reproducing women's unpaid labor, and despite feeling that that they were finally being compensated for work they were already doing at home, they were saving the factory costs associated with hiring employees for maintenance jobs.

We might expect that the conflicting efforts of faster productivity by the dark-skinned women and slower productivity by the light-skinned women would cancel each other out. Neoclassical economists have long argued that discrimination is not productive. Therefore in this case pitting dark- and light-skinned women against each other should not be profitable. This may well be true if we are looking at the short-term interests of the corporation. However, I argue that dividing dark- and light-skinned women by forcing them to compete with each other through flirtation serves a long-term interest. In this case, dividing the women workers and creating mistrust on the shop floor trumps the argument that discrimination is not productive. In short, discrimination serves to maintain labor control, which in the long term is profitable.

On another level, managers and supervisors occupy contradictory class positions. They are after all not the owners of the factory and are not reaping all the profits. Therefore, managerial control is only partly about productivity in the factory—because managers have to report to people above them—but it is not exclusively about productivity. Managers and supervisors gain something else from sexual harassment: power. The fact that managers and supervisors at Hacienda BC have so much control over women's lives, particularly job stability, makes them feel extraordinarily powerful. Managers, in particular, made comments to me about feeling like they had no control over their own working conditions. Several of them felt that they were on call twenty-four hours a day, seven days a week. Ramón said, "They [bosses] feel like they can call me at any time. They don't care that I have a family." Supervisors think that even though this is a well-paying job, they have to give up a lot of independence. Efraín said, "I thought that being a supervisor meant that I would have a lot of independence. In reality I'm just another worker." The one thing all supervisors said they had control over was the workers. Having substantial, if not complete, control over workers in the factory allowed these managers and supervisors to take out their frustrations about their own working conditions on workers, particularly women. Furthermore, managers and supervisors believe that they can sexually harass the women because there are few if any repercussions for their actions.

Why does management at Hacienda BC use competition between women as one of its main forms of coercion? And why does such rampant sexual harassment exist on the shop floor? In short, competition between women serves to divide the workforce over job stability and allows managers to maintain shop-floor control. Sexual harassment, on the other hand, gives managers the sense of power, when in their own jobs they often feel powerless. These conditions are interconnected with the complex relationship between state policies and the local labor market.

State Politics

Political Economy of Hacienda BC's Location   Hacienda BC is located in the Mexican state of Baja California. By 2000, the date of the last census, the population of the city had exploded; it nearly quadrupled in thirty years (Cross Border Business Associates 2003). The increase in population is both a result of the city's proximity to the U.S. border and work opportunities in the maquiladora industry. When Mexico began its maquila project in 1965, this was one of the first cities to have a factory. Since then the number of maquilas has grown rapidly. As of 2002 the city had 647 maquiladoras, a full 61 percent of all maquiladoras in the state of Baja California. Its key maquila industries are electronics, auto, and garment. The number of maquilas in the city and other border regions, such as Ciudad Juárez, has attracted thousands of workers from all over Mexico. In fact, nearly 50 percent of the city's population comes from other parts of Mexico, with most coming from Jalisco (Crossborder Business Associates 2003). Many workers have been displaced from their lands and forced to migrate to the border regions where they can find industrial work. Maquila owners have tried to recruit primarily young women to work in their factories. However, in the last several decades this has been changing, and increasingly, men work in the maquiladoras as well. This trend has been documented by Catanzarite and Strober (1993) and Salzinger (2003).

The most recent upsurge in maquila employment took place after the passage of NAFTA. Despite the huge employment boom in the mid-1990s, since 2001 the maquila industry in the city has slowed down substantially. In the "race to the bottom," many maquilas have moved to the interior of Mexico or other developing nations, particularly China, where wages are lower (Iritani and Boudreaux 2003; Cross Border Business Associates 2003).

State and Labor Market Influences on the Shop Floor   The role of the state at Hacienda BC is different from that at Hacienda CA. While in the California factory we saw how state policies were more directly used in shop-floor control; at Hacienda BC the state plays a more indirect role in shaping shop-floor politics. The exception is the centrality of immigration policy on both sides of the border. At Hacienda CA, state intervention, through policies and laws, shapes the immigration regime. At Hacienda BC, the role of the state is more complex because of the multifaceted interactions between the U.S. state and the Mexican state. At Hacienda BC, both U.S. immigration policies and Mexican economic development policies and practices work together to create opportunities for those managers to maintain a gender regime.

The United States and Mexico have had a long and complex relationship negotiating foreign capital and emigration (Caulfield 1998; De la Garza 2003a). Over the last one hundred years, Mexico has fluctuated between economic nationalism and complete state sovereignty to a strategy of attracting foreign capital and privatizing certain national industries (Caulfield 1998). The United States has fluctuated in its immigration policies by opening and closing its doors to Mexican immigrants. the Bracero Program, Operation Wetback, the Immigration Reform and Control Act, and Operation Gatekeeper are all examples of this fluctuation. However, in the last thirty years, Mexico has maintained a consistent process of export-led development, a development strategy that seeks to reorient the economy toward producing goods for the export market. This is particularly highlighted by its participation in the General Agreement on Trade and Tariffs in 1983 and NAFTA in 1994 (Middlebrook 1995; Bensusán and Cook 2003). In other words, Mexico is a prime example of the globalization process.

Globalization has led to serious social problems in developing countries. Specifically, it has increased the proletarianization of indigenous and rural peoples who used to rely on subsistence agriculture. This shift from subsistence agriculture to wage labor has caused internal and external migration, the deterioration of culture, erosion of the countryside, and the exploitation of workers (Sassen-Koob 1984; Sklair 1993; Lee 1998; Tobar 2006).

Studies predicted that the liberalization of corn prices would displace thousands of small farmers (Hinojosa-Ojeda and Robinson 1992). This was certainly the case for Margarita, a production worker at Hacienda BC. María said, "My family has a long history in the corn industry. My entire family used to grow corn in Guerrero. In 1998 my father had to abandon the farm that we all grew up on. He could no longer compete with the cheap U.S. corn that was coming into Mexico. We [the children] moved to Baja California to find maquila employment. I worked as a garment worker for two years, but then the factory closed. So that is how I came to work for Hacienda BC."

Margarita is not the only worker who experienced this kind of displacement. Most of the women said they had to migrate because there was no longer any opportunity for their families in their hometowns. According to CIESAS (Center for Research in Social Anthropology), the migration rate increased from 14 percent to 20 percent from 1970 to 1990. While people from Guerrero used to migrate to the coastal region for work in coffee plantations, over the last ten years migration has shifted northward to places such as Mexico City and the border. This is a result of a variety of causes, including lack of services and the economic crisis. As a result of this displacement, many people from rural communities were forced to migrate to cities, often taking maquila jobs. In fact, maquila employment rose after the passage of NAFTA. In 1995 the industry employed 648,263 people. At its peak in 2000, it employed 1,291,232 people (Instituto Nacional de Estadistica Geografía e Informática 2003c; Pastor and Wise 2003). However, by 2003 employment in the maquila sector in Mexico as a whole had fallen to 1,062,105 (Instituto Nacional de Estadistica Geografía e Informática 2003c). In Baja California the situation was more drastic, as the number of maquilas rapidly declined from a peak of 1,235 maquiladoras in 2001 to 888 establishments in 2004, even though the population continued to increase. While the unemployment rate in the city is relatively low at 2 percent (Secretaría del Trabajo y Previsión Social 2003a), it has increased since 2001, when it was only 1 percent (Secretaría del Trabajo y Previsión Social 2003a). The low unemployment rate in the city can be attributed to lack of state-supported unemployment benefits. Since people cannot afford to subsist when unemployed, they are driven into underemployment (De la Garza and Salas 2006). Here we see an interesting parallel between the processes of proletarianization on the Mexican side of the border and welfare reform on the U.S. side. In both cases, neoliberal policies have created a pool of displaced and often desperate workers. This allows employers to be even more unscrupulous in their labor control tactics.

Nearly all the women I interviewed had migrated to Baja California with their husbands and small children. Half of these women came from rural areas, while the others came from small cities. Today, most of these women are single mothers with no family in the area. Their husbands crossed the border. Some of them are missing, others are dead, and yet others can't afford to bring their families to the United States. Rosa said, "I haven't been in communication with my husband for five years. When he crossed to the other side, our daughter was six months old. I stayed here in Baja California without any family, waiting for him." Isabel said, "My husband made it across the border okay, but he hasn't been able to send enough money to bring our family to the United States. It's too expensive and more dangerous by the day. He would rather not see me, and know that I am alive. We talk on the phone every week."

This is the role that U.S. state policies play in shaping the local labor market in the border region. The militarization of the border in the United States has prevented many families from crossing the border. Most of the women that I interviewed said that their husbands were afraid to have the whole family cross the border, particularly because many of them had heard about deaths due to increased enforcement. Xochitl said, "My husband told me it would only be a few months. He would go earn some money, come back and bring us all to the U.S. It has now been over seven years. I heard from him for the first couple of months and never again."

The attraction of foreign capital to the border region, along with U.S. state policies that limit migration and employer preferences for women, has produced a local labor market with many single women (Anderson and Dimon 1999). Hacienda BC has been able to attract these single women into their labor force because of the stability of the tortilla industry compared with maquilas. Because these women, particularly single mothers, prize stable jobs above wages and other working conditions, managers and supervisors can be unscrupulous in their exploitation of women. Much like at Hacienda CA, at Hacienda BC we also see the centrality of immigration policy in labor control.

The State, Unions, and Constitutional Rights   Another way in which the state plays a role in giving Hacienda BC managers the tools to maintain a coercive regime is by the lack of enforcement of Mexican labor law, and more fundamentally, by how labor law and practice was institutionally developed. As we saw in Chapter 3, the Mexican constitution is one of the most progressive in the world. Written in 1917 during the Mexican Revolution of 1910–1920, it promises workers unprecedented labor protections. Article 123, the provision that delineates workers' rights, includes minimum wage standards, the right to form a union, nondiscrimination (including sexual harassment), health and safety protections, overtime pay, health insurance, and paid vacation, among other benefits. However, as Bensusán and Cook (2003, 235) argue, "despite the generally protective character of labor legislation, the strong state role in labor relations has allowed successive governments to modify and even violate these protections in order to adapt to changing demands of a more market oriented economy." These conditions are especially true along the border. In order to attract foreign investment, many local officials choose to turn a blind eye to violations of labor law and constitutional rights.

Once again, the parallels with the United States are striking. Over forty years, the United States has seen a significant erosion of labor law protections. Most recently, this erosion has been manifested in the form of *Hoffman Plastics v. NLRB,* where some of the NLRA protection of immigrants was gutted because the Supreme Court deemed immigration law to supersede labor law.

As Aiwa Ong (1999) suggests, the border is often a zone of graduated sovereignty. It is a place where states give up some of their sovereignty to attract foreign capital. This is also true in Mexican border cities. However, in Mexico, as a result of NAFTA, border zone benefits were extended to companies (including those that are Mexican owned) throughout the country. In signing NAFTA the Mexican government gave up some of its rights to control the flow of capital and trade. However, it also opened up privileges to Mexican-owned companies. Hacienda BC benefited from this process, especially because it is located in a border zone where government officials routinely turn a blind eye to violations of labor law. Managers are well aware that regulations are not followed and use the opportunity to sexually harass women workers.

Another way that the company is able to abuse its power is through network connections with national leaders, including former presidents, as well as with the local government. There is also a strong relationship between the union and the company. On my first visit to Hacienda BC, I asked the production manager if there was a union in the factory. He looked at me suspiciously and said, "Yes and no. The CTM (Confederación de Trabajadores Mexicanos)[6] represents a factory in another state, and supposedly this union also has jurisdiction over the factory, but not really. In any case, we like it this way, because if anyone tries to start something, I can show him that a union represents him. If anyone ever started making trouble and tried to get a union, [moves hand across throat as in cutting the throat]. We are a business, not a charity, and I am the only one who controls these workers." The manager made it very clear that the union, which is supposed to represent workers, does not in fact do so. He and other executives in the company are overtly antiunion. They believe that unions cut into their profits and their ability to manage workers. When I raised the issue of unions, the production manager's good nature (at least with me) changed. It was particularly striking that he moved his hand across his neck as a symbol of cutting a throat, as if to imply that anyone participating in the union could be injured. My impression was that he was not simply joking by using that gesture. Independent unions are extraordinarily difficult to form in Mexico and despised by management.

When I first noticed sexual harassment on the shop floor, I asked the women why they didn't file a grievance with their union. Most of them rolled their eyes at me. Marta said, "The union is not a union for workers. They are always on management's side. They are sympathizers of the same political party as the owners of the company so they help each other out. We don't go to the local arbitration boards, because we know that the state will also protect the union and the company, since they helped them [political party] get into power." Most workers correctly believe that if they try to file a complaint with local arbitration boards, not only will they lose the arbitration, but they will very quickly lose their jobs and be blacklisted. Ximena commented, "There was a girl who worked with us, Juana was her name. She went to the union once to complain about the harassment. The very next day she was fired. What kind of confidence does that give us?" Management at Hacienda BC can count on the union siding with them. They can count on the state siding with them. I want to make clear here that the lack of enforcement of labor law in Mexico and ghost unions who do not represent workers are not gendered issues; these practices affect all workers. However, women tend to be the lowest-paid and most mistreated workers and therefore have the most to gain from genuine legal protections. These policies particularly affect women at Hacienda BC because they make up the majority of the workers in the factory and have to endure constant sexual harassment, something that men in the factory are not exposed to. Women at the Hacienda BC plant are compelled to sell their labor power because social policies that would allow them to withhold their labor from the market are not in place or are not enforced (Burawoy 1985). While there are constitutional provisions that protect them, the state does not enforce these, leaving no buffer between women and the corporation. Furthermore, the economic instability of the area, a product of the race to the bottom, gives them few options for leaving to work in the surrounding maquilas.

Wage Inequality between Hacienda CA and Hacienda BC

One of the most striking differences between the California and Baja California factories is the distinct level of wage inequality. Using the nominal currency exchange rate, we see that wages at the California plant ($8.79 per/hr) are 7.6 times greater than wages in the Baja California plant (1.15 per/hr). Even when adjusting for cost of living by using the purchasing power parity index (PPP),[7] I found that workers at Hacienda CA are still making five times as much, in actual purchasing power terms, as workers at Hacienda BC.[8] I also evaluated the price that Hacienda can get for its product at their respective locations. If Hacienda can sell their products for more money in the United States, then they can afford to pay higher wages there. In 2003 a package of ten Hacienda flour tortillas in a Baja California supermarket cost Mex$9.60 (U.S.$0.96). The same package in a U.S. supermarket is priced at $0.99. This illustrates that the prices of Hacienda tortillas is basically similar in both countries. Thus prices clearly cannot account for the huge wage disparity.

The wage disparity between the two plants can largely be attributed to the border. Border restrictions and militarization make it impossible for

TABLE 2. Wages in flour tortilla manufacturing

	Hacienda CA (dollars/hr)	Hacienda BC (pesos/day)	Hacienda BC (dollars/hr)
Wages	$8.79	$86.00*	$1.15

* Exchange rate and hour conversion factor: $86/8 hr = 10.75/hr; exchange rate = 0.1068. Exchange rate is from 1/22/02, the date of the interview at which these wages were reported.
Source: Data from company records.

the wage rate to equalize between the United States and Mexico. While there is some mobility of labor on the border, Mexicans still cannot freely cross the border to sell their labor for higher wages.

Conclusion

I have argued that Hacienda BC operates using a gender regime. Free trade has created numerous social problems in Mexico, particularly the displacement of families from their small farms. This has created both internal migration in Mexico and external migration to the United States. Many of the women workers at Hacienda BC moved to the border with their spouses and children to seek better opportunities. The increased militarization of the U.S. border prevented many families from crossing the border, but it has not stopped migration, because men continue to cross. Women were left alone with their children and no other familial networks. While waiting for their husbands, many of these women began to work in the border's maquiladoras. The increasing economic instability in the area, due to an ever-increasing race to the bottom, has forced women to look for more stable work in national industries.

Managers at Hacienda BC take advantage of women's vulnerable position in the local labor market, and their cheap wages compared with those of men, to create a competitive shop-floor environment. The gender regime serves several purposes. First, it allows managers to maintain control of the shop floor with coercion. Second, it increases the productivity of the factory. Third, it gives managers and supervisors power to control women workers' bodies. Furthermore, the role of the state in Mexican labor relations (Bensusán and Cook 2003) continues to provide managers with opportunities to get away with a sexualized work environment.

6

Fighting Back?

Resistance in the Age of Neoliberalism

> Our struggle is not easy. Those who oppose our cause are rich and powerful
> and they have many allies in high places. We are poor. Our allies are few. But
> we have something the rich do not own. We have our bodies and spirits and
> the justice of our cause as our weapons.
>
> Cesar Chavez, 1968

Over the course of this book we have learned how macro-level policies impact the daily lives of workers on the shop floor. In particular, I have focused on how state policies give managers the tools of coercion and how race, gender, and class are produced at the point of production. Very little attention has been paid to how workers fight against anti-immigrant policies and oppression on the shop floor. This is the subject of this chapter. However, remember that resistance is a complex phenomenon. In some ways this chapter is as much about a lack of resistance as it is about fighting back. Here, I analyze how resistance operates in the Hacienda CA and Hacienda BC factories. I find that resistance operates differently in each location.

In the mid-1990s Carlos, a truck driver at Hacienda CA, and 150 of his co-workers went on strike. As a result of the difficult, yet successful action, truck drivers were able to negotiate a contract. Most importantly, they successfully fought back the company's attempt to convert the drivers into independent contractors.

In 1997 Felipe, a production worker, and several of his co-workers formed a group to discuss organizing production workers at Hacienda CA. Felipe was first contacted to discuss unionization by organizers from the Manufacturing Organizing Project (MOP). As a result of an immigrant worker organizing boom in California in the 1990s and the successful Hacienda truck driver strike, the International Brotherhood of Teamsters (IBT) and MOP partnered to organize tortilla production workers industrywide. There was a mixed response about unionization from workers. Nevertheless, Felipe and MOP organizers began to form organizing committees at Hacienda CA. However, the MOP-IBT partnership fell though soon after initial organizing, and the production worker organizing drive ultimately failed.

Since 1997, there has been almost no union organizing in the California tortilla industry. No other union has attempted to organize production workers at Hacienda CA. At the time of my interviews, there was no collective resistance among production workers. What did exist was sporadic individual-level resistance such as eating tortillas off the line, even though this was against company policy.

On the other side of the border, at Hacienda BC, worker actions were also taking place. In 1996, the same year that the truck drivers struck the Hacienda CA factory, over 50 percent of the production workers at Hacienda BC went on strike. Women workers walked off the job to protest poor safety standards. Five workers had been seriously injured on the production floor the month before, and management had done nothing to improve working conditions on the shop floor despite many complaints from workers. Workers also tried to file a formal complaint with the union, but to no avail. The union had been formed in secret cooperation with management even before the factory opened. The walkout at Hacienda BC lasted only a few days. When workers returned to work, managers continued to deny their demands. As a result a significant percent of production workers left the factory to go to work in the surrounding maquila industry.

Since the 1996 walkout, there has been no collective resistance at Hacienda BC, but workers engage in more consistent individual resistance than do workers at the Hacienda CA factory. That being said, resistance in general is at a low point. Furthermore, calling the kind of individual-level actions workers engage in *resistance* is questionable. In fact, I will argue below that this resistance is part of the managerial strategy in the factory.

What explains the boom of organizing and resistance in the 1990s versus the lack of organizing and resistance in the 2000s at both the California and Baja California factories? This chapter will explore how state policy and the labor market played a significant role in both the boom and bust of the resistance cycle at each location. I argue that the truck driver contract campaign was successful because they already had a union, effectively engaged the public, and didn't have to contend with anti-immigrant policies. In contrast, production workers at Hacienda CA were going to have to organize a union from scratch, they were a mix of documented and undocumented workers, and most importantly, there was an ideological difference in organizing strategy between the IBT and MOP. This difference resulted in the loss of funding for the campaign. I argue that since 2000 resistance has all but disappeared among production workers at Hacienda CA because immigration policies, particularly the militarization of the border and the criminalization of immigrants, have become much more severe, leading to substantial fear of deportation. These new policies and the institutionalization of immigration policies in the 1990s have generally affected immigrant organizing in California. In fact, while there is an abundance of immigrant activism *inside* unions and worker centers, very few *new* immigrant workers are being organized in California.[1]

State policy and law has had similar effects in Baja California. The 1996 walkout by Hacienda BC workers was possible, at least in part, because of labor market conditions in Baja California in the 1990s. At that time, the maquila industry was booming, especially after the passage of NAFTA in 1994. As a result, there were a lot of opportunities for employment in the maquiladora sector. At the time of the walkout, the heightened militarization of the border was so recent that it wasn't possible to fully evaluate its effect on migration. Furthermore, NAFTA's implementation was still in the early stages, and thus displacement as a result of NAFTA was not fully visible. As a consequence, workers felt that they could take the risk of walking off the job with little consequence to their economic well-being.

Since 2000, the situation has changed. Displacement as a result of NAFTA has become a serious trend. The militarization of the border has become institutionalized, making it even more dangerous to cross, and the once-booming maquila industry has slowed down, with factories moving to China. Institutionalized state policies, as well as the instability of the maquila industry, have created less economic security for workers and more danger for those crossing the border. I argue that there is a direct connection between the more militarized environment and the immigration regime implemented at Hacienda CA. The immigration regime is also connected to lack of resistance and mobilization on the shop floor. Losing one's job has become a more serious risk, one that few workers at Hacienda BC are willing to take. Resistance at Hacienda BC in the twenty-first century has been at a low point. In the following sections we analyze the California and Baja California campaigns.

The California Immigrant Worker Organizing Boom

The 1990s was the decade for immigrant worker organizing in California. The state had never seen anything like it in its history, nor has the organizing boom been re-created since. In the 1990s, immigrant worker organizing took two main forms, strategic organizing and hot shop organizing.[2] These two types of organizing practices were being hotly debated inside the labor movement. In strategic organizing, a union consciously decides to organize an industry (e.g., garment manufacturing), after gaining an understanding of the particular industry, its importance to the economy, and the feasibility of organizing it. Strategic organizing is important in the globalized economy because the union attempts to organize an entire industry. So, even if one factory closes down, all the other factories in the industry are unionized. This model of organizing protects workers in an entire industry, rather than just one factory. One of the most successful examples of strategic organizing in the 1990s was the Justice for Janitors campaigns developed by the Service Employees International Union (SEIU) (Milkman 2006).

Hot shop organizing, on the other hand, begins with the workers. Workers having problems at a particular worksite engage in a variety of actions on the job, sometimes including walkouts, to try to push management to resolve the problem. These workers sometimes look for a union that is willing to help organize them. Oftentimes, unions are not willing to work on such a campaign because the worksite is not part of the strategic industry of a union's focus. On other occasions multiple unions all try to organize the same worksite. In a hot shop campaign, when a company shuts down, the campaign is over, and individual workers lose as does the union, which loses the resources invested in the campaign. On the other hand, in strategic organizing, while individual workers may lose if a company shuts down, workers in the industry as a group have gained something if the entire industry is unionized.

The debate surrounding strategic versus hot shop organizing is particularly sharp in the dramatically changed political economy of recent decades. In the last thirty years, organizing in the United States has been challenging because of contracting systems (both internal to the United States and offshore); antiunion labor law; and new, effective union-busting strategies used by employers. As a result, it takes a lot of union resources to organize and win campaigns. Therefore, it often makes sense for unions to use strategic organizing so that unionization is ensured across a sector rather than at a single worksite. In the 1990s three very visible and large-scale campaigns were Justice for Janitors, American Racing Equipment, and the drywallers. The Justice for Janitors was a strategic campaign, the American Racing Equipment campaign was a hot shop campaign, and the drywallers campaign was a mix of both. These campaigns demonstrated to immigrant workers and the labor movement that immigrants can indeed be organized.

Justice for Janitors

SEIU had a long history of success in the janitorial industry after World War II, peaking in the late 1970s. Union membership in 1978 was about five thousand, and wages were about $12 an hour by the early 1980s (Fisk, Mitchell, and Erickson 2000). However, after the recession of the 1980s and the extreme antiunionism of the Reagan era, unionization and wage rates in the janitorial industry fell dramatically. By 1985 janitorial union membership in Los Angeles had fallen to nearly two thousand. This dramatic decline was also a result of industrial restructuring and changes in the workforce. The industry moved to a model of subcontracting, where building owners no longer directly employed janitors. Instead, janitors were now employed by cleaning contractors who were nonunion. While the janitorial industry was increasing at an unprecedented pace because of the number of buildings built after 1980, these jobs were essentially all nonunion contract jobs. The vast majority of these contracted jobs were going to Latina immigrants from Mexico and Central America. The number of African Americans workers, who had been 31 percent of the unionized workforce, declined to about 12 percent after subcontracting and deunion-ization. Local 399, the local SEIU union, had all but given up on organiz-ing and maintaining janitors in the union, but SEIU International stepped in and imposed the Justice for Janitors campaign on the local level (Fisk, Mitchell, and Erickson 2000).

The Justice for Janitors campaign strategically targeted building owners and managers even though workers were technically employed by clean-ing contractors. The goal of the SEIU was to get building managers to use unionized cleaning contractors who were paying union wages. While the campaign initially made slow gains, in June of 1990 the union decided to strike. Strikers were brutally attacked by the police department during a peaceful march with supporters and family. The attack was caught on camera and received national media attention. As a result of the public outrage, support from the Mayor of Los Angeles, and support from other SEIU locals, workers won the campaign. The contract included raises of thirty cents an hour, bringing the average wage to $5.20. While this was still much lower than the industry wage in the early 1980s of $12 an hour, it was a victory for workers because the union had found a way to re-unionize the entire sector. This meant that most of the building owners felt enough pressure to hire only unionized contractors, which in turn meant that many nonunion contractors chose not to fight unionization.

The campaign received national media attention and highlighted the labor movement to many immigrant workers who had previously had little or no interactions with unions. The campaign also proved to the American Federation of Labor-Congress of Industrial Organizations (AFL-CIO) that organizing immigrants was not only possible, but necessary. Addi-tionally, it showed the labor movement that immigrant workers could be equally militant, if not more militant, than native-born workers. Further-more, Justice for Janitors captured the hearts of many nonimmigrants and brought sweatshop conditions to the attention of the public. The campaign was ultimately successful because it organized an entire industry instead of focusing only on a few cleaning contractors.

American Racing Equipment

A little over a month after the Justice for Janitors victory, nearly one thou-sand workers at American Racing Equipment (ARE), a manufacturer of automobile wheels, walked off the job. They were frustrated with their boss because new technology was introduced into the factory with little training. Furthermore, this new technology sped up the pace of work. Workers were also frustrated by new work rules that required them to ask permission before using the bathrooms (Zabin 2000). Being worried about the safety of the new technology and the speedup (with no extra pay), workers in the foundry were the first to walk off the job. By the end of the three days, the vast majority of workers in the factory refused to cross the picket line (Bacon 1995). During the three-day strike, a variety of unions tried to get the workers to organize with them. However, workers decided that they were better off without a union at the time. After the strike, workers returned to work with a clear message to their employer that they were willing to organize and strike. The workers at ARE, who were mainly first-generation Mexican immigrants, eventually decided to unionize with the International Association of Machinists and Aerospace Workers (IAM). The various different unions who were interested in the ARE workers had to go through their own process to figure out who was best suited to organize these workers. When the IAM committed a quarter of a million dollars to the organizing drive, other unions backed away from the campaign (Zabin 2000). Despite support from workers, the union had its work cut out for it. Workers were divided, and management hired a union-busting consulting firm to try to destroy the campaign. Despite these challenges, on December 20, 1990, workers voted in favor of the union by a clear majority. The success of the campaign was largely attributed to workers taking ownership of the organizing and the union allowing workers to run their own campaign. In the end, management at ARE recognized the union, and the workers won their first contract a little over one year after their initial strike (Zabin 2000).

The organizing campaign at ARE was dramatically different from the Justice for Janitors Campaign. First of all, immigrant workers at ARE went on strike on their own, with no union involvement. Second, unlike the janitorial industry, ARE was a manufacturer that could have potentially closed and moved its operations offshore. Finally, workers (and eventually the union) were not organizing an entire industry; they focused on one shop. This campaign was a more traditional form of hot shop organizing. Nevertheless, workers and the union demonstrated that a traditional union campaign still had possibilities for success.

Drywallers

Two years after the Justice for Janitors and American Racing Equipment organizing drives, thousands of Mexican immigrant drywall hangers went on a five-month strike for higher pay and union recognition. The strike halted residential construction from Santa Barbara (north of Los Angeles) to the San Diego-Mexican border (Milkman and Wong 2000; Milkman 2006). According to Bacon (1995, 7), "they finally forced building contractors to sign the first agreements covering their work in decades, the first union contracts won by a grassroots organizing effort in the building trades anywhere in the country since the 1930s."

In the 1960s and 1970s, the residential drywall industry was 80 percent unionized, and wages were high. However, much as in the janitorial industry, construction employers went on the attack in the 1980s. The Association of Builders and Contractors initiated a nationwide campaign to deunionize the industry. By 1990 union density in construction nationwide was cut in half. The residential construction sector suffered an even greater loss of union density. Deunionization was in large part responsible for cutting drywall wages by half. As a result, many native-born (mostly white) union members in California left residential construction for the more stable and unionized commercial construction. Immigrants came into the industry in large numbers as unionized native-born workers left. In fact, in 1980, 87 percent of drywallers were native born (mostly white, but some Latina/os and Blacks); by 1990 the percentage had dropped to 43 percent. Foreign-born Latina/os comprised 35 percent of the workers (Milkman and Wong 2000; Milkman 2006).

Organizing for better wages and working conditions began when a drywaller was cheated out of part of his wages for three weeks in a row. He contacted the United Brotherhood of Carpenter's union (UBC). The union offered the worker a meeting space, and he began making on-site visits to organize his fellow workers. While the drywall workers were having regular meetings at the local UBC, the campaign leading up to the strike and the strike itself emerged from a rank-and-file movement, without union affiliation or involvement. During the long months of the strike, the labor movement, in particular the UBC, provided extensive financial and legal assistance to the striking workers. As a result, the drywallers chose to affiliate with the UBC. After the strike's crippling effect on the industry, the

Pacific Rim Drywall Association (representing all major drywall firms north of San Diego) recognized the UBC and provided higher piece rates, medical benefits, and preferential hiring rights to the workers (Milkman and Wong 2000).

The drywallers' campaign represents a hybrid form of organizing tactics. It had elements of both a strategic campaign and a hot shop campaign. On the one hand, the organizing drive was industry based, and a large part of the industry became unionized (except San Diego). On the other hand, the campaign was started by workers who were frustrated by their wages and working conditions. While workers received financial and legal support from various unions, it was not until almost the end of the strike that workers chose to affiliate with the UBC. In that sense, the campaign resembled hot shop organizing.

All three of the campaigns highlight the energy and momentum of immigrant worker organizing in California in the 1990s. Even though each campaign had a different method, all three were successful endeavors that created a buzz in the labor movement around the issue of immigrant workers.

Strategic Organizing at Hacienda CA

The truck drivers' strike at Hacienda CA occurred on the coattails of the successful campaigns detailed above. In order to understand the genesis of the truck driver contract campaign, we must first understand where some of the resources for the campaign came from. In the midst of the immigrant worker organizing occurring in California, a group of union organizers formed the MOP. The goal was to promote organizing in California's manufacturing industries. MOP had three basic principles: first, manufacturing is important because California is the largest manufacturing center in the United States; second, issues of poverty in California cannot be addressed effectively without jobs that offer a living wage; and third, unions are agents of change that can improve wages and working conditions of immigrant workers who are not linked to political and economic power. The primary vision of MOP was to do strategic, industry-wide organizing in the manufacturing sector. This led to a multiunion, multiemployer, community-based organizing project (Delgado 2000).

By early 1995 MOP consisted of nine unions that each agreed to contribute $25,000 to the project.[3] Initially, the goal was to create a separate
entity into which workers would be organized, but many of the unions reacted negatively to this idea. By 1996, many of the unions had dropped out
of the project. The main union funding the project was the IBT. The IBT
alerted MOP to the contract struggle of truck drivers in the tortilla industry, and MOP jumped at the opportunity to work on the campaign. With a
strategic, tortilla industry-wide campaign in mind, MOP worked with the
IBT to help truck drivers at Hacienda CA win their contract campaign.

Los Troqueros and Company Restructuring

In the 1990s *los troqueros*[4] working for Guadalupe Tortillas formed a union
and won a contract. Workers under this contract owned their own trucks
but got a base salary, health insurance, and a gas allowance from the company. While Guadalupe did put up a battle in the unionization of these
workers, it was not nearly as terrible as some of the antiunion campaigns
seen in the past. The workers were able to get recognized and win their
first contract without a strike.[5] Several years later, Guadalupe was bought
out by TortiUS. When Hacienda took over the company, it wanted to turn
all of the truck drivers into independent contractors not covered by a collective bargaining agreement. Under this new arrangement the truck drivers would have lost their base salary, health insurance, and gas allowance.
They would have worked on commission alone, based on their sales totals
for the week. When the truckers' contract expired, Hacienda tried to move
this agenda. The truck drivers fought back by organizing.

El Chupacabras and Ethnic-Based Organizing

In developing a strategy for the truck drivers' contract campaign, organizers with MOP (who were mostly Latina/os) decided that an important approach to use to win this campaign would be to "use the common bonds
of ethnicity, nationality and culture to empower workers as we organize
them into the labor movement."[6] Because almost all of the truck drivers
were Mexican, one way to get them active in the campaign was to expose
Hacienda CA for what the company really was. This was also a way to garner Latino community support. Organizers at MOP did extensive research

on the tortilla industry and the company. As a result of this research, they found that the company was a large transnational whose executives had significant ties to the former president of Mexico, Carlos Salinas de Gortari. Salinas's party, the Partido Revolucionario Institucional (PRI), was the ruling party in Mexico for seventy-one years, until Vicente Fox with the Partido de Acción Nacional (PAN) came into power in 2000. The PRI was well known among workers in both countries for its corruption and the vast patronage system it had constructed. When workers discovered the close ties between Hacienda CA and the PRI, they quickly understood the politics of the company. Through its corporate research, MOP organizers successfully tied Hacienda CA to Mexican corruption and corporate greed. As one organizer told me, "Salinas was symbolic of the draining of the working class in Mexico." Workers and the Mexican community were already very sophisticated in their understanding of Mexican politics, so understanding the link between the company and the Mexican state created a lot of support for the union.

As a way to garner support and enthusiasm from other workers and the community, truck drivers and MOP organizers started using the term *El Chupacabras* to refer to the company. El Chupacabras in Spanish literally means "the goat sucker." El Chupacabras is a mystical creature in Latin America that has been known to suck all the blood from goats and other animals (the closest approximation in English would be a vampire). Nixtamal workers in Mexico had accused the owner of Tortimundo of having "sucked" subsidies from CONASUPO (recall Chapter 2). Through its subsidiary Hacienda CA, the corporation was bleeding the workers dry on the U.S. side of the border. In other words Tortimundo had become a binational Chupacabras.

After recognizing the corporate greed at Hacienda CA and what was at stake if the company successfully reclassified them as independent contractors, 150 truck drivers at Hacienda CA decided to go on strike. The strike began with a picket line in front of the company. Knowing that the company was going to pull out all of its union-busting tactics, the workers and the union knew that in order to have a successful strike they needed to have a multipronged campaign. In addition to the corporate campaign (exposing the company for its ties with corrupt Mexican officials), workers and organizers recognized that the strike would not be effective unless there was community, labor, and political support. In order to get these other types of support, organizers began a generalized boycott campaign.

This campaign included paid publicity, free media utilization, outreach, and strategic leafleting.[7]

The first step was to make the community, labor, and politicians aware of what was going on at Hacienda CA. Newspaper ads were placed in community newspapers and *La Opinion* (the largest Spanish language newspaper in the state). To gain access to free media coverage, organizers and workers held a press conference announcing the boycott. The press conference was attended by labor, politicians, and community leaders and covered by both the English and Spanish language media. On the outreach front, workers and organizers reached out to the labor movement, Latina/o politicians, the Latina/o community at large, local city governments, community organizations, and non-Latina/o leaders. The labor movement supported the effort by sending mailings to its members and having labor leaders attend press conferences. Workers and organizers asked Latina/o elected officials to send mailings to their constituencies and attend the workers' press conferences and rallies. The Latina/o community more broadly was asked to support the boycott, sign pledge cards, and attend rallies. Community organizations were asked to make presentations to their constituencies and get their members to sign pledge cards. In addition to outreach to these different constituencies, one of the most important aspects of the boycott was strategic leafleting. Leaflets were passed out after mass at churches, at Mexican Independence Day events, and at selected supermarkets and fast-food chains selling or using Hacienda products. The leafleting created an enormous amount of visibility for the boycott.

Essentially, the strategy for the boycott was to get the Latina/o community engaged and involved in these workers' struggle. Therefore, the campaign became about Latina/o empowerment. The following messages were used to capture the hearts and minds of the community: The success of the strike will help future struggles by Latina/os; every Latina/o worker should have the support of his/her community; the tortilla industry is one of a few in which the community can make its power felt; and Latina/o workers should get some of the benefits made possible by Latina/o consumers in a mostly Latina/o industry.[8] Organizers also consciously made the truck drivers' strike part of the larger immigrant-organizing efforts in California by referring to the janitors', drywallers', and farm workers' struggles.

Each of these messages made explicit how the truck drivers' struggle was essential for the empowerment and advancement of the entire community. The messages evoked feelings of ethnic solidarity against a common enemy. What was difficult about this kind of ethnic messaging was that the employer, a Mexican company, was trying to evoke in the workers the same kind of ethnic solidarity with the company. However, most workers and the community were not persuaded because of the connections that MOP made between the company and the former president of Mexico, Salinas de Gortari. The "Chupacabras Binacional" was a very effective slogan that resonated with the community's understanding of Mexican politics.

In the early part of the strike, the company responded by telling the media that the strike was having no impact on its distribution of tortillas. However, as the strike and boycott became more successful, Hacienda CA started using more serious union-busting tactics. These included forcing workers to attend captive audience meetings. During these meetings workers were told by the company that the union was corrupt and that the union was just using them because they wanted to make money off workers' dues. The company also sent a letter to truck drivers stating that drivers could return to work and be protected for not striking. The letter also said that "employees who choose not to strike also have a legal right, if they wish, to resign their union membership before returning to work in order to avoid potential fines by the union. To avoid a fine, the law requires that a written resignation be received by the union before the employee returns to work."[9]

Several truck drivers who had been involved in the strike and boycott also told me that the company hired thugs to follow their cars and break the windows of their homes. One man was allegedly beaten and mugged by one of these thugs. Several weeks into the strike, security guards hired by the company followed a caravan of workers going to do strategic leafleting at a fast-food chain. The caravan was forced off the freeway, and workers were attacked with pepper spray. The California Highway Patrol explained to a reporter, "A videotape of the incident, clearly shows the security guards forcibly stopping the convoy on the freeway and discharging some kind of liquid at the IBT member driving his vehicle."[10] In addition to physical threats, the company also tried to co-opt workers by offering better positions in Hacienda CA if they stopped striking. Carlos Moreno, a truck driver, commented, "They [the company] called me to tell me that they knew that I did not want to strike, but that the union was threatening me. They told me they would give me a supervisor position if I did not stay on strike.... I told them that I could think on my own and that nobody would tell me what to do." Ricardo Martínez said, "they offered me $900 per month to be a manager, I told them yes, if I could be a manager and in the union. They said that managers could not be in the union, and so I told them that I could not be a manager." These workers and other truck drivers held their ground.

After nearly seven hard weeks on the picket line, the strike ended and the contract was settled. The new five-year contract included a wage increase over five years that amounted to 24 percent if base pay and commission are combined. Workers also won a 1 percent increase in commission on all sales of $2,000 or more, and a new paid holiday, their birthday. Most importantly, the new contract prohibits the company from contracting out the work of route drivers during the term of the contract. Furthermore, new routes must be first offered to existing drivers according to seniority before new drivers are hired (MOP internal files). The drivers were not successful at eliminating the copay on medical insurance, nor did they eliminate the $2,000 per week sales minimum before the 6 percent commission kicks in. All in all, the truck drivers considered the strike and boycott a success.

Why was the truck drivers' strike successful? There were two main reasons. First, workers engaged in a militant strike that disrupted the company's production system. The truck drivers put up twenty-four-hour picket lines at the company's locations and followed replacement workers to their delivery destinations. The disruption cost the company over $1 million in fees for rental trucks, replacement workers, and security. Second, there was substantial community and political support. The community really related to the fact that these were Mexican workers, distributing a Mexican product (the tortilla). The slogan Chupacabras Binacional also resonated with the community, because they understood what it meant for this Mexican company to be tied to the Mexican state. Furthermore, many politicians (especially Latina/os) signed a pledge to boycott Hacienda CA. This was particularly important because it signaled to Hacienda CA that it was increasingly isolated, even among politicians who had accepted campaign contributions from the company in the past.[11] But how does this success compare with production worker organizing?

Organizing on the Shop Floor

After the successful strike held by Hacienda CA truck drivers, MOP and the IBT began to focus on production worker organizing in 1997.

By that time the MOP project with multi-union involvement had fallen apart. The only remaining organization to fund the project was the IBT. Nonetheless, MOP continued with its strategic, industry-wide strategy and shifted to organizing tortilla workers. A lot of research was done on the tortilla industry in Southern California. However, the first target for the campaign was Hacienda CA. This approach made sense for a couple of reasons. First, it was the largest tortilla-manufacturing operation in the region, and second, the truck drivers had just completed a successful strike. While Hacienda CA production workers had not significantly participated in the truck driver strike (a couple went to picket lines), production workers definitely knew about the strike and its success. They also knew about the intimidation and threats. During the truck driver strike Hacienda managers had forced production workers to attend captive audience meetings to hear negative propaganda about the union. Production workers were well aware of the negative consequences of unionization (despite the success of the truck drivers).

The first step for MOP organizers was to figure out the lay of the land inside the factory. They needed to understand how many workers worked in each shift, what products were being produced, what major complaints workers had, and the different departments inside the factory. Organizers discovered that the biggest complaints by workers were staffing cuts, speedups (as a result of staff being cut), accidents, gender discrimination, insufficient or bad physical protection equipment, starting work twenty to thirty minutes before clocking in without being compensated, and supervisor favoritism. Injury rates were of particular concern to workers. Even though safety standards were getting better, production workers were quick to remember eleven finger amputations and one hand amputation caused by factory injuries between 1990 and 1994.[12] Another very common concern was that the company expected workers to produce at 100 percent capacity. Production workers were already producing at 96 percent capacity, but to expect 100 percent at a time when the company was reducing staff was impossible.

Next, organizers needed to identify some worker leaders who would be interested in the campaign. After developing some relationships with workers on the shop floor, the IBT began holding underground meetings with a group of production workers who were interested in unionization. There were worker committees at two of the factories in California. This signified the potential of a huge organizing campaign, with a combined workforce of one thousand workers in the two plants. The worker leaders of the organizing effort began to talk to other workers on the inside, but they were constantly discouraged by the lack of mass support for unionization. Many workers were afraid of getting fired from relatively good jobs, especially after a hard recession in the mid-1990s in Southern California; other workers witnessed what the company thugs did to the truck drivers and feared for their lives. A few workers mentioned fear of deportation. While workers were sympathetic to the idea of a union, they were not ready for the kind of mobilization it would take to win a unionization campaign. Furthermore, as mentioned in Chapter 4, the union-busting firm that Hacienda CA hired during the strike recommended to the company that it implement some strategies to ensure that production workers would not organize. As a result of these recommendations, Hacienda raised production wages, started offering health insurance benefits, and developed a limited pension plan for workers. It also started training supervisors not to use favoritism. So, as a result of the truckers' strike, and without having to take any risks, production workers' conditions improved overnight. These improvements in working conditions also operated as a deterrent to unionization. In many ways, the truck driver campaign was easier because those workers were already unionized and were fighting to keep their union. Production workers, on the other hand, would have to start from scratch.

MOP organizers commented that, in addition to the difficulties of building worker-led organizing committees on the shop floor, there was significant tension centered on organizing strategy between MOP and the IBT. MOP was trying to build the campaign slowly and as organically as possible. They understood that if they could bring down the biggest company, they would have a good chance of unionizing the entire industry with less effort. On the other hand, the IBT, which was fully committed to the project, but was used to the hot shop-organizing model explained above, had little patience for the slow building of a campaign. The IBT wanted to go into the factory, get workers to sign union cards, and then have a recognition election. MOP wanted to think strategically about the industry. They wanted to build a base and build worker capacity to ensure a successful unionizing campaign. In the middle of the production worker campaign, the differences in strategies created a rupture in the relationship between the two organizations. Sensing that something was wrong in the organizing campaign, some of the workers on the organizing committee dropped out. Shortly after, the IBT ceased funding for the campaign, and the organizing drive (which was never on solid footing) dissipated.

While a few of the workers on the organizing committee felt that the union had abandoned them, most went on with their work as though nothing had happened. Seven years after the strike and underground organizing efforts, some workers still want a union. Other workers are still disgruntled about the organizing campaign. Yet others feel that the political climate today is much more hostile than in the past and fear the consequences of organizing. There has been no collective organizing inside the plant since the 1997 effort.

When workers cannot resist oppressive conditions collectively, they often turn to other methods of defense. These methods have been called "the weapons of the weak" (Scott 1985). Some common ways that workers in other workplaces engage in acts of resistance are arriving late to work, talking, taking bathroom breaks, and slowing down equipment. These practices are nearly impossible at Hacienda CA because of the heavy level of video surveillance in the factory. Furthermore, the lack of trust between workers in the factory makes it even more difficult to engage in these acts of resistance because workers feel that they never know who will report them to managers. Nonetheless, workers do sporadically engage in breaking the rules by eating tortillas off the line, confronting supervisors, and taking long bathroom breaks.

State Policy, the Labor Market, Union Politics, and Resistance

How can we explain the success of the truck drivers' strike, the failure of the production worker organizing campaign, and the lack of resistance in the factory since the late 1990s? I argue that the explanation lies in a combination of state policy, labor market conditions, and internal union politics.

The truck drivers' strike occurred on the heels of successful organizing by immigrant janitors, wheel manufacturers, and drywallers. The campaign was not a new organizing drive, but rather one to save the union and improve conditions. This fact made it less risky and a bit easier for workers to engage in collective action. Anti-immigrant state policies did not hinder the truck driver campaign for several reasons. First, most of the truck drivers were not undocumented. Second, anti-immigrant policies were not as institutionalized as they are in 2008 (sometimes even affecting permanent residents). Finally, some of the worst anti-immigrant policies did not yet exist at the time of the immigrant upsurge in California.

For the most part, truck drivers at Hacienda CA were not undocumented immigrants. While most of them were first-generation immigrants, many of them had been in the United States for a number of years. Some of them were homeowners, and all of them owned their trucks (which they used for the distribution of tortillas). As a result, anti-immigrant policies targeting undocumented immigrants did not really apply to the truck drivers. Hacienda CA could not threaten truck drivers with deportation. Nevertheless, these truck drivers certainly had undocumented family members, friends, and co-workers laboring in production who could have been affected by the anti-immigrant legislation of the time.

It is also true that anti-immigrant policies were not as institutionalized in the 1990s as they are today. For example, the janitors', drywallers', and American Racing Equipment's campaigns were not affected by Proposition 187, because these campaigns occurred before the proposition was passed by California voters in 1994. Recall from Chapter 3 that Proposition 187 sought to deny education and access to health care to undocumented immigrants and their children. A massive social movement forced the issue into court, and ultimately the California Supreme Court found these provisions to be unconstitutional. Despite not being directly affected by this legislation, truck drivers and the broader immigrant community were empowered by the defeat of the proposition. This is a markedly different situation from today, where workers at Hacienda CA, especially undocumented workers, labor under a system of coercion because of immigration policies implemented after the mid 1990s.

The militarization of the border through programs such as Operation Gatekeeper did not begin until 1994. This program did not directly affect the truck drivers because they were not worried about being deported or their ability to leave and re-enter the United States. If it had been passed earlier, the Illegal Immigration Reform and Responsibility Act of 1996 (IIRRA) could have seriously impacted some of the truck drivers, because some of the legislation's provisions apply to U.S. permanent residents. Recall that the law took a big step toward the criminalization of immigrants by allowing immigrants who are permanent residents of the United States to be deported for prior, lesser felonies such as driving while drunk. However, this legislation did not pass until the end of September 1996, and the truck drivers' strike ended in the middle of September. Other immigrant organizing drives at the time, such as the home health-care workers campaign in 1997, were equally unaffected by this policy because it was not yet firmly institutionalized. Finally, many of the harshest anti-immigrant proposals and policies of recent times were developed (or escalated) in the post-9/11 environment. Immigrant workers in the 1990s were not seriously affected by the Social Security No-Match letters. They were not affected at all by the *Hoffman Plastics v. NLRB* decision. In short, because the truck drivers were mostly documented and anti-immigrant policies were not fully institutionalized at the time of the strike, state policies did not impact their ability to organize a successful contract campaign. The other immigrant organizing projects of the time were also equally unaffected by anti-immigrant state policies because these policies either did not exist during their campaigns or were not yet fully institutionalized.

How then do we explain the failure of the production workers' campaign in the context of a boom in immigrant worker organizing? I argue that the fundamental reason that this campaign failed was because of the rupture in the relationship between MOP and the IBT. MOP organizers could not build a significant base of production worker leaders fast enough. The IBT lost patience with the slowness of the campaign and moved its financial resources elsewhere. It is impossible, of course, to predict if the campaign would have been successful had the IBT not withdrawn, but spending more time building the campaign would have provided a clear perspective on the potential for success.

There are also other reasons for the failure of the campaign. First, labor market conditions contributed to its failure. Many workers had been seriously affected by the recession of the early and mid-1990s and did not want to lose their relatively good jobs. Times were still difficult in the post-recession period, and decent jobs were not easy to come by. Furthermore, a significant number of workers were homeowners and had other financial commitments that would make it hard for them to go on strike to win a unionization battle. By contrast, the recession did not seriously impact the striking truck drivers; these workers were already unionized and felt that the union would protect them against unjust firings. Production workers, on the other hand, would have only weak protections from the NLRA.

Second, production workers were a mix of documented and undocumented immigrants. Fear of deportation was more present than in the truck drivers' campaign, but according to MOP organizers, still relatively insignificant. Anti-immigrant policies that could have affected production worker organizing largely did not. For example, had Proposition 187 not been defeated in the courts, it could have had a negative impact on production worker organizing. However, as a result of the mass movement that forced Proposition 187 into the Supreme Court, it was a nonissue. Another law that could have hurt production worker organizing was the IIRRA of 1996, which was in place during the production worker organizing campaign. This law did not affect production organizing for a couple of reasons. First, the law had only passed about four months before the production worker campaign began. Therefore, it was only in the early stages of becoming institutionalized. Second, the production worker campaign was not public, and so this policy was not something that managers could use against workers because they were unaware of the worker campaign. Finally, production workers had not yet felt the effects of the militarization of the border, and therefore were not as concerned with this issue.

Since 2001, however, anti-immigrant state policies have impacted the ability of workers to collectively resist. While workers I interviewed during the course of my fieldwork were very sympathetic to the idea of a union, they were also very quick to express feelings of fear. Many of them felt that the political environment was too dangerous for organizing and that public sentiment was too anti-immigrant. As Andres, a worker, pointed out, "now it is very difficult to challenge the boss, because it means we would also have to challenge the policies that allow the boss to do his job. We need more than five hundred people to win this battle." By this Andres means that workers at Hacienda CA would not merely be fighting their employer. They would also have to fight against all of the anti-immigrant state policies that their employer uses to maintain shop-floor control. A single tortilla factory with five hundred workers cannot change these policies.

Workers' feelings of fear were, in fact, justified, since many of the policies in the late 1990s and the policies post-9/11 became strongly institutionalized during the time I was in the field. For example, as discussed in Chapter 4, Hacienda CA managers used Social Security No-Match letters and *Hoffman Plastics v. NLRB* to maintain shop-floor control. Workers believed that if they tried to unionize, they would definitely be fired and might be deported. Furthermore, policies such as the IIRRA, which were not yet fully institutionalized at the time of the production worker campaign, have since become normalized. Moreover, the workers now feel the effects of the militarization of the border. As illustrated in Chapter 4, many undocumented workers feel that they are trapped in the United States, because if they try to go back to Mexico, they do not know if they will be able to return. Workers were certainly not blind to the employer's tools for using coercion on the shop floor. The institutionalization of these policies shows the extent to which state policies have helped employers create a chilling effect on organizing on the shop-floor after 2000. But how have state policies affected organizing and resistance in Baja California?

Organizing as a Response to Globalization in Baja California

Organizing within the Mexican political economy is extremely difficult. Even though the Mexican constitution has remarkable support for workers' rights, the enforcement mechanism is very weak and has become increasingly weaker with globalization. In order to attract foreign capital, the Mexican state has been all too willing to turn a blind eye to labor law violations. Moreover, the prevailing interpretations of provisions in the Mexican constitution have made it very difficult for independent unions to challenge the corrupt charro unions that exist in the country. It is difficult to organize an independent union in general and nearly impossible to do so in a workplace that already has a union (no matter how ineffective or corrupt that union is).

Most labor and community organizing efforts in Baja California have been connected in one way or another to the maquiladora industry. This is the case for a number of reasons. First, the maquiladora industry is supremely important to the border region's economy and one of its largest employers. Second, the industry has created very unhealthy and unsafe working conditions. Finally, the industry is in large part responsible for environmental devastation in the city. The organizing approach in the maquiladora industry has predominantly been to organize the community in which the maquiladora is situated first and then to figure out the feasibility of organizing the actual maquila.

Such an approach is necessitated by the unusual obstacles to organizing in the maquilas directly. In most cases the maquila already has a charro union, and in many instances union contracts were signed even before workers were hired at the maquila. This makes it nearly impossible to engage in independent union organizing. By beginning with organizing the community, organizations build relationships and trust with people in that neighborhood and also with the maquila workers (who often live in the same area). Organizations focus on organizing around issues that are deeply affecting the population, such as health, sexual harassment, and environmental justice. Because maquilas tend to be big polluters, communities are often affected by toxic dumping. The results of toxic dumping have been devastating on multiple levels. For example, toxic chemicals can cause birth defects and other serious health illnesses. They also impact the availability of clean water and safe air quality. These organizing campaigns do a lot of work to make the connections between globalization and bad working conditions, pollution, and poor health. Community organizations have been particularly critical of NAFTA and other free-trade agreements that have eroded the standard of living for many of Baja California's residents.

The community, cross-border groups, and campaigns discussed below all play an incredibly important role in neighborhoods surrounded by maquiladoras. These organizations often provide the only recourse workers and the public have. However, the organizations have been less effective at successfully organizing the maquila sector. While there have been some successful independent union campaigns in Mexico, there have been none, to my knowledge in the city where Hacienda BC is located. Furthermore, because of their scarce resources, these organizations have not been able to focus much attention on the conditions of workers in national or non-maquila industries in the region. As such, places such as Hacienda BC can slip through the cracks.

The community, cross-border groups, and campaigns continue to work on behalf of workers in Baja California.

Han Young

In June 1997, workers at Han Young, a maquiladora that welds chassis for Hyundai, joined the Union of Workers in the Metal, Steel, Iron and Connected Industries (STIMAHCS), one of Mexico's largest independent unions. Workers' main complaints concerned low wages and life-threatening health and safety conditions. Skilled welders were only earning $4 a day for eleven-hour shifts. Workers were also worried about inadequate safety equipment and a lack of ventilation for toxic gases. As a result of these poor working conditions (that the existing union did nothing about), workers went on strike for two days. Nine labor activists were fired during the strike (Bacon 1997).

As the election for the recognition of their independent union approached, workers were intimidated and threatened. Management also tried to co-opt workers by offering them higher wages if they agreed not to fight for an independent union. The state also played a significant role in trying to derail the election. In early September, about a month before the election, a state representative ordered that all TV stations in Baja California stop covering the story of the Han Young workers. U.S. observers of the election process helped break the media blackout. Both the Mexican state and the maquila industry were worried about a possible victory for this independent union campaign. The state was worried that it would have a harder time attracting foreign capital if the campaign was successful, and the industry was worried about the potential for a widespread movement. Despite many attempted derailments, the election occurred on October 6, 1997 (Bacon 1997).

During the election, workers had to publicly and openly (according to law) state their preference for either the Authentic Labor Front (FAT, the labor federation to which STIMAHCS belongs) or the Revolutionary Confederation of Workers and Peasants (CROC, the company union). While workers were voting, a group of people who the Han Young workers had never seen in the factory showed up to vote in the election. Han Young employees and FAT became suspicious that these people had been sent by the company to ensure a win for the CROC. Despite this, Han Young workers voted fifty-five to thirty-two in favor of the independent union, the FAT. This was a historic election because Han Young became the first U.S.-Mexico border maquiladora in which workers voted for an independent union (Bacon 1997). At the October 9 certification hearing, the Mexican labor board (the Conciliation and Arbitration board) did not certify the election. It was only after a twenty-six-day hunger strike by workers and supporters that the election results were finally certified. During the struggle for independent unionism, there was substantial support from Mexican community organizations and international organizations (including many unions) from the United States, Canada, and even Korea. Despite certification of the election, the company continued to refuse to bargain with the independent union. Furthermore, the company brought in new employees from Veracruz and also allowed the CROC back into the factory to have meetings with all the factory workers (a clear violation of the certification agreement). Five months after certification the Han Young workers went on strike again, this time to demand that the boss negotiate with the new independent union (La Botz 1998). In the end, after a two-year campaign, the Han Young workers were never able to achieve a contract.

Factor X—Casa de la Mujer

Factor X is a Baja California women's group that helps organize maquila workers. The group was started in 1989 after Mexican police attacked an abortion clinic in Mexico City. Factor X responded by building a self-sufficient grassroots movement to help women organize, educate, and empower themselves. From its inception Factor X has been involved in organizing around women workers' issues. It offers programs that support battered women, workshops on sexual harassment and labor organizing, and classes on reproductive and workplace health. It also has a legal clinic.[13]

Most recently, Factor X has been involved in organizing fourteen-week sessions to train women workers to become workplace organizers (promotoras). During the fourteen weeks, women learn about globalization and feminism. They gain an understanding of how the global economy operates and why wages along the border have stagnated. They also get substantial training on workplace rights. The idea for the promotora program is not simply for these women to get extensive training as individuals, but rather for these women to go back into their communities and workplaces and organize other workers. When the program has trained a good number of promotoras, organizers hope to be able to launch campaigns targeting specific maquilas.

Centro de Información para Trabajadoras y Trabajadores

Much like Factor X, Centro de Información para Trabajadoras y Trabajadores (CITTAC) is an association of men and women who support workers' struggles for better living and working conditions, especially in the maquiladora industry. They also hold classes and training on workplace rights. CITTAC is particularly interested in promoting autonomous, democratic, worker-run organizations. For example, it was a strong supporter of the Han Young workers in their struggles for an independent union. CITTAC also provided support and solidarity to a campaign against Sara Lee organized by ENLACE and Servício, Desarollo y Paz (SEDE-PAC, an independent union). CITTAC works with numerous community and cross-border organizations such as the Coalition for Justice in the Maquiladoras and the San Diego Maquiladora Workers' Solidarity Network.

The Environmental Health Coalition San Diego

The Environmental Health Coalition (EHC) has a Border Environmental Justice campaign in coalition with a variety of community-based organizations in the border region, including Factor X and CITTAC. They also work with smaller, less well-known community organizations in the area. One of EHC's most significant campaigns deals with the abandoned Metales y Derivados maquila. In 1972, a San Diego-based metals company initiated lead-smelting operations in Tijuana. The company's operation consisted of recovering lead, copper, and phosphorous from lead acid batteries and other scrap metals (Environmental Health Coalition San Diego). Even though Mexican law requires that waste produced in maquiladoras be returned to the country in which the company is based, Metales accumulated all the waste from its operations in Tijuana. In 1994, the Mexican government forced Metales y Derivados to close because of the maquila's violations of Mexican environmental laws and complaints from the community, Colonia Chilpancingo. Colonia Chilpancingo, located directly down the hill from Metales, was particularly concerned about contaminated water and residents' eye and skin irritations. When the maquila closed, the owners abandoned the site and returned to the United States, where they are still operating, but leaving tons of lead sag, waste byproducts, sulfuric acid, and heavy metals behind in Tijuana (Environmental Health Coalition San Diego).

For years after Metales closed, the Mexican government did not clean up the toxic waste site. Because the site was not marked as a dangerous and toxic, many people in surrounding communities started taking some of the heavy metals from the site to build squatter communities. They were not aware that these metals were extremely hazardous. The community below Metales continued to be the most affected. Birth defects increased, and the community believes that they are a direct result of the abandoned Metales factory.

The EHC worked with community organizations around the Metales y Derivados maquila to inform and educate community members about the toxic waste site. As a result of this collective project, community organizations were successful in pressuring the Mexican government to do something about the toxic environment. The government only covered up the problem, building a brick wall around Metales and placing a polyurethane top to stop air exposure. The EHC and community organizations filed a case under the NAFTA environmental side agreement to expose the effects of maquilas in Tijuana. Metales y Derivados still has not been satisfactorily cleaned up, and the EHC and community organizations continue to fight.

It's important to note here that most of these campaigns were carried out at a time when workers, especially women workers, had alternatives in the booming maquiladora industry. Conditions have changed and today women have fewer alternatives.

The campaigns and organizations discussed above are doing impressive work given the political economy of Mexico and the hardships faced in engaging in even the most basic organizing. These campaigns and organizations have had a significant impact on workers in the maquiladora sector. Many of these organizations do not have the time or resources to focus on all workplaces in Baja California. As a result, factories that are not horrendous, but nevertheless have poor working conditions—such as Hacienda BC—are often ignored.

Resistance at Hacienda BC

Resistance at Hacienda BC has taken a very different trajectory from that of the organizing done at the Hacienda CA factory. According to interviews with several managers, when the Baja California plant opened in 1994, management at Hacienda headquarters in Mexico signed a contract with

the Conferderación de Trabajadores Mexicanos (CTM) before workers
even started working at the factory, following a well-established pattern
in many Mexican factories. This collective bargaining agreement covers all
employees in the factory, including the truck drivers. The contract is re-
newed every three years, without worker input or knowledge of negotia-
tions. Union leaders, who are not part of the workforce, negotiate contracts
behind closed doors. The first act of resistance at Hacienda BC involved a
collective walkout in 1996 by workers concerned about health and safety in
the factory. This was a very unusual situation and has never been repeated
in the factory. More commonly, and much more consistently than at Hacienda CA, workers in the factory engage in individual resistance.

Walking Out for Our Health

According to the production manager, in 1996 a few production workers started talking about unionization. They threatened management with
unionization during a particularly bad month in which five workers were
seriously injured on the job and management did nothing for them. When
workers threatened to unionize, the plant manager at the time told them
that they could not, because they were already represented by the CTM.
When the workers tried to contact their union to file a grievance against
management, they were told that the union was based in another state.
During my fieldwork at Hacienda BC, one of the few employees who had
been working at the factory in 1996 told me that workers in 1996 made
many attempts to file a grievance against the company, but the union never
responded to them.

   Frustrated by their experience with the so-called union and angered by
management's response to their problems, over 50 percent of workers in
the factory walked off the job. The walkout lasted several days. When the
workers returned to work, managers still had not met workers' demands
for better health and safety. As a result, most of the women workers who
walked out decided to leave Hacienda BC and go work in the maquila industry. At that time, the maquiladora industry was very stable and offered
better wages and benefits. Since the 1996 walkout, there has been no mass
worker collective action at Hacienda BC. Workers also dropped the idea
of organizing an independent union. Josefina told me, "It's not that we
don't want an independent union. We do. We want a union that will fight

for our rights. We don't want to live in constant fear. But we will have to be patient and wait to organize. Times have changed, and the situation for women workers is much more difficult today than eight years ago."

As Josefina suggests, the labor market in Baja California significantly changed between the time of the original walkout and the time of my fieldwork. Women have had to find other ways to fight back.

Weapons of the Weak?

At the time of my fieldwork, workers at Hacienda BC were much more likely to engage in individual resistance than collective resistance. In his book, *Weapons of the Weak,* James C. Scott (1985) makes a persuasive argument for how agency can take many different forms. Often, when workers lack the ability to resist collectively because repression is too great, they find ways of individually fighting this repression. While I argue that workers at Hacienda BC do resist in some ways, I think it is important not to overstate this claim. In general, resistance in the workplace is at a low point. However, when women workers find their conditions insufferable, they do act. Whether these actions can be called "resistance" is debatable. The women that I interviewed cited various individual actions that they engage in to make the day pass faster. For example, Marta said, "I take many bathroom breaks during the day. This bothers the managers because they have to move someone from another part of the factory to keep my place on the assembly line while I go to the bathroom. I do this because it makes the day go faster; I get more chances to rest. They [managers] complain that I use the bathroom too much. What will they do? People have to use the bathroom."

Taking bathroom breaks is not uncommon among the women I interviewed. Many of them told me that they did the same thing and that other women in the factory also engaged in this activity. Managers are also well aware that women take frequent bathroom breaks, but as one of them said to me, "it's all part of the price you pay when you are running a business. If doing that [going to the bathroom frequently] makes them feel powerful, what can I say?" Unlike managers in California who very intensively monitor workers' every move, the managers I spoke with at the BC factory clearly seemed relaxed about bathroom breaks. Given that managers see this kind of resistance as part of their operating costs, one could make the argument that this is part of management's co-optation strategy. In other words managers and workers are playing a game that is really much more about consent than resistance.

Women also viewed arriving at work late as a form of challenging the power structure. They know that they will not be penalized for arriving late, so they take their time getting to work. Ximena and Rosa said, "Why should we give them [managers] an extra fifteen minutes of our sweat, when we get paid the same if we come on time or are fifteen minutes late. We are so busy that it is hard to get to work on time. This way we have a little extra time. We can't leave the factory early, so we take advantage of the fact that we can come late." Occasionally, women will engage in spontaneous collective action inside the factory. Sometimes a small group will all have to take a break, or drink water, or go to the bathroom at the exactly the same time. When this occurs managers, slow down the machines for a few minutes until everyone is back in their places. This kind of resistance does in fact impact the productivity of the factory and irks managers much more. However, this kind of action is rare. One supervisor told me, "when they start slowing down production in groups, we know we've taken it too far." In other words, managers know when they have either engaged in too much sexual harassment or sped up the assembly line too much. Their response to this kind of small collective action is to back off the workers until things have cooled down. Later, managers resume to their normal way of operating until the next action. Once again, it is important not to overstate the resistance that takes place in the factory. These small collective actions are a form of resistance, but they are extremely limited in their effectiveness. Instead, they seem to be part of a negotiation strategy between managers and workers.

Women workers would like to do more organizing in the factory, and they hope that in the future conditions will be better in Baja California so that they can do more collective work. Women in the factory were particularly interested in organizing around health and safety issues, including sexual harassment. They want to work in a cleaner and safer environment. However, any kind of collective organizing is viewed by management as threatening. As long as resistance is about these small acts, things are fine. But as one manager put it, "we worry that these small acts could get out of control." In order to launch an effective campaign, workers' would need to fight the company, the union, and the local state. This is extraordinarily hard for women workers in Baja California who are single mothers with little support.

Neoliberal Policies, Labor Market Changes, and Resistance

How can we explain the difference in the kinds of resistance among women workers at Hacienda BC between the 1990s and the early years of the twenty-first century? I argue that state policies and changes in the local labor market explain the lack of collective resistance, or any kind of "real" resistance for that matter, in the 2000s.

In the 1990s women workers at Hacienda BC were able to protest their unsafe working conditions. While they were not able to successfully obtain a resolution to their demands or organize an independent union, they had the ability to quit their jobs in search of other opportunities. This illustrates that at that time women workers had some power vis-à-vis their employer. They were able to leave Hacienda BC because the labor market in Baja California was booming. In particular, the maquiladora industry flourished after the United States and Canada signed NAFTA. Women workers were able to simply leave their job at Hacienda BC and go to work in the maquila industry, often for higher wages than those they had been earning. The risks involved in leaving the factory were few. Women quickly found other work. Furthermore, most women workers at that time were either from Baja California or surrounding areas. This meant that they had family and friend networks in the area. As a result, they were able to seek help while they looked for other jobs.

The situation for women workers at Hacienda BC drastically changed between 1996 and early 2003 when I finished my field research. First, labor market conditions had significantly changed in Baja California due to shrinking numbers of maquiladoras and maquila employment. The labor market for low-skill jobs was becoming increasingly slack.

Second, the slack labor market was coupled with the fact that most women working in the factory were no longer from Baja California (as the previous generation had been), but rather from the interior of Mexico. By 2000, internal migration and displacement as a result of NAFTA was in full effect. Recall from Chapter 5 that several women I interviewed had come from corn farmer families. When U.S. corn flooded the Mexican corn market, many of these farms closed. As a result, these families had to migrate to other parts of Mexico. Often hoping to migrate to the United States, many families migrated to Baja California. However, it was difficult to get a good job in a maquila, so many women opted to work at Hacienda BC.

Third, since the late 1990s, and especially in the twenty-first century, the militarization of the border became a much more serious project. This has led to migration at more dangerous border-crossing locations, such as the Arizona desert. When families migrated to Baja California as a result of displacement from NAFTA, they were confronted with a more militarized border. The dangerous nature of border crossing led some families to decide that only one or two individuals should cross the border rather than the whole family. Most often these individuals were men, leaving women and children behind in border cities with few or no familial networks. The resulting effect was that women could not simply quit their jobs in a slack labor market, especially since they had no support.

Changes in the labor market, policies such as NAFTA, and the militarization of the border have made it nearly impossible for women at Hacienda BC to engage in collective resistance today. Women are simply not able to take the risks of losing their jobs given the political economy of Baja California. Therefore, women have had to find other ways of challenging their employers. This comes by way of individual resistance, but as discussed above, managers and workers collectively decide how this resistance works. Resistance therefore serves as a gauge for how far each party can push the other. State policies and a changing labor market played a crucial role in creating a chilling effect for resistance at Hacienda BC. Managers have been able to use this effect to maintain coercion on the shop floor.

Conclusion

In this chapter, we have explored resistance and the lack thereof at both Hacienda CA and Hacienda BC. At Hacienda CA there was one successful campaign (the truck drivers), one unsuccessful campaign (production workers), and a general lack of resistance in the twenty-first century. The success of the truck drivers' campaign was a result of an already unionized workforce; documented immigration status; and a public, community-supported campaign. The failure of the production worker organizing was largely a result of the rupture in the relationship between MOP and the IBT. Finally, the lack of resistance after 2000 can be attributed to institutionalized state policies that have allowed managers to maintain coercive shop-floor environments. The immigration regime in the factory has served the purpose of dividing and intimidating the workforce and successfully curtailing strong, collective mobilization.

On the other hand, at Hacienda BC the ability of women workers to walk off the job in the 1990s was a result of a flourishing local labor market and familial networks in the area. Similar to Hacienda CA, the lack of collective resistance after 2000 was deeply impacted by state policies such as NAFTA and the more severe militarization of the border. Furthermore, a slacker labor market made it difficult for women to find better opportunities elsewhere. Managers at Hacienda BC have been able to effectively use the gender regime to restrict effective collective resistance to oppression on the shop floor.

In conclusion, we see that collective resistance has occurred in the two factories, but it has become increasingly difficult as a result of neoliberal and anti-immigrant state policies. While resistance in the age of neoliberalism is not impossible, it is much more difficult, especially at the worksite level.

Shop-Floor Politics in the Twenty-First Century

The philosophers have only hitherto interpreted the world
in various ways; the point, however, is to change it.

KARL MARX, *Theses on Feuerbach*

How does the labor process work in the twenty-first century at the
height of neoliberalism? Why should we care about managerial control?
In this book we have traveled through two shop floors of a Mexican transnational tortilla manufacturer along the U.S.-Mexico border. These factories serve as sites for exploring the interconnections between state policies,
labor market conditions, and shop-floor politics. In the previous chapters,
I have argued that the labor process under neoliberal capitalism cannot
be explained without looking at the role of the state and the intersection
of race, gender, and class at the point of production. These changes in the
functioning of the labor process, and the control it gives managers on the
shop floor, has important implications for creating a more just society.
In other words, we should care about managerial control because it has
implications for organizing workers on both sides of the U.S.-Mexico border. We should care because workers, organizers, and activists need the
tools and knowledge to effectively challenge both hegemonic and coercive shop-floor regimes. Let me first recap some of the central findings

with regard to changes in the labor process, then discuss the prospects for organizing.

One of the central findings of this book has been that, on the U.S.-Mexico border, plant managers construct different modes of labor control according to the vulnerabilities of each workforce. Mexican managers and workers themselves produce and reproduce race, class, and gender hierarchies at the point of production. Managers do this by invoking the different state polices at their disposal and also by using workers' racialized and gendered statuses in society. Workers also use existing ideas about identity to reproduce race and gender hierarchies in the factory. In each factory regime despotism and hegemony are used differently. Hacienda CA is characterized by an immigration regime that uses a two-tier structure of labor control. Documented workers labor under a more hegemonic system of control, while undocumented workers endure coercive control. Hacienda BC is characterized by a gender regime, where hegemony and despotism also coexist, but the overall character of the regime in this case is coercive.

At Hacienda CA, 75 percent of workers are immigrant Latino men. About half of the workforce is undocumented. In the shop floor at Hacienda CA, managers pit documented and undocumented workers against each other using the *Hoffman v. NLRB* decision and Social Security No-Match letters to intimidate undocumented workers. They also provide undocumented workers with lower wages, bad schedules, and little upward mobility in the factory's internal labor market. Managers are, in part, successful because they solicit allegiance and commitment by exploiting sentiments of national solidarity since they are a Mexican company. They also use the racialized status of both documented and undocumented workers to keep wages low, compared with other baked-foods industries. Even workers with legal status are not entitled to welfare benefits because many of them have not been residents of the United States for more than five years. This also limits the buffer between those workers and the employer.

Hacienda also uses gender to enforce shop-floor control. It predominantly hires male immigrant labor that is just as cheap as female immigrant labor but is less likely to have additional familial responsibilities. This gives managers the ultimate flexibility in assigning shifts, in particular by forcing undocumented male workers to work the graveyard shift (10 P.M.–6 A.M.). Managers at the factory also use their hiring practices to divide male and female workers on the shop floor. The corollary to constructing tortilla manufacturing as men's work is that the work is not considered appropriate for women. This creates a set of socially produced and context-specific attitudes. Men in the factory do not understand why women work there, and women often feel threatened by the number of male workers in the factory. Women workers' husbands express feelings of protectiveness and defensiveness about their wives' vulnerability. These tactics, coupled with the number of signs warning about sexual harassment in the factory, lead to essentially no communication between men and women in the factory.

Managers at Hacienda CA use direct and indirect state policies and racialized and gendered hierarchies to enforce shop-floor control. In this way they aim to produce a certain kind of worker—predominantly an undocumented Latino man. Divisions in the factory along both immigration and gender lines allow managers to maintain shop-floor control because there is a lack of trust between workers in the factory, and workers live in constant fear that they will be fired or deported.

Across the border, at Hacienda BC, 72 percent of workers are women. According to managers, 90 percent of them come from other parts of Mexico. Several workers that I interviewed were forced to migrate to Baja California after their small farms failed as a result of price deregulation. Workers at Hacienda BC fit the maquila worker stereotype. They are predominantly young, single women, and mothers. Not unlike managers of the various large maquilas in the area, Hacienda managers also argue that these women are better suited for assembly line work than their male counterparts. They state that this is particularly the case in the tortilla industry, as tortillas are products that have traditionally been the responsibility of women. As a result of constructing tortilla work as women's work, managers at Hacienda BC can hire mostly women workers who work a full $2 per day cheaper than their male counterparts.

At Hacienda BC the use of state policies to enforce shop-floor control is more indirect than those at the California factory. This is mainly because there are no specific laws or policies such as those we saw in the United States (*Hoffman v. NLRB*, Social Security No-Match letters) that directly affect employers' ability to control workers on the shop floor, despite the fact that immigration policy is equally central to the regime in Mexico. The relationship between the state and the factory in Mexico is more hidden, but nonetheless important. There are several ways in which state policies in Mexico impact the shop floor at Hacienda BC. First, state policies such as export-led industrialization in Mexico and U.S. immigration policies have created a feminized labor market in Baja California. Second, efforts to attract foreign capital to Mexico have involved reducing the labor protections and standards for workers.

Export-led industrialization has involved reducing and nearly eliminating protective tariffs on national industries in Mexico. The result has particularly impacted the corn market by driving down prices, making production nearly impossible for Mexican farmers. As a result, many farmers have lost their small farms and have had to migrate to Mexico's urban centers (Zabin, Hughes, and Wiley 1995). Many wind up along the border in cities such as Ciudad Juárez. Families wishing to cross the border to obtain employment in the United States have found that it is nearly impossible, especially after the implementation of border control policies such as Operation Gatekeeper. As a result, many men cross the border, leaving their families behind in Baja California. This is the perfect labor market for transnational corporations looking for the fantasy docile and complacent female assembly line worker. It is also the perfect labor market for Mexican corporations that are currently benefiting from the decline in maquilas along the border caused by cheaper production and better labor incentives in other parts of the Global South.

Second, companies routinely violate even those policies that all corporations are required to abide by, such as sexual harassment policies. State officials, ghost unions, and the higher-level managers at Hacienda BC all turn a blind eye to rampant sexual harassment. The nonenforcement of women's constitutional rights and the role of the state in labor relations in Mexico are other ways in which the state influences the labor process at Hacienda BC.

Mexican state policies in Baja California and U.S. immigration policy allow managers at Hacienda BC to create a despotic shop-floor labor regime regulated by a competitive and sexualized shop-floor environment. Neoliberal state policies, which have encouraged nonenforcement of workers' constitutional labor protections, and U.S. immigration policies, which make it difficult to cross the border safely, have given managers at Hacienda BC opportunities for coercion. Managers at Hacienda BC are dealing with a labor force that has little access to labor markets with higher wages and better benefits. Furthermore, women's need for stable employment in an unstable labor market allows managers significant control over women in the factory.

Workers at both Hacienda CA and Hacienda BC have had varied responses to managerial control. In the mid-1990s, truck drivers at Hacienda
CA and production workers at Hacienda BC went on strike. Their ability to engage in this kind of collective resistance can be largely attributed
to the fact that institutionalization of many of the immigration policy reforms and other neoliberal policies that were institutionalized in the late
1990s (e.g., NAFTA in 1994 and immigration reform in 1996) were not yet
in place. Production workers at Hacienda CA were not successful in their
brief attempt at unionization. However, as we learned in Chapter 6, this
can be attributed more to internal union politics than state policies. By the
new millennium, there was essentially no collective resistance in either of
the factories. In fact, the only kind of resistance that existed was at the individual level. This kind of resistance was seen by management as simply
a normal part of their labor costs, so it is questionable whether we should
even think of it as resistance at all.

Comparison across these two factories points to the centrality of state
policies in labor control and the construction of race, class, and gender at
the point of production. Why are these two factors critical to understanding shop-floor politics in the twenty-first century?

Globalization and Labor

Globalization and Tortimundo's never-ending thirst for expansion have
impacted both the culture and the tradition of tortilla making and labor
control on the shop floor. In short, shop-floor politics in the twenty-first
century is not only about managerial control but also about the relationship between production and consumption. Neoliberalism operates both
at the workplace level and at the cultural level. Nowhere is this more evident than in the U.S. consumption of this ethnic food group. In the United
States, the consumption of tortillas has exploded. The tortilla went from
its humble beginnings as an ethnic food, mainly consumed by Latina/os, to
a deracialized food entity that morphed into wraps and that now has the
versatility of most other bread products. Consumers, fast-food chains, restaurants, and supermarkets can now purchase low-calorie and low-fat tortillas and tortillas and wraps in a myriad of flavors such as spinach, red
pepper, and habañero chili.

On the Mexican side of the border, some communities are fighting to preserve traditional tortilla making. They are not simply fighting to maintain part of their cultural heritage but also to preserve the nutritional values contained in nixtamalized tortillas. Corn flour, known as *masa,* is increasingly becoming a substitute for nixtamalized corn. Masa is less nutritious, but has a longer shelf life and is faster to work with. Large transnational corporations such as Tortimundo have flooded the Mexican tortilla market with this processed corn flour in an attempt to re-create the Mexican palate. These corporations are most interested in steering Mexican consumers to purchase packaged supermarket tortillas. They are trying to convince Mexican consumers that these tortillas taste just as good as, and are just as nutritious as, homemade tortillas or tortillas bought in small neighborhood tortillerias. In essence, they want to commercialize tortillas and tortilla production.

Globalization has also affected U.S. and Mexican tortilla workers. Workers at Hacienda CA and Hacienda BC endure primarily despotic labor control strategies because the workers have essentially no alternatives other than relying on their employers to purchase their labor power. This occurs because workers in each of these factories do not have a buffer (union, welfare state protections, etc.) between themselves and their employers and because workers have no exit route from their employment (no viable alternatives).

The lack of a buffer and an exit route is a result of two macro-structural conditions. First, over the past thirty years, we have witnessed a shift from the Keynesian state to the neoliberal state. This has resulted in the undermining of unions and other safety nets, but it has also resulted in closing off alternative job prospects. For example, the shift to neoliberalism has wiped out subsistence farming in Mexico and has diminished job creation in both the United States and Mexico. Second, globalization, racism, and sexism push workers into secondary and informal labor markets. At the same time, shifts in immigration policy reduce the range of jobs available to undocumented immigrants in the United States (therefore exit becomes difficult for men at Hacienda CA) and make crossing the border a treacherous and costly alternative for workers in Mexico (reducing the exit route for women at Hacienda BC).

Neoliberalism certainly has its contradictions. For example, the state is growing weaker in terms of labor protections, but stronger with regard to border enforcement. While this is a contradiction in terms of the stated logic of neoliberalism, it is nonetheless consistent with the business inter-ests that drive neoliberal policy.[1] Neoliberalism has put all workers in both the United States and Mexico at a disadvantage. In the United States this shift is marked by dwindling protections for workers. Under the Keynesian state, workers were able to access welfare programs when they were fired or laid off work. Under neoliberal reforms these protections are decreas-ing, and many restrictions are placed on access to services. In 2008, workers can access welfare benefits for a total of only five years under the welfare reform act passed during the Clinton administration. Furthermore, in the past thirty years, unionized workers have had to give many concessions to employers who routinely threaten to move offshore. Concessions have included decreased wages, reductions in health benefits, and restrictions on noneconomic rights such as seniority. These concessions reduced the power of the labor movement and workers. The neoliberal state has partic-ularly impacted workers without legal immigration status. These workers do not have access to protections such as welfare and unemployment insur-ance. Furthermore, they often do not have unions to fight for their rights (even with concessions). Moreover, anti-immigrant sentiment puts them in a vulnerable position with employers and in their communities. It is these workers who ultimately have the most to lose. While documented work-ers still have some legal protections, creating a very thin buffer between workers and employers, undocumented workers have essentially no such buffer. They are completely reliant on their employers. This vulnerability is exacerbated by the immigration policies that have the consequences of pushing workers to the bottom of the labor market, with very little mobil-ity between jobs.

In Mexico, the transition from import substitution to neoliberalism has also taken the form of loss of worker protections, particularly in the ma-quila sector, but increasingly in other sectors as well. The state, in its at-tempt to attract foreign capital to the country, has turned a blind eye to the enforcement of labor protections under the Mexican constitution and labor law. State-imposed reduction of rights for workers along the border essen-tially eliminates the buffer between workers and employers. While there are many unions along the Mexican side of the border, they often play no role in creating a buffer between workers and employers, because most of them are company unions. All of these issues are exacerbated by the fact that U.S. immigration policies do not give these workers the ability to cross the border and work where wages are higher. Once again we see the parallels with the United States, where labor law protecting immigrants has been severely eroded over the last decade, creating a similarly weak buffer between workers and employers.

In the United States institutionalized racism and sexism have forced people of color and women into the secondary and informal labor markets, where wages are low and workers have to endure poor working conditions. Real average hourly wages for production workers have fallen from a peak of $8.99 in 1972 to $8.27 (constant 1982–84 dollars) in 2003 (Economic Report of the President 1995). Furthermore, studies show that involuntary part-time work rose 100 percent between 1970 and the late 1980s (Callaghan and Hartman 1992).[2] Contingent work continues to be on the rise. Undocumented immigrants of color are at particular risk of being pushed into these sectors, because they do not have legal documents that allow them to work for employers in the primary labor market. They often work for small corporations and ethnic businesses. Even those who do manage to get jobs in large manufacturing plants, such as meatpacking factories, are faced with a deunionized industry and lower wages. State policies, such as those described in Chapter 3, limit undocumented workers' mobility within the firm and different labor markets and between countries as well.

In Mexico, globalization has played an important role in stimulating both internal and external migration (Sassen Koob 1984; Sassen 1988). Workers from the interior of the country, who have been displaced from their lands, are often forced to migrate to border cities where they can obtain work in the local economy (often in maquiladoras). Employment in maquiladoras is, however, also changing as transnational corporations scour the planet in search of cheaper labor. Since 2001 there has been a decrease in the number of maquiladoras in Baja California from 1,235 to 888 (Instituto Nacional de Estadistica Geografía e Informática 2004). So, available work in border cities is shrinking, and there is growing unemployment. As discussed in Chapter 5, unemployment in Baja California has doubled since 2001.

As mentioned above, the shift from Keynesianism to neoliberalism significantly reduces the buffer between workers and employers. Moreover, state policies and institutionalized racism and sexism force people of color and women into the secondary and informal labor markets in the U.S.

These conditions are exacerbated for undocumented immigrants, who have even less of a buffer between themselves and employers and have even more restricted mobility within and between labor markets. These conditions give managers tools of coercion, particularly in immigrant industries in the United States and border industries in Mexico. Many studies on transnational corporations focus on the role of U.S. or Western exploitation of the Global South. It is easy to demonize these processes as a particular U.S. (or Western) phenomenon. However, in this book, I demonstrate that the transnational company's country of origin is relatively inconsequential. Ultimately, about the problem lies in capitalism and the power that corporations (from all over the world) have gained through neoliberalism.

Toward an Intersectional Analysis

Global politics, however, cannot be divorced from the internal production machinery of the factory. The key in any analysis of transnational shop floors must be to create an intersectional analysis. In this book I have tried to construct an intersectional analysis on two levels. First, I have developed a discussion of the dynamic link between the macro-politics of globalization and neoliberalism, meso-level labor market conditions, and the micropolitics of the shop floor. Second, I have demonstrated how race, class, and gender are all produced at the point of production.

For some years, prominent scholars such as Angela Davis (1983), Patricia Hill Collins (1990, 2006), and bell hooks (1981, 2000) have proposed a theory of *intersectionality*. By this term they mean that race, class, and gender are not distinct categories that can be analyzed or experienced separately. In other words, they are not additive processes. Instead, these scholars and others argue that race, class, and gender are experienced in an intersectional or interlocking way. For example, a middle-class white woman experiences the world through a lens of class and race privilege on one hand and gender oppression on the other. The lack of an intersectional approach can be widely seen in the older labor process literature where "worker" has often implicitly translated into "white, male, blue-collar worker." Starting the analysis from the perspective of a white, male, blue-collar worker has obviously yielded an analysis that has typically privileged class identity.

Critiques of that approach have yielded excellent shop-floor analyses of women workers and the centrality of gender to the production process (Lee 1998; Freeman 2000; Salzinger 2003). However, these studies have privileged gender and class without looking at the centrality of ethnicity and race in the labor process. In general, the role of race and ethnicity has been undertheorized in the labor process literature. However, some notable examples of integration of race and ethnicity into the analysis are seen in Chun (2001), Kwong (1999), and Webster (2001).

In this book, I have created an intersectional analysis that highlights the centrality of race, gender, and class at the point of production. Intersectional theory gives us the tools to produce this kind of analysis on several levels. First, the concept of intersectionality allows us to see the very institution of the factory as a site where the construction and reproduction of race, gender, and class takes place. As Lee (1998) has argued, "gender is a primary organizing principle of production politics... production relations rely on gender ideology, organization, and identity, factors that also shape the terms and forms of production politics." Shop-floor politics at Hacienda CA and Hacienda BC are clearly driven by gender. This is most notable in the fact that managers insist on hiring men on the U.S. side of the border and women in Mexico. Work is therefore constructed as men's work in the United States and women's work in Mexico. This has serious implications for the construction of gender at each site. For example, undocumented men working on the assembly in the California plant are often ridiculed by managers and co-workers because they work with women and have the "easy" jobs. *Easy* is translated to mean the work that women do. Women workers do not exclusively work on the assembly line at Hacienda CA. They also work in other areas of the factory, with the exception of trucking and the warehouse. This demonstrates that the stereotype used to construct workers' gender is not based in material reality but is actually ideological. At the Baja California plant, women work almost exclusively on the assembly line, and work in the factory is constructed as women's work. Here they are forced to deal with a sexualized work environment driven by managerial fantasies.

This gendered system of labor, however, cannot be understood without also looking at how race and class intersect with it. Race and class intersect with gender in unique ways at each plant. At Hacienda CA immigration status is central to labor control. As we saw in Chapter 4, both documented and undocumented workers are disadvantaged by working in an ethnic industry that pays significantly lower wages than the baked goods industry standard. Furthermore, managers use immigration policies to push undocumented workers to the margins of factory life.

Both managers and documented workers classify undocumented workers through a race and class analysis. In the eyes of managers and documented workers, undocumented workers become dark, poor, dirty, and uneducated. These differences between documented and undocumented workers are seriously exaggerated. Documented workers have a vested interest in creating these differences to maintain their privileged status in the workplace.

At Hacienda BC, race and class intersect with gender differently. Here skin tone plays a prominent role in the creation of a gender regime. As you will recall from Chapter 5, light-skinned women are pitted against darker-skinned women for managerial attention. Attention from managers is important because of women's perceptions and managers' creation of the sense that complying with sexual harassment will lead to greater job stability. However, skin tone becomes a complicated issue when it is not clear who is "light" and who is "dark." Here, skin tone becomes complicated by class status. For instance, darker-skinned women who come from an educated family are often considered to be light, while lighter-skinned women who come from a poor background can often be considered dark.

It is evident that in these two case studies race, class, and gender are dynamic and fluid. They are influenced by external race, class, and gender hierarchies, but both managers and workers reproduce these hierarchies on the shop floor and assign them their own characteristics.

Second, intersectional theory helps us understand that race, class, and gender are not stagnant categories; rather, they can be fluid and changing. This is evidenced by several unique factors discussed in this book. First, managers construct the same kind of work in different ways on each side of the border. Second, managers construct ethnicity differently on each side of the border. At Hacienda CA the racialized status of Latina/os in the United States plays out in shop-floor politics. Furthermore, managers pit documented and undocumented workers against each other. In the process, both managers and workers racialize illegality. In Baja California, however, skin tone is the primary way through which ethnic identity is defined. Class status also works differently on each side of the border. At

Hacienda CA "poor" is central to the construct of undocumented, even though there are no real differences in the class position of documented and undocumented workers in the factory. At Hacienda BC, class status is interlocked with skin tone. Both within each factory and between factories we see how race, gender, and class are socially constructed. Of particular importance is that the construction of race, class, and gender are significantly influenced by changing immigration laws that shift the significance of being a woman or an undocumented man in the border region.

Is Another World Possible?

Must these factory regimes be organized in the manner in which they are in order to be productive and generate profits? Are there ways of organizing work that could create more humane conditions on the shop floor within a capitalist system where profit motive is paramount? Is another world possible? In short, I argue yes. The opportunities and possibilities for cross-border labor solidarity between U.S. and Mexican workers employed by this transnational corporation provide hope for the future. Of course, this cause is not something workers at Hacienda CA and Hacienda BC can take up on their own; rather, it must be a large-scale social movement. That being said, their particular location in a strategic industry could be a starting point.

Despite the numerous problems with both the U.S and Mexican labor movements and the challenges that this particular workforce faces, there is still a possibility for international worker solidarity. There are several reasons why a cross-border organizing campaign in this industry (but particularly between these plants) is possible.

First, factories on both sides of the border are exclusive providers to large fast-food chains. A consumer boycott of the product and of fast food companies that use the product could have a significant effect on the profitability of the company. This tactic has generated numerous successes in the garment industry, as illustrated by the Nike and Gap campaigns; in agriculture, through the United Farm Workers' grape boycott; and through the coalition of Immokalee workers' campaign against Taco Bell.[3] Furthermore, Hacienda cannot just pick up and move to another location, since it produces a perishable product that must be delivered to their customers within 24 hours. Capital mobility, therefore, is not as much of a challenge in this industry as it is in other manufacturing industries.[4] There are dozens of Hacienda factories in both the United States and Mexico, and a multicountry contract could have an effect on wages and working conditions across the border. A cross-border organizing campaign against this corporation could serve as a model for international worker solidarity. The leverage created in these two factories would make it much easier to organize Hacienda's other factories in the United States, Mexico, and international locations.

Second, the independent union movement in Mexico is growing and succeeding despite repression from state-backed unions. One of the most enlightening examples was the recent victory at the Kuk Dong factory in Puebla, where an independent union successfully organized several hundred garment workers. Another example is the coalition between the FAT (Frente Autentico Del Trabajo) in Mexico and the UE (United Electrical Radio & Machine Workers of America) in the United States.[5] Independent unions that break with the corporatist ties of the large unions in Mexico provide evidence of change and the building of democracy in the Mexican labor movement.

Third, U.S. unions, though having been hesitant about immigrant organizing, have learned many new tactics from the immigrants they have organized. U.S. unions today are more aware of the unique challenges of immigrant organizing, and they are more willing to take the risks necessary to organize these workers. This change in the labor movement was first witnessed in 2000, when the AFL-CIO changed its anti-immigrant position and advocated for amnesty for all immigrants. More recently, the building trades, considered to be some of the most reactionary unions, have also taken a position advocating for amnesty and organizing. These changes in the U.S. labor movement have led to more immigrant worker organizing but also an interest in labor solidarity across borders.

I am not suggesting a cross-border campaign run solely by U.S. unions,[6] in other words, a campaign that involves a U.S. union organizing in Mexico. I am suggesting a truly international campaign in which unions on both sides of the border work together to address the issues of their different workforces. In the case of Hacienda, U.S. unions could provide a good deal of financial backing in such a campaign, and the Mexican union could organize a strike that halts the flow of Hacienda fried products into the United States. A boycott could be waged on both sides of the border. A truly international organizing effort, in which unions on each side of the border work together, would better serve the interests of workers on both sides of the border.

Despite cautious optimism for cross-border labor solidarity, I am not optimistic that another world is possible along the U.S.-Mexico border if real immigration reform is not achieved in the United States. Workers at Hacienda CA and Hacienda BC are connected to the political economy of the border. La Línea and U.S. policies about it are the principal division by which managers can coerce undocumented workers in the California factory and women workers in the Baja California factory. This will not change if current immigration policy is not changed. We need a just immigration system in the United States that will not deny workers basic rights. We need a policy that will not grant employers free reign over immigrant workers. Most importantly, we need a policy that is not punitive and inherently exploitative.

In our journey through the shop floors of Hacienda CA and Hacienda BC, I have examined the relationship between race, class, gender, and the state in the construction of labor regimes. I have demonstrated that race, class, and gender are not only external to the production process but an integral part of production relations. We have also witnessed how Hacienda managers not only use existing racialized and gendered hierarchies to enforce shop-floor control but also have directly and indirectly used state policies and labor market conditions to produce and reproduce new gendered and racialized labor practices.

As we continue to witness the dismantling of labor and social protections, the further decline in union density, and the consolidation of neoliberalism, we will see an ever-increasing number of coercive labor regimes worldwide. These coercive regimes are most likely to impact workers who lack formal and substantive citizenship rights. However, these trends can be challenged. In recent years we have witnessed the rise of social movements, including the antiglobalization, antisweatshop, and antiwar movements. We have also seen the emergence of the World Social Forum, a modest, but hopeful beginning toward a global challenge to neoliberalism. Another world is possible. The end of this chapter in history is not yet written.

Notes

1. The Tortilla Behemoth and Global Production

1. The names of the corporation, its subsidiaries, and all workers have been changed to protect confidentiality. In addition, I have also avoided disclosing the cities where the factories are located. I call the transnational corporation Tortimundo. It has subsidiaries in the United States and Mexico. I refer to these as TortiUS and TortiMX. I refer to the factory in the United States as Hacienda CA and the factory in Mexico as Hacienda BC.

2. At the beginning of my fieldwork, the agency was still called INS; after the implementation of the Department of Homeland Security, its name changed to Immigration and Customs Enforcement (ICE). Both terms are used throughout the book.

3. This is a pseudonym, not the name of a real organization.

4. Weiss (1998); Ong (1999); Sassen (1996); O'Riain (2000); Gilpin (2000); McKay (2006).

5. According to Robinson (2004, 87), "This Transnational State (TNS) apparatus is an emerging network that comprises transformed and externally integrated national states, together with supranational economic and political forums and has not yet acquired any centralized institutional form. The economic forums include the International Monetary Fund (IMF), the World Bank, the World Trade Organization (WTO), the regional banks, and so on. The political forums include the Group of Seven countries and the larger Group of Twenty-two countries, among others, as well as the United Nations system, the Organization of Economic Cooperation and Development (OECD), the European Union, the Conference on Security and Cooperation in Europe (CSCE), and so on."

6. Martínez (1996); Anzaldúa (1987); Ruiz and Tiano (1987); Sánchez (1993).

7. Some recent examples of the literature include Ward (1990); Gonzalez et al. (1995); Nash (1995); Kopinak (1996); Moghadam (1996); Fernandes (1997); Peña (1997); Prieto (1997); Lee (1998); Cravey (1998); Collins (2003); Salzinger (2003).

8. Here I am directly borrowing from Burawoy's (1985) concept of factory regime. The factory regime is the set of political and ideological mechanisms by which workers are controlled and production is organized.

9. I use the term neoliberalism in the way that Harvey (2005, 2–3) defines it: "A theory of political economic practices that proposes that human well-being can be best advanced by liberating individual entrepreneurial freedoms and skills within an institutional framework characterized by strong private property rights, free markets, and free trade.

10. Cohn (2000); Green (2001); Milkman (1987); Gordon, Edwards, and Reich (1982).

11. No-Match letters are sent by the Social Security Administration to employers whose workers have social security numbers that do not match those in the SSA's system. While the administration claims not to be targeting immigrant workers, these letters have had huge repercussions on these workers. In fact, a recent study by the Center for Urban Economic Development at the University of Illinois at Chicago showed that a full 53.6 percent of employers who received No-Match letters responded by firing their employees (Mehta, Theodore, and Hincapié 2003).

12. According to Harvey (2005, 138) "Mexico lost 200,000 jobs in just two years as China (in spite of NAFTA) overtook it as a major supplier of the US market in consumer goods."

13. For an excellent review of this kind of ethnography see Burawoy et al. (2000); Burawoy (1998); and Burawoy et al. (1991).

14. National Institute for Statistics and Geography.

2. The Political Economy of Corn and Tortillas

1. Torres (1996); Pujol (1996); Sheridan (1996); Ribeiro (2005).

2. Author's translation from a document in Spanish.

3. In order to protect the confidentiality of the company as much as possible I am using Major Metropolitan Newspaper for all articles that name the corporation.

4. At the time of writing, the 2002 Economic Census had just come out. While there is general information about the industry as a whole, there is no specific data. I rely on the 1997 census for specific information on employment and wages.

5. This comment came from several small tortilleria owners who attended the Tortilla Industry Association Meeting in 2000.

6. This information comes from the internal files of the Manufacturing Organizing Project (I'm using a pseudonym here).

3. A Tale of Two Countries

1. There is no perfect term that captures what the U.S.-Mexico border looks like. In some parts it is a tightly woven chain-link fence, and in others it is a wall pieced together out of corrugated metal with a jagged top. In many places these fences are reinforced with fixed and mobile monitoring technology.

2. There are many possible errors that can take place using this system. These can include human error (illegible handwriting), employer error (employer mixing workers up and reporting incorrect Social Security numbers), and EEVS computer error.

3. My emphasis.

4. Reisler (1976); Barrera (1979); Glenn (2002); Ngai Mae (2004); Zolberg (2006).

5. I borrow this term from Ngai (2004).

6. There is a large market in counterfeit immigration documents at least in part because of employer sanctions.

7. My emphasis.

8. This is the wording of the actual Social Security No-Match letter. The document can be downloaded at www.nilc.org.

9. The number of immigrants not eligible for legalization would be quite large. The costs of legalization in terms of fees and fines could be prohibitive. Furthermore, any immigrant who has committed a crime such as using a fake Social Security number would be ineligible for the legalization program.

10. Fernandez-Kelly (1983); Caulfield (1998); Cowie (1999); United States General Accounting Office (2003); Salzinger (2003).

11. The term *maquiladora* primarily refers to export-processing factories that assemble parts produced in the United States and other countries for sale in the U.S. market. Since the passage of NAFTA, Mexican national industries have also acted as maquiladoras (in terms of assembly and organization of labor). Maquilas are not exclusively dominated by U.S. capital. Other countries also have a presence. For the purpose of this book, I will maintain the distinction and use the term maquiladora or maquila to refer to export-processing factories.

12. According to Salzinger, they got the idea from Southeast Asian countries.

13. This is clearly not what Robinson (2004) means when he talks about the transnational state. Robinson argues that there is a transnational state in formation, and it operates on a macro-level. Actors that form part of this transnational state are the United Nations, G7 and G22 countries, the World Bank, and IMF, etc. I am merely trying to illustrate the way in which the United States erodes Mexican sovereignty by imposing state policies that have a direct impact on Mexico.

14. For a more detailed analysis of Mexican labor history see Caulfield (1998); Middlebrook (1995); Collier and Collier (1991); Hathaway (2000).

4. Hacienda CA

1. Most of my research took place in the original Hacienda CA plant, although I also visited the second one numerous times. In this book, when I talk about Hacienda CA, I mean the original plant.

2. Managers were careful to state that they had no information regarding undocumented workers but that they suspected about half of the workers inside the factory were undocumented.

3. I use the terms manager and supervisor interchangeably throughout the text to provide additional confidentiality to these participants.

4. The workers that I interviewed felt the health insurance was too costly. They were paying an average of $160 per month for a family of four.

5. This information comes from a brief interview with the antiunion consulting firm hired by Hacienda.

6. The ISO is the International Standards Organization.

7. There is no team structure at this plant; therefore, production workers other than those who become line leaders or supervisors are not directly involved in decision making.

8. Nixtamal is the process by which dry corn is soaked in water and powdered limestone so that the kernels swell and the walls break down. This is an extremely time-consuming procedure that few tortilla manufacturers still follow. It is, however, what makes a tortilla taste authentic and homemade. Today most tortilla manufacturers and small tortillerias just use corn flour (masa harina or Maseca) to produce tortillas.

9. The documented workers in the factory are legal residents, but most of them are not U.S. citizens.

10. The INS is no longer an agency. After 9/11, the Immigration and Naturalization Services (INS) became Immigration and Customs Enforcement (ICE). This new agency falls under the purview of the Department of Homeland Security.

11. Before *Hoffman,* workers were entitled to receive back wages on "wages not earned." This means that if they were fired illegally and thus became unemployed for a certain amount of time, they would receive compensation for the time they were unemployed.

12. Even though Coyotes are hired by immigrants, they are often seen as vultures in immigrant communities. They often mistreat the people they are bringing to the United States. Immigrants also tell stories of how they were exploited, blackmailed, and sexually assaulted.

13. It is important to make clear that not all native-born people have equal access to the social safety net. African Americans and other native-born people of color have long been subject to discrimination in this process.

14. Legal permanent residents have a Social Security number and are therefore eligible for unemployment benefits.

15. There are no statistics that actually state that most workers in the tortilla industry are foreign born. However, according to managers, about 80 percent of the workers at Hacienda CA are foreign born and the other 20 percent are born in the United States and are of Latina/o descent. Hacienda is one of the largest tortilla manufacturers in the world, so I am assuming that if this is the case for the largest corporation, it is reasonable to predict that it is an industry-wide phenomenon.

16. The Canadian border has become more militarized since September 11, 2001, but not nearly at the same levels as the U.S.-Mexico border.

17. The translation for *indio* is technically Indian. In Latin America this is often used as a derogatory term. Indios are considered to be backwards, stubborn, and of course dark skinned.

5. Hacienda BC

1. The shifts operate from 6 A.M. to 2 P.M. and 2 P.M. to 10 P.M.

2. I specifically use this term to mean hiring through a network of family or friends.

3. This was calculated using the nominal exchange rate as of January 22, 2002.

4. They earn 118 pesos per day. I used the average exchange rate for the year 2003 to calculate the average hourly dollar wage.

5. For a fuller discussion of pigmentocracy and the complications of skin color among Latina/os see Duany (2002).

6. The CTM is considered a "charro" union. It is tied to both the company and the former ruling party of Mexico, the PRI.

7. PPPs are "currency conversion rates that both convert to a common currency and equalize the purchasing power of different currencies. In other words, they eliminate the differences in price levels between countries in the process of conversion" (www.oecd.org).

8. This number is calculated by dividing the Hacienda BC workers' hourly wage (10.75 pesos) by the PPP index for Mexico from 2001 (6.36). This gives us an adjusted per hour income for Hacienda BC workers of $1.69 in terms of purchasing power as opposed to $1.15, which we obtained from the nominal exchange rate. Thus, when we divide $8.79 per hour by $1.69 per hour, we find that workers in Los Angeles make five times the wage of workers at the Baja California plant.

6. Fighting Back?

1. This is not because immigrant workers are unorganizable. For an excellent dispelling of this myth, see Delgado (1994).

2. There were many organizing campaigns in this decade. Covering all of them is outside of the scope of this book. I only discuss those that garnered the most media attention.

3. The unions were the United Auto Workers (UAW); United Brotherhood of Carpenters (UBC); United Food and Commercial Workers (UFCW); International Ladies' Garment

Workers' Union (ILGWU); International Longshoremen's and Warehousemen's Union (ILWU); International Association of Machinists, Oil, Chemical and Atomic Workers (OCAW); United Steelworkers of America (USWA); and the International Brotherhood of Teamsters (IBT).

4. Troqueros is the Spanish term for truck drivers.

5. The details of this campaign came from workers who helped organize the first strike and MOP internal files.

6. MOP internal files.

7. MOP internal files.

8. MOP internal files.

9. MOP internal files.

10. MOP internal files.

11. MOP internal files.

12. MOP internal files.

13. Information on Factor X came from a meeting with the group through a 2001 Global Exchange Border Reality Tour in which I participated.

7. Shop-Floor Politics in the Twenty-First Century

1. While some corporations and newspapers have been advocating open borders, most of the business elite in recent times have been arguing for liberalized immigration. I argue that the business elite want enough border control that it makes it difficult to come in and weak labor laws so that immigrant workers have essentially no protection thus are completely vulnerable (hence the call for more guest-worker programs). If there were no border control, then there would be few risks in entering and leaving the country (for example, when conditions are difficult in the workplace). This decreased risk would create an instability in the cheap immigrant labor force and less incentive to stay in the United States when an immigrant doesn't need to. Corporations want to keep immigrants in the United States, trapped so that they have no rights, and unable to leave.

2. The part-time work is involuntary because these workers would prefer to obtain full-time employment. However, they have to settle for part-time jobs.

3. This is not to imply that there are not serious faults with the boycott as a tactic. However, it can be useful when it is used in conjunction with other strategies.

4. The strategic locations of the factories would not allow the company to shut down operations in one location within the United States and move to another.

5. For a thorough discussion see Hathaway (2000).

6. For a thorough discussion of cross-border organizing see Armbruster (2005).

REFERENCES

Alexander, Robin, and Dan La Botz. 2003. "Mexico's Labor Law Reform." *Mexican Labor News and Analysis* 8, no. 4 (March 2004). www.ueinternational.org.

Almaguer, Tomás. 1994. *Racial Fault Lines: The Historical Origins of White Supremacy in California.* Berkeley: University of California Press.

Alonso-Zaldivar, Ricardo. 2004. "Bush Would Open U.S. to Guest Workers: Immigrant Advocates and Some in the GOP Assail His Plan." *Los Angeles Times,* January 8, p. A1.

American Civil Liberties Union. 1997. "Federal Judge Says States May Not Set Immigration Policy." (June 2000). http://archive.aclu.org/news/n111497c.html.

Anderson, Joan B., and Denise Dimon. 1999. "Formal Sector Job Growth and Women's Labor Sector Participation: The Case of Mexico." *Quarterly Review of Economics and Finance* 39: 169–191.

Anzaldúa, Gloria. 1987. *Borderlands/La Frontera: The New Mestiza.* San Francisco: Spinsters/Aunt Lute.

Appelbaum, Eileen, and Rosemary Batt. 1994. *The New American Workplace: Transforming Work Systems in the United States.* Ithaca, NY: ILR Press.

Armbruster Sandoval, Ralph. 2003. *Globalization and Cross-Border Labor Solidarity in the Americas: The Anti-Sweatshop Movement and the Struggle for Social Justice.* New York: Routledge.

Aspin, Chris. 1996. "New Revolution: Tortilla Prices." *Chicago Sun Times,* August 18, Sunday News, p. 54.

Associated Press. 2007. "Mexico Tortilla March Organizers Sideline Leftist Leader." *International Herald Tribune,* January 31. www.iht.com/articles/ap/2007/01/31/america/LA-GEN-Mexico-Tortilla-March.php.

Bacon, David. 1997. "Tijuana Workers Continue Hunger Strike to Force Recognition of Their Union." http://www.pacificnews.org/jinn/stories/3.25/971210-union.html (accessed May 2006).

———. 1995. "Rising from Below: The Coming Labor Earthquake in Los Angeles." http://dbacon.igc.org/Unions/30LARising.htm (accessed May 2006).

Barrera, Mario. 1979. *Race and Class in the Southwest: A Theory of Racial Inequality.* Notre Dame: University of Notre Dame Press.

BBC News. 2007. "Mexicans Stage Tortilla Protest." February 1. http://news.bbc.co.uk/go/pr/fr/-/2/hi/americas/6319093.stm (accessed June 2007).

Bendesky, León. 2005. "Del Comal a la Producción en Masa." *La Jornada,* January 17. www.jornada.unam.mx/2005/ene05/050117/secara.html (accessed March 2005).

Bensinger, Ken. 2004. "Attention Turns to Mexico's Weak Immigration Policy." *Washington Times,* January 15. www.washtimes.com/world/20040114-113024-7362r.htm.

Bensusán, Graciela. 2000. *El Modelo Mexicano de Regulación Laboral.* México: Universidad Autónoma Metropolitana.

Bensusán, Graciela, and Maria Cook. 2003. "Political Transition and Labor Revitalization in Mexico." In *Labor Revitalization: Global Perspectives and New Initiatives,* edited by Daniel B. Cornfield and Holly McCammon, 229–268. London: JAI Press.

Bonacich, Edna, and Richard Appelbaum. 2000. *Behind the Label: Inequality in the Los Angeles Apparel Industry.* Berkeley: University of California Press.

Buchanan, Pat. 2000. "Trouble in the Neighborhood." Speech at the San Diego World Affairs Council, April 28, San Diego, CA. www.buchanan.org/pa-00-0428-troubleintheneighborhood.html (accessed January 2004).

Burawoy, Michael. 1976. "The Functions and Reproduction of Migrant Labor: Comparative Material from Southern Africa and the United States." *American Journal of Sociology* 18 (5): 1050–1087.

———. 1979. *Manufacturing Consent: Changes in the Labor Process under Monopoly Capitalism.* Chicago: University of Chicago Press.

———. 1985. *The Politics of Production.* London: Verso.

———. 1998. "The Extended Case Method." *Sociological Theory* 16 (4).

Burawoy, Michael, Joseph A. Blum, Sheba George, Zsuzsa Gille, Teresa Gowan, Lynne Haney, Maren Klawiter, Steven H. Lopez, Seán Ó Rian, and Millie Thayer. 2000. *Global Ethnography: Forces, Connections, and Imaginations in a Postmodern World.* Berkeley: University of California Press.

Burawoy, Michael, Alice Burton, Ann Arnett Ferguson, Kathryn J. Fox, Joshua Gamson, Nadine Gartrell, Leslie Hurst, Charles Kurzman, Leslie Salzinger, Josepha Schiffman, and Shiori Ui. 1991. *Ethnography Unbound: Power and Resistance in the Modern Metropolis.* Berkeley: University of California Press.

Bureau of Labor Statistics. 2001. *Current Population Survey, 2000.* Washington D.C.

Bush, George. 2004. "President Bush Proposes New Temporary Worker Program: Remarks by the President on Immigration Policy." Speech in the White House East Room. Washington, D.C.: January 7. http://www.whitehouse.gov/news/releases/2004/01/print/20040107-3.html (accessed January 2004).

Calavita, Kitty. 1992. *Inside the State: The Bracero Program, Immigration, and the I.N.S.* New York: Routledge.

California Rural Legal Assistance Foundation. 2003. "Operation Gatekeeper Fact Sheet." www.stopgatekeeper.org (accessed February 2004).

Callaghan, Polly, and Heidi Hartmann. 1992. *Contingent Work: A Chart Book on Part Time and Temporary Employment.* Washington, D.C: Economic Policy Institute.

Carroll, Susan, and Daniel González. 2003. "Border Death Toll Varies Due to Multiple Counting Methods." *Arizona Republic,* October 16. http://www.azcentral.com/news/border/articles/1016deaths-difference.html (accessed Febuary 2004).

Catanzarite, Lisa M., and Myra H. Strober. 1993. "Gender Recomposition of the Maquiladora Workforce in Ciudad Juárez." *Industrial Relations* 32 (1): 133–147.

Caulfield, Norman. 1998. *Mexican Workers and the State: From Porfiriato to NAFTA.* Fort Worth: Texas Christian University Press.

Chang, Grace. 2000. *Disposable Domestics: Immigrant Women Workers in a Global Economy.* Cambridge, MA: South End Press.

Chavez, Cesar. 1968. "Statement by Cesar Chavez on the Conclusion of a 25 Day Fast for Non-violence." http://www.laprensa-sandiego.org/archieve/march28-03/cesar3.htm (accessed December 2006).

Chavez, Leo R. 1998. *Shadowed Lives: Undocumented Immigrants in American Society.* Fort Worth: Harcourt Brace.

Chun, Jennfier J. 2001. "Flexible Despotism: The Intensification of Insecurity and Uncertainty in the Lives of Silicon Valley's High-Tech Assembly Workers." In *The Critical Study of Work: Labor, Technology, and Global Production,* edited by Rick Baldoz, Charles Koeber, and Philip Kraft, 127–154. Philadelphia: Temple University Press.

Cohn, Samuel. 1985. *The Process of Occupational Sex Typing: The Feminization of Clerical Labor in Great Britain.* Philadelphia: Temple University Press.

———. 2000. *Race and Gender Discrimination at Work.* Boulder: Westview Press.

Collier, Ruth, and David Collier. 1991. *Shaping the Political Arena: Critical Junctures, the Labor Movement, and Regime Dynamics in Latin America.* Princeton: Princeton University Press.

Collins, Jane L. 2003. *Threads: Gender, Labor, and Power in the Global Apparel Industry.* Chicago: University of Chicago Press.

Cornelius, Wayne. 1998. "The Structural Embeddedness of Demand for Mexican Immigrant Labor: New Evidence from California." In *Crossings: Mexican Immigration in Interdisciplinary Perspectives,* edited by Marcelo Suárez-Orozco, 114–144. Cambridge, MA: Harvard University Press.

Cowie, Jefferson. 1999. *Capital Moves: RCA's Seventy-Year Quest for Cheap Labor.* Ithaca, NY: Cornell University Press.

Cox, Robert W. 1996. "A Perspective on Globalization." In *Globalization: Critical Reflections,* edited by John H. Mittelman, 21–30. Boulder: Lynne Rienner Publishers.

Cravey, Altha J. 1998. *Women and Work in Mexico's Maquiladoras.* Lanham, MD.: Rowman and Littlefield.

Crossborder Business Associates. 2003. "Tijuana-San Diego Border Facts: An Overview of History, Trade, and Social Demographics of the Region." www.crossborderbusiness.com (accessed March 2003).

Davies, Scott. 1990. "Inserting Gender into Burawoy's Theory of the Labour Process." *Work, Employment and Society* 4 (3): 391–406.

Davis, Angela Y. 1983. *Women, Race, and Class.* New York: Vintage Books.

Davis, Mike. 1999. *Magical Urbanism: Latinos Reinvent the U.S. City.* London: Verso.

De La Garza, Enrique T., and Carlos Salas, eds. 2006. *La Situación del Trabajo en México.* México: Plaza y Valdés.

De la Garza, Enrique T. 2003a. *Refleciones Sobre la Reforma Laboral.* Universidad Autónoma Metropolitana, México.

———. 2003b. "Mexican Trade Unionism in the Face of Political Transition." In *Labor Revitalization: Global Perspectives and New Initiatives,* edited by Daniel B. Cornfield and Holly McCammon, 207–228. London: JAI Press.

De Genova, Nicholas. 2005. *Working the Boundaries: Race, Space, and "Illegality" in Mexican Chicago.* Durham, NC: Duke University Press.

Delgado, Héctor L. 1994. *New Immigrants, Old Unions: Organizing Undocumented Workers in Los Angeles.* Philadelphia: Temple University Press.

———. 2000. "The Los Angeles Manufacturing Action Project: An Opportunity Squandered?" In *Organizing Immigrants: The Challenge for Unions in Contemporary California,* edited by Ruth Milkman, 225–238. Ithaca, NY: Cornell University Press.

Doeringer, Peter B., and Michael J. Piore. 1971. *Internal Labor Markets and Manpower Analysis.* Lexington, KY: Heath.

Duany, Jorge. 2002. *The Puerto Rican Nation on the Move: Identities on the Island and in the United States.* Chapel Hill: University of North Carolina Press.

Economic Report of the President. 1995. "Hours and Earnings in Private Nonagricultural Industries." Table B-47. http://www.gpoaccess.gov/eop/2005/2005_erp.pdf (accessed June 2006).

Enriquez, Sam. 2007. "Inflation Fears All Rolled Up in Tortilla Prices." *Los Angeles Times,* February 9, Foreign Desk, Part A.

Environmental Health Coalition. "Border Justice Campaign: The Case of Metales y Derivados." http://www.environmentalhealth.org/cec.html (accessed March 2005).

Fernandes, Leela. 1997. *Producing Workers: The Politics of Gender, Class, and Culture in the Calcutta Jute Mills.* Philadelphia: University of Philadelphia Press.

Fernandez-Kelly, Maria P. 1983. *For We Are Sold, I and My People: Women and Industry in Mexico's Frontier.* Albany: State University of New York Press.

Fisk, Catherine L., Daniel J. B. Mitchell, and Christopher L. Erickson. 2000. "Union Representation of Immigrant Janitors in Southern California: Economic and Legal Challenges." In *Organizing Immigrants: The Challenge for Unions in Contemporary California,* edited by Ruth Milkman, 199–224. Ithaca, NY: Cornell University Press.

Freeman, Carla. 2000. *High Tech and High Heels in the Global Economy.* Durham, NC: Duke University Press.

Fröbel, F., J. Kreye, and O. Heinrichs. 1980. *The New International Division of Labor.* New York: Cambridge University Press.

Fuentes, Annette, and Barbara Ehrenreich. 1983. *Women in the Global Factory.* Cambridge, MA: South End Press.

Gilpin, Robert. 2000. *The Challenge of Global Capitalism: The World Economy in the 21st Century.* Princeton: Princeton University Press.

Glenn, Evelyn Nakano. 2002. *Unequal Freedom: How Race and Gender Shaped American Citizenship and Labor.* Cambridge, MA: Harvard University Press.

Goldfrank, Walter L. 2003. "The Mexican Revolution." In *Revolutions: Theoretical, Comparative, and Historical Studies,* 3rd ed., edited by Jack A. Goldstone, 213–223. Belmont, MA: Thomson and Wadsworth.

Gonzalez, Soledad, Olivia Ruiz, Laura Velasco, and Ofelia Woo. 1995. *Mujeres Migración y Maquila en la Frontera Norte.* Tijuana, México: El Colegio de la Frontera Norte.

Gordon, David M., Richard Edwards, and Michael Reich. 1982. *Segmented Work, Divided Workers: The Historical Transformation of Labor in the United States.* New York: Cambridge University Press.

Green, Eric. 2007. "Immigration Bill Defeat Lamented by Bush, Congressional Leaders." International Information Programs, June 29. http://usinfo.state.gov/xarchives/display.html?p=washfileenglish&y=2007&m=June&x=200706291319321xeneerg 0.4296839 (accessed June 2007).

Green, Venus. 2001. *Race on the Line: Gender, Labor, and Technology in the Bell System 1880–1980.* Durham, NC: Duke University Press.

Harvey, David. 2005. *A Brief History of Neoliberalism.* Oxford: Oxford University Press.

Hathaway, Dale. 2000. *Allies across the Border: Mexico's "Authentic Labor Front" and Global Solidarity.* Cambridge, MA: South End Press.

Hill Collins, Patricia. 1990. *Black Feminist Thought: Knowledge, Consciousness, and Politics of Empowerment.* Boston: Unwin Hyman.

———. 2006. From Black Power to Hip Hop: Racism, Nationalism, and Feminism. Philadelphia: Temple University Press.

Hinajosa-Ojeda, Raul, and S. Robinson. 1992. "Labor Issues in a North American Free Trade Area." In *North American Free Trade: Assessing the Impact,* edited by Nora Lustig, Barry P. Bosworth, and Robert Z. Lawrence, 69–98. Washington, DC: Brookings Institution.

Hoffman Plastics Compounds v. National Labor Relations Board, 535 U.S. 137 (2002). Lexus Nexus (p.10).

Hondagenu-Sotelo, Pierrette. 1994. *Gendered Transitions: Mexican Experiences of Immigration.* Berkeley: University of California Press.

hooks, bell. 1981. *Ain't I a Woman: Black Women and Feminism.* Cambridge, MA: South End Press.

———. 2000. *Feminist Theory: From Margin to Center.* 2nd ed. Cambridge, MA: South End Press.

Hossfeld, Karen J. 1988. "Division of Labor, Divisions of Lives: Immigrant Women Workers in Silicon Valley." Ph.D. diss. University of California, Santa Cruz.

Immigration and Naturalization Service. 1997. "Illegal Immigration Reform and Immigrant Responsibility Act of 1996." *U.S. Department of Justice Fact Sheet.* http://uscis.gov/graphics/publicaffairs/factsheets/948.htm (accessed May 2004).

———. 1998. "Operation Gatekeeper: New Resources, Enhanced Results." *U.S. Department of Justice Fact Sheet.* http://uscis.gov/graphics/publicaffairs/factsheets/opgatefs.htm (accessed January 2003).

Instituto Nacional de Estadística Geografía e Informática. 2003a. "Población Emigrante a Estados Unidos de América por Entidad Federativa Según Sexo." *XII Censo General de Población y Vivienda.* www.inegi.gob.mx (accessed May 2004).

———. 2003b. "Porcentaje de Población Emigrante a Estados Unidos de América por Entidad Federativa Según Sexo." *XII Censo General de Población y Vivienda.* www. inegi.gob.mx (accessed May 2004).

———. 2003c. "Personal Ocupado en la Industria Maquiladora de Exportación Según Tipo de Ocupación." *Estadística de la Industria Maquiladora de Exportación.* www. inegi.gob.mx (accessed February 2004).

———. 2004. "Principales Características de la Industria Maquiladora de Exportación." *Estadística de la Industria Maquiladora de Exportación.* www.inegi.gob.mx (accessed February 2004).

Iritani, Evelyn, and Richard Boudreaux. 2003. "Mexico's Factories Shift Gears to Survive: Competing with Asia, the Sector Is Investing in Technology and Seeking New Customers." *Los Angeles Times,* January 5, C1.

Kopinak, Kathryn. 1996. *Desert Capitalism: Maquiladoras in North America's Western Industrial Corridor.* Tucson: Arizona University Press.

Kwong, Peter. 1999. *Forbidden Workers: Illegal Chinese Immigrants and American Labor.* New York: New Press.

La Botz, Dan. 1992. *Mask of Democracy: Labor Suppression in Mexico Today.* Cambridge, MA: South End Press.

———. 1998. "Hyundai Under Pressure to Recognize Han Young Union." Mexican Labor News and Analysis 3(16). http://www.ueinternational.org/vol3no16.html.

Lee, Ching Kwan. 1998. *Gender and the South China Miracle: Two Worlds of Factory Women.* Berkeley: University of California Press.

Maher, Kristen Hill. 2002. "Who Has a Right to Rights? Citizenship's Exclusions in an Age of Migration." In *Globalization and Human Rights,* edited by Alison Brysk, 19–43. Berkeley: University of California Press.

Major Metropolitan Newspaper, 1996a.

Major Metropolitan Newspaper, 1996b.

Malkin, Elisabeth. 2005. "Science vs. Culture in Mexico's Corn Staple." *New York Times,* March 27, Section 1, Column 1, Foreign Desk p. 10.

Martínez, Oscar J. 1996. "Introduction." In *U.S.-Mexico Borderlands: Historical and Contemporary Perspectives,* edited by Oscar J. Martinez, xiii–xix. Wilmington, DE: Jaguar Books.

Massey, Douglas S., Jorge Durand, and Nolan J. Malone. 2002. *Beyond Smoke and Mirrors: Mexican Immigration in an Era of Economic Integration.* New York: Russell Sage Foundation.

McKay, Steven. 2006. *Satanic Mills or Silicon Islands? The Politics of High-Tech Production in the Philippines.* Ithaca, NY: Cornell University Press.

McKinley, James C. 2007. "Cost of Corn Soars, Forcing Mexico to Set Price Limits." *New York Times,* January 19, Section A, Column 1, Foreign Desk.

Mehta, Chirag, Nik Theodore, and Maria Elena Hincapié. 2003. "Social Security Administration's No Match Letter Program: Implications for Immigration Enforcement and Workers' Rights." Report: Center for Urban Economic Development. Chicago: University of Illinois.

Middlebrook, Kevin. 1995. *The Paradox of Revolution: Labor, the State, and Authoritarianism in Mexico.* Baltimore: Johns Hopkins University Press.

——, ed. 1991. *Unions, Workers, and the State in Mexico.* San Diego: Center for U.S.-Mexican Studies, University of California, San Diego.

Milkman, Ruth. 1987. *Gender at Work: The Dynamics of Job Segregation by Sex during World War II.* Urbana: University of Illinois Press.

——, 2006. *L.A. Story: Immigrant Workers and the Future of the U.S. Labor Movement.* New York: Russell Sage Foundation.

——, ed. 2000. *Organizing Immigrants: The Challenge for Unions in Contemporary California.* Ithaca, NY: Cornell University Press.

Milkman, Ruth, and Kent Wong. 2000. "Organizing the Wicked City: The 1992 Southern California Drywall Strike." In *Organizing Immigrants: The Challenge for Unions in Contemporary California,* edited by Ruth Milkman, 169–198. Ithaca, NY: Cornell University Press.

Moghadam, Valentine, ed. 1996. *Patriarchy and Economic Development: Women's Positions at the End of the Twentieth Century.* New York: Clarendon Press.

Nash, June. 1995. "Latin American Women in the World Capitalist Crisis." In *Women in the Latin American Development Process,* edited by Christine E. Bose and Edna Acosta-Belen, 151–167. Philadelphia: Temple University Press.

National Immigration Law Center. 2005. "House Passes Border and Immigration Enforcement Bill: Immigrants, Noncitizens, Even Citizens Face Unprecedented Assault on Rights." *Immigrant Rights Update* 19 (8): December 22. http://www.nilc.org/immlawpolicy/CIR/cir002.htm#intro (accessed May 2006).

——. 2007a. "State and Local Proposals That Punish Employers for Hiring Undocumented Workers Are Unenforceable, Unnecessary, and Bad Public Policy." http://www.nilc.org/immsemplymnt/ircaempverif/employersanctionsTPs_2007-02-22.pdf (accessed May 2007).

——. 2007b. "NILC's Statement on the Senate-White House Immigration Reform Proposal: Secure Borders, Economic Opportunity and Immigration Reform Act of 2007. http://www.nilc.org/immlawpolicy/CIR/cir022.htm (accessed June 2007).

National Immigration Project. 2006. "Comparison of Immigration Proposals." http://www.nationalimmigrationproject.org/immigration_bills_comparison_chart_6.5.06_final.pdf (accessed in September 2006).

Nevins, Joseph. 2002. *Operation Gatekeeper: The Rise of the "Illegal Alien" and the Making of the U.S.-Mexico Boundary.* New York: Routledge.

Ngai, Mae M. 2004. *Impossible Subjects: Illegal Aliens and the Making of Modern America.* Princeton: Princeton University Press.

Ochoa, Enrique C. 2000. *Feeding Mexico: The Political Uses of Food Since 1910.* Wilmington, DE.: Scholarly Resources.

Ohmae, Kenichi. 1996. *The End of the Nation State: The Rise of Regional Economies.* New York: Free Press.

Omi, Michael, and Howard Winant. 1994. *Racial Formation in the United States: From the 1960s to the 1990s.* 2nd ed. New York: Routledge.

Ong, Aihwa. 1999. *Flexible Citizenship: The Cultural Logics of Transnationality.* Durham, NC: Duke University Press.

Ono, Kent A., and John M. Sloop. 2002. *Shifting Borders: Rhetoric, Immigration, and California's Proposition 187.* Philadelphia: Temple University Press.

O'Riain, Sean. 2000. "The Flexible Developmental State: Globalization, Information Technology, and the 'Celtic Tiger.'" *Politics and Society* 28 (3): 3–37.

Organisation for Economic Co-operation and Development. Definition of Purchasing Power Parity. www.oecd.org

Orsi, Peter. 2007. "Mexican Consumers Pressed by Rising Tortilla Prices." January, 13. www.azstarnet.com/allheadlines/164391 (accessed June 2007).

Parenti, Christian. 1999. *Lockdown America: Police and Prisons in the Age of Crisis.* London: Verso.

Parker, Mike, and Jane Slaughter. 1988. *Unions and the Team Concept.* Cambridge, MA: South End Press.

Pastor Manuel, and Carol Wise. 2003. "Picking Up the Pieces: Comparing the Social Impacts of Financial Crisis in Mexico and Argentina." Department of Latin American and Latino Studies, University of California Santa Cruz. Unpublished manuscript.

Peña, Devon G. 1997. *The Terror of the Machine: Technology, Work, Gender, and Ecology on the U.S.-Mexico Border.* Austin: The Center for Mexican American Studies University of Texas at Austin.

Piore, Michael. 1979. *Birds of Passage: Migrant Labor and Industrial Societies.* New York: Cambridge University Press.

Prieto, Norma Iglesias. 1997. *Beautiful Flowers of the Maquiladora: Life Histories of Women Workers in Tijuana.* Austin, TX: University of Texas Press.

Pujol, José F. 1996. "Racionalización de Subsidios y Liberalización de Precios del Sector." In *La Industria de La Masa y La Tortilla,* edited by Felipe Torres, Ernesto Moreno, Isabel Chong, and Juan Quintanilla, 39–49. México D.F.: Universidad Autónoma de México.

Reese, Ellen, and Elvia Ramirez. 2002. "The New Ethnic Politics of Welfare: Struggles Over Legal Immigrants' Rights to Welfare in California." *Journal of Poverty* 6 (3): 29–62.

Reisler, Mark. 1976. *By the Sweat of their Brow: Mexican Immigrant Labor in the United States 1900–1940.* Westport, CT: Greenwood Press.

Ribeiro, Silvia. 2005. "Amenazas al Maíz." *La Jornada,* January 17. www.jornada.unam.mx/2005/ene05/050117/secara.html (accessed March 2005).

Robin, Gabriella. 2003. "*Hoffman Plastic Compounds, Inc v. National Labor Relations Board:* A Step Backwards for All Workers in the United States." Unpublished Manuscript.

Robinson, William I. 2004. *A Theory of Global Capitalism: Transnational Production, Transnational Capitalists, and the Transnational State.* Baltimore: Johns Hopkins University Press.

Roig-Franzia, Manuel. 2007. "A Culinary and Cultural Staple in Crisis; Mexico Grapples With Soaring Prices for Corn—and Tortillas." *Washington Post,* January 27, Section A.

Rosas Peña, Ana María. 2005. "Un Mercado Hecho Bolas." *La Jornada,* January 17. www.jornada.unam.mx/2005/ene05/050117/secara.html (accessed March 2005).

Ruiz, Vikki L. 1987. *Cannery Women, Cannery Lives: Mexican Women, Unionization, and the California Food Processing Industry 1930–1950.* Albuquerque: University of Mexico Press.

Ruiz, Vicki L., and Susan Tiano. 1987. Introduction to *Women on the U.S. Mexico Border: Responses to Change,* edited by Vicki L. Ruiz and Susan Tiano, 1–13. Boston: Allen & Unwin.

Sabel, Charles F. 1982. *Work and Politics: The Division of Labor in Industry.* New York: Cambridge University Press.

Salas-Porras, Alejandra. 1996. "The Mexican Business Class and the Process of Globalization: Trends and Counter Trends." Ph.D. diss., London School of Economics and Political Science.

Salzinger, Leslie. 2003. *Genders in Production: Making Workers in Mexico's Global Factories.* Berkeley: University of California Press.

Sánchez, George. 1993. *Becoming Mexican American: Ethnicity, Culture, and Identity, in Chicano Los Angeles, 1900–1945.* New York: Oxford University Press.

Sassen-Koob, Saskia. 1984. "From Household to Workplace: Theories and Survey Research on Migrant Women in the Labor Market." *International Migration Review* 18 (4): 1144–1166.

Sassen, Saskia. 1988. *The Mobility of Labor and Capital: A Study in International Investment and Labor Flow.* New York: Cambridge University Press.

———. 1996. "Beyond Sovereignty: Immigration Policy Making Today." *Social Justice* 23 (3): 9–21.

Scott, James C. 1985. *Weapons of the Weak: Everyday Forms of Peasant Resistance.* New Haven, CT: Yale University Press.

Secretaría del Trabajo y Previsión Social. 2003a. "Tasa de Desempleo Abierto 32 Áreas Urbanas." *Encuesta Nacional de Empleo Urbano e Indicadores de Empleo y Desempleo, INEGI.* www.stps.gob.mx (accessed May 2004).

———. 2003b. "Salarios Medios Pagados a los Obreros en la Industria de la Maquiladora de Exportación por Entidad Federativa." *Estadística de la Maquiladora de Exportación, INEGI.* www.stps.gob.mx (accessed May 2004).

———. 2003c. "Salarios Medios Pagados a los Obreros en la Industria de la Maquiladora de Exportación por Producto Procesado." *Estadística de la Maquiladora de Exportación, INEGI.* www.stps.gob.mx (accessed May 2004).

Sheridan, Mary Beth. 1996. "'Luxury' Tortilla Shops May Signal End of Subsidies; Mexico: The Stores Sell Nation's Staple at Twice the Controlled Price. But Authorities are Treading Carefully." *Los Angeles Times,* September 30, 1.

Sklair, Leslie. 1993. *Assembling for Development: The Maquila Industry in Mexico and the United States.* San Diego: Center for U.S. Mexico Studies.

———. 2001. *The Transnational Capitalist Class.* Oxford: Blackwell.

Skocpol, Theda. 1985. "Bringing the State Back In: Strategies and Analysis in Current Research." In *Bringing the State Back In,* edited by Peter B. Evans, Dieter Reuschemeyer, and Theda Skocpol. New York: Cambridge University Press.

Smith, Vicki. 1997. "New Forms of Work Organization." *Annual Review of Sociology* 23: 315–339.

SourceMex. 2004. "Tortilla Consumption Continues to Decline in Mexico but Grows Steadily Overseas." http://ladb.unm.edu/sourcemex/(accessed June 2006).

Strange, Susan. 1996. *Retreat of the State: The Diffusion of Power in the World Economy.* New York: Cambridge University Press.

Thompson, Ginger. 1999. "In Mexico, Children, and Promises, Unkept." *New York Times,* June 2, Section A, p.1, Column 3, Metropolitan Desk.

Tobar, Héctor. 2006. "Divergent Visions for a Divided Nation: The Two Front-Runners in Mexico's Presidential Race Have Built Support Bases That Are Split Along Economic, Regional and Social Lines." *Los Angeles Times,* July 2, 1.

Torres, Felipe T. 1996. "Antecedentes del Debate Actual Sobre el Maíz en México." In *La Industria de La Masa y La Tortilla,* edited by Felipe Torres, Ernesto Moreno, Isabel Chong, and Juan Quintanilla, 19–29. México D.F.: Universidad Autónoma de México.

Torriente, Anna L., ed. 1997. *Mexican and U.S. Labor Law and Practice: A Practical Guide for Maquilas and Other Businesses.* Tucson: National Law Center for Inter-American Free Trade.

Tortilla Industry Association (TIA). 2003. *TIA News: The Latest News in the Tortilla Industry,* XXII (3): 3.

——. 2003. "Study Finds Tortillas Second Most Popular in America." *TIA News: The Latest News in the Tortilla Industry,* 22 (3): 1.

——. 2002. "Registration Materials for Annual Conference." TIA Industry Association, City of Industry, CA April 2002

Tortimundo. 2003. Annual Financial Report.

Tucker, Robert C., ed. 1978. "Theses on Feuerbach by Karl Marx." In *The Marx-Engels Reader,* 2nd ed., 143–145. New York: Norton.

United States Census Bureau. 1997. *Economic Census: Manufacturing in California.* http://www.census.gov/epcd/ec97/ca/CA000_31.HTM#N311 (accessed March 2003).

United States Census Bureau. 2002. *Economic Census: Manufacturing in California.* http://www.census.gov/econ/census02/data/ca/CA000_31.htm.

United States General Accounting Office. 2003. "International Trade: Mexico's Maquiladora Decline Affects U.S.-Mexico Border Communities and Trade; Recovery Depends in Part on Mexico's Actions." http://www.gao.gov/new.items/d03891.pdf (accessed August 2003).

Vallas, Steven P. 2003. "The Adventures of Managerial Hegemony: Teamwork, Ideology, and Worker Resistance." *Social Problems* 50 (2): 204–225.

Velázquez, Ricardo B. 2005. "Nuestro Maíz." *La Jornada,* January 17. www.jornada.unam.mx/2005/ene05/050117/secara.html (accessed March 2005).

Waldinger, Roger, and Michael L. Lichter. 1999. "Network, Bureaucracy, and Exclusion: Recruitment and Selection in an Immigrant Metropolis." In *Immigration and Opportunity: Race, Ethnicity, and Employment in the United States,* edited by Frank D. Bean and Stephanie Bell-Rose. New York: Russell Sage Foundation.

——. 2003. *How the Other Half Works: Immigration and the Social Organization of Labor.* Berkeley: University of California Press.

Ward, Kathryn, ed. 1990. *Women Workers and Global Restructuring.* Ithaca, NY: ILR Press.

Warman, Arturo. 2003. *Corn and Capitalism: How a Botanical Bastard Grew to Global Dominance.* Trans. Nancy L. Westrate. Chapel Hill: University of North Carolina Press.

Webster, Edward. 2001." Manufacturing Compromise: The Dynamics of Race and Class Among South African Shop Stewards in the 1990s." In *The Critical Study of Work: Labor, Technology and Global Production,* edited by Rick Baldoz, Chuck Koeber, and Phil Kraft, 127–154. Philadelphia: Temple University Press.

Weiss, Linda. 1998. *The Myth of the Powerless State.* Ithaca, NY: Cornell University Press.

Wells, Miriam J. 1996. *Strawberry Fields: Politics, Class, and Work in California Agriculture.* Ithaca, NY: Cornell University Press.

Wilson, William J. 1996. *When Work Disappears: The World of the New Urban Poor.* New York: Random House.

Zabin, Carol. 2000. "Organizing Latino Workers in the Los Angeles Manufacturing Sector: The Case of American Racing Equipment." In *Organizing Immigrants: The Challenge for Unions in Contemporary California,* edited by Ruth Milkman, 150–168. Ithaca, NY: Cornell University Press.

Zabin, Carol, Sallie Hughes, and James Wiley. 1995. "Economic Integration and Labor Flows: Stage Migration in Farm Labor Markets in Mexico and the United States." *International Migration Review* 29 (2): 395–423.

Zolberg, Aristide R. 2006. *A Nation by Design: Immigration Policy in the Fashioning of America.* New York: Russell Sage Foundation.

Index